Ambiguity and the Presence of God

AMBIGUITY
AND THE
PRESENCE
OF GOD

Ruth Page

SCM PRESS LTD

British Library Cataloguing in Publication Data

Page, Ruth
   Ambiguity and the presence of God.
   1. Theology   2. Deconstruction
   I. Title
   230'.01   BT83.8

ISBN 0–334–00022–X

First published 1985
by SCM Press Ltd
26–30 Tottenham Road, London N1

Phototypeset by Input Typesetting Ltd
and printed in Great Britain by
Billing & Sons Ltd
Worcester

Contents

Foreword

It is not an uncommon experience to come away from the reading of a work of theology dissatisfied, not because of any shortcoming in the stylistic clarity or intellectual rigour of the work, but because the world with which it deals does not seem to correspond to the world we know. Theologians speak of the world as 'contingent', thereby acknowledging that it does not fit tidily into any formal system of theology. But however good the intentions of such a designation, it seldom seems to be worked out in a way that does justice to the messiness and chanciness of the world as we experience it. As a result many otherwise impressive works of theology leave us with an uneasy sense of their irrelevance and inapplicability to our everyday experience.

Whatever the reactions to Dr Page's book, they will not be of that kind. The difficult concept of the 'ambiguity' of the world is carefully analysed. We are left in no doubt that the world she is talking about is the world we actually live in. But 'ambiguity', unlike 'paradox', is not a concept which lends itself naturally to the development of a positive theological position. Yet this is what Dr Page here undertakes to do, in relation both to the understanding of God and to Christian spirituality and practice.

Her thesis is a challenging one, and in developing it she draws on a wide range of philosophical knowledge and practical experience. Not everyone will agree with her argument. But no one could read this book without in the process being made more sensitive to the problems and possibilities of a contemporary faith. A theological work that achieves that result achieves a lot more than most theological writing. To suggest that this was a 'definitive' study of its subject would be a self-contradictory claim. What it does do is to give valuable philosophical, theological and religious expression to some of the

basic problems concerning Christian faith today, which I believe
are widely felt but seldom find appropriate articulation. I hope
it will be widely read and discussed.

Maurice Wiles

Acknowledgments

There are many people I should like to thank for their help in making this book possible. My initial debt is to the organizers of the Ecumenical Consultation on Rural Ministry in New Zealand, who in 1977 provoked me into taking ambiguity seriously for the first time. They immersed me in the activities of a country community for a week, then asked for a theology of nature derived specifically from that varied and polyvalent experience. From such a beginning only an empirical and pragmatic theology could emerge!

Professor John McIntyre and Professor Maurice Wiles have been kind enough to read and comment on parts of the draft manuscript. I am grateful for their interest and their assistance, and owe a further debt to Professor Wiles for his willingness to write a foreword. Numerous friends have argued constructively with me at various points, but I am particularly indebted to the observations of Mary Hall, John Lindsay and Fergus Smith. Yet, as I argue in my last chapter, the influence of friends and companions does not remove my responsibility for the final presentation. I wrote the main draft on sabbatical leave in New Zealand, and I should like to thank the Staff at the Theological Hall and at Salmond Hall, Dunedin for their encouragement and hospitality. John Brewster and James Fields gave valuable assistance with the Index.

Edinburgh, June 1985   Ruth Page

1

Introduction: The Interpretation of Experience

The experience with which this book is concerned is that of complexity and incalculability: it is the experience of interacting changes which often have unpredictable effects, the experience of having to choose among variously imperfect courses and accept the consequences of the decision, the experience of competing interests and explanations yielding different interpretations. The problem is to interpret a changing, unfinished world of diverse and polyvalent experience and to declare its relationship with God.

Part of the confusion of contemporary life comes from the variety of opinion, expert or lay, which flourishes on every issue from nuclear disarmament to abortion. Rarely, if ever, is one clear course of thought or action universally perceived, and even when an approach wins majority approval its implementation is usually complicated by contingent circumstances. Moreover it has become the commonest truism that we live in an age of accelerating change, with technology, for instance, altering patterns of industry while domestic life is rearranged around unemployment or working wives. In the midst of change it is hard to evaluate the difference it makes or to gauge its direction and momentum. Population estimates, for instance, have knock-on effects in provision for food and energy consumption, but in 1954 informed opinion predicted a world population of 3500 million in the year 2000; by 1975 the United Nations projection was 7000 million. Current estimates are that world population will reach 11000 million soon after 2000.[1]

The whole matter of interpreting and not merely predicting experience is further complicated by the interrelationship of events: an increase in American interest rates (which will have its own reasons) leads to a fall in the value of sterling, which is good for exports but bad for imports and has further implications for interest rates in Britain with all that entails; cheaper coffee on European shelves results not only in less return for the producers but also, among other things, in the inability of their country to repay its debt to the first world. Choices and decisions, even on a much more local and personal scale than these examples, often have such wide-ranging, unintended but inter-related repercussions. The picture is not all gloom – some changes benefit some people – yet it is undoubtedly perplexing. As a result of such perceptions of variety, change and incalculability life appears to be a precarious process involving a multitude of interacting variables whose effects are uncertain and whose interpretation is at best provisional.

In spite of all these formidable difficulties, however, John Oman's observation, first made in the uncertain days of 1928, still holds good: 'Every age has its own task of interpreting its own experience and no age has found it to need less than all its faith and all its labour. The impression, so generally received, that our age is of a singular perplexity may, therefore, only be because we live in the midst of it.'² The complex, shifting nature of contemporary life, insecure because we are still 'in the midst of it' is certainly experienced as 'of a singular perplexity'. It calls for interpretation by theologians as much as by anyone else, since the world in all its variety, change and inter-relationship is believed to depend on God for its very existence and to be related to a Creator who cares for every temporary variable in its constitution. To relinquish the task of interpreting current experience is to create a divide between faith and life so that God appears to be connected only with less complicated private 'spiritual' experiences of individuals and not with the complexities of the world at large. Yet interpretation which neither simplifies nor devalues the diversity, intricacy, change and unfinished nature of the experienced world requires, as Oman noted, all one's faith and all one's labour.

There are different ways of going about such interpretation. One is to take each issue or group of issues piecemeal – world poverty, say, or the welfare state – presenting the background, present condition and probable implications from particular religious, moral, social or political points of view. In this way information is spread, consciousness raised, and possible lines of action are indicated. Such interpretation is clearly necessary to understand our own time, however partially and however much disagreement there may be between points of view. But a very different manner of interpretation is intended initially in this book, one which does not supersede cumulative investigation, but rather endeavours to go behind all individual issues to ask in general how the world comes to be so complex and confusing and in particular how a world with these characteristics is related to God and God to such a world. Only after that may particular issues of interpretation and action arise.

To express this intention another way: the first requirement in interpreting experience is the delineation of a metaphysic which gives a credible picture of the way the world goes and of ourselves as actors in that world. Without such a picture experience fragments into unrelated moments of tenuous meaning; alternatively, we have to inhabit a number of worlds, religious and secular, for example, or at home and at work, which are no longer connected by one overarching conception of how things are. To know where we are in any particular sense we need to know the nature of the map on which we are seeking co-ordinates. A metaphysic supplies such a map with its explanation.

The most complete metaphysical framework ever devised operated in the late Middle Ages, when the world was in an important sense 'coherent, luminous, intellectually secure and dependable' on that account, for then people knew who they were and what was possible.[3] The power of that framework is vividly rendered in a theatrical moment from Brecht's play *Galileo Galilei* when actors with banners demonstrate mediaeval cosmography. One man stands firm in the centre of the stage to represent the stable Earth while others gradually move into place round him as planets circling in their orderly paths. The action is simultaneously a representation of society with the Pope, the Vicar of Christ, central and unmoving while in relation to him other clergy and lay classes in their degrees from royalty to beggars rotate in their fixed orbits. As the procession goes round and round it is clear that the only movement is cyclical along a preordained path. What has been will be; as one is so one will remain. The inclusive orderliness of the spectacle may be disquieting in its confident authoritative rigidity, yet it has also the aesthetic appeal of simplicity and completeness. No doubt actual life in the Middle Ages could be as complex and incalculable as ours today, but the complexities could still be located within an orderly conception of how things were, indeed of how God had ordered everything, a conception which both supported and restricted thought and action.

It is an old story that changes in belief, science and society entirely destroyed the late mediaeval synthesis. But the story is often told in terms of pure gain: advance in place of rotation; experiments in place of authorities; power in the hands of that intelligent and flexible class, the bourgeoisie. But however one evaluates the gains, there is loss to be reckoned with as well, for with the restriction went also the support of the framework. In confident times the loss was scarcely noticed, for progress itself became the dominant conception into which thought, action and belief could be fitted. But when such social self-confidence has gone, as it has in the West today, there remains no general understanding of how things are by which to interpret the variety and change of experience.

The mediaeval synthesis was inspired and legitimated by the belief that God had ordered everything, so that it was the divine will that everything had a place and only that place. Belief in God's ordering of the world still persists, a matter I shall return to challenge, but where it endures it has become increasingly abstract and general in face of the variety, change and polyvalence of experience, to the point where it is often more formal than material. In many areas it has disappeared in any effective sense and has not been replaced. In his novel *How Far Can You Go?*, David Lodge provides the opposite picture to Brecht's. He follows the experience of middle-class English Roman Catholics from the 1950's to the 1970's, and in so doing charts,

> the fading away of the traditional Catholic metaphysic – that marvellous complex and ingenious synthesis of theology and cosmology and casuistry, which situated individual souls on a kind of Snakes and Ladders board, motivated them with equal doses of hope and fear, and promised them, if they persevered in the game, an eternal reward. The board was marked out very

clearly, decorated with all kinds of picturesque motifs, and governed by intricate rules and provisos. Heaven, hell, purgatory, limbo. Mortal, venial and original sin. Angels, devils, saints and Our Lady Queen of Heaven. Grace, penance, relics, indulgences and all the rest of it. Millions of Catholics no doubt still believe in all that literally. But belief is gradually fading. The metaphysic is no longer taught in schools and seminaries in the more advanced countries and Catholic children grow up knowing little or nothing about it. Within another generation it will disappear, superseded by something less vivid but more tolerant.[4]

The metaphysical maps of other Western churches, never so full or so highly coloured, are fading too. Yet it is far from clear that all maps can be dispensed with. 'Something less vivid but more tolerant' may do very well for a generation raised in the tradition, but it does not itself give a tradition to hand on, nor a coherent understanding for the present. If God can no longer be seen as the deviser of immutable order, the sanction or goal of progress, or the Boardmaster of spiritual Snakes and Ladders, how is the divine-human relationship to be perceived? For if that is not discerned and articulated, no current, understandable, livable relationship will be apprehended.

This book will therefore be concerned with a metaphysic in general, a theistic metaphysic in particular and a way of understanding God's relationship with the world. Such reflection is no more new in theology than 'singular perplexity' is a condition of our age alone. The supreme example is Augustine's *City of God*, which put Alaric's sack of Rome into a total metaphysical perspective embracing the world and the church from creation to consummation. Yet as the world changes, understanding changes also. The Middle Ages had no value for change and therefore their total and finely-wrought metaphysic of God, the church, nature, the heavens and society denied any possibility of alteration. But a multiplicity of actual changes overthrew the whole conceptual system and there is no return to that kind of fixed finality. There may be a sense in which the human condition of personal lives in pilgrimage from birth to death remains broadly comparable from age to age; moreover we believe that God remains unswerving in love and concern for the world. Yet our understanding of our social and psychological selves, of technology and science, of history and society, of knowledge and information, has changed profoundly since Augustine wrote in the fifth century or Galileo rebelled in the seventeenth. The theological interpretation of experience in broad metaphysical lines as well as on individual issues remains an unending task.

In the next chapter, therefore, I have drawn a metaphysical sketch. It is not so much a framework for the neat disposition of orderly thought like the mediaeval synthesis as an action *Gestalt* of the way the world goes as I see it. 'A likely story' was what Plato called his metaphysic in the *Timaeus*, aware as he was of his finitude in a changing world.[5] The most likely story I can tell of the world concerns experience of and reasons for its ambiguity, which I have taken as the key, though not the only, characteristic. Since every orderly explanation of the world is sooner or later upset or rearranged by change and variety, I have made these conditions basic to the interpretation.[6] If the world is ambiguous in this way, however, the nature and status of knowledge and the sense that can be given to 'truth' become pressing questions. The third chapter is therefore devoted to their consideration. Only after that are the implications for belief drawn; and the theology which follows is written in the light of the metaphysic and epistemology.

This order may seem to put the philosophical cart before the theological horse. But doctrine is never thought through in a vacuum sealed off from all outside influences. Truth and knowledge, in the way we normally understand these terms, are at issue in it. Even the representation of religion's relation to the world as an intertwined double helix separates off theological thought too decisively from thought in general. The spiral of interpretation is nearer the mark in that the Christian tradition, itself a product of various ages and places, is studied, absorbed and interpreted by one who has Christian beliefs but is also a person living at a certain time with a certain experience of the world. The beliefs and the experience have to make sense *together* if Christianity is to be a lived faith, rather than doctrine and spirituality divorced from the complexity of experience I have described.

Although the metaphysical and epistemological descriptions are taken first, that is only so that they can be clarified before they are wedded with theological interpretation. If such matters are not specifically worked out, they will be implicitly presupposed in a theology, for assumptions concerning how the world is and what it is to know are inescapable and will affect the tone and emphases of the theology itself. It is therefore better to be as clear on these issues as possible. Doctrine can then interact with and give point to the this-worldly perspective which emerges, although it may not simply endorse it. At that point it may be possible to have a totality of life and faith.

That interaction of doctrine and experience will be explored primarily in the way of conceiving the relationship between God and creation, a relationship which is not to be seen as an extra 'something' happening only outside and apart from the tensions of existence, nor one which removes these tensions. Moreover the relationship has to be conceived in such a way that on our human side it can be understood, lived through and acted upon in daily life, while on the divine side God's absolute attributes as well as his relative care have to be accounted for. The full picture will be painted in piece by piece in the second part of the book, but the theme there will be that God is present *with* creation in the role of companion, and is thus part of every situation in its complexity, a source of values and perspective on the world. Belief in God does not make the processes of living any more simple, nor does it ensure that the best thing will always be done. But just as tradition describes God as Immanuel and his people as pilgrims, so God may be understood as companioning humanity while it wrestles with ambiguity, giving direction and meaning to the struggle.

Another preliminary explanation required here is that this is a book of Christian theism but does not at any point dwell at length on Jesus Christ. That is an anomalous but not impossible position. The decision was taken because any proper discussion of his role would involve too many extra areas of argument in what is already a broad enough field. Without proper discussion, references to Jesus Christ may be clouded by undisclosed assumptions. In one sense, therefore, christology is bracketed out of the following theology which concentrates on the relationship between God and the world. In another sense, however, such bracketing is impossible since the God of the Christian faith is the one known in and through Jesus Christ. It is the particular role of Christ

himself which is left temporarily out of account, although this
limits the comprehensiveness of the discussion. A further reason
for leaving christology aside at the moment is that although
Christians have continued to see in Christ the focus of God's
relationship with the world, the understanding of Christ's person
and work has varied from the very beginning. Ambiguity is amply
illustrated by the history of christology. Current christology, in
that case, requires behind it a theology which has already come
to terms with change and diversity.

There is a sense in which I can scarcely lose with a thesis of
ambiguity, for those who disagree with my constructions simply
illustrate its prevalence. But that is a trivial kind of victory. There
is another sense in which it is hard to win, for I wish not only to
display ambiguity as the state of the world, but also to argue a
case for what one does in and with that state. Yet the tools for
making the case and the point of view from which it is presented
are themselves ambiguous. As I shall argue later, values, decisions
and commitment do give direction and an ordering of priorities
in an ambiguous world. But the serious recognition of diversity
and mutability leads to according an argument the status of a
recommendation or persuasion among possibilities rather than a
demonstration of the one true state of affairs. There is a constant
tension between the case made and the ambiguity of experience
it interprets. I have endeavoured to maintain this tone and tension
even when arguing strongly, but they are not advertised at
all points because of the sheer tediousness of repeating their
necessity. Yet if the world is indeed ambiguous and not simply
lapsed from one original divinely-given order, all expression,
even of religious commitment and values, cannot escape the
effects of the condition.

2

The Ambiguous World

Order and chaos

What kind of world is this?

That is the question which metaphysics seeks to answer in its widest scope, giving an overall world-view which we inhabit as truly as we inhabit the physical world, for it interprets that world in general terms to us. Traditional answers concerning the nature of all-that-is have assumed that the first and ultimate decision is on the choice between order and chaos. The world in its totality either exhibits some comprehensible patterns and structure which we may understand and flourish in, or it is void of order, sterile, meaningless and inconsequential. Chaos, however, even when it has been defined less starkly than this, has never been a live option in any sense and has served rather as the bad symbol which highlights the goodness of order, the fear of its loss, or the impulse to disrupt it. Since no third possibility has been advanced, most have concluded with Hume's Philo: 'How could things have been as they are were there not an original inherent principle of order somewhere, in thought or in matter?'[1] Even those who are not given to metaphysical speculation still assume that order in their lives, their society and the world at large is both normal and right: that order represents not only how things usually are, but how they ought fundamentally to be. Without order the world's components would not cohere in a stable manner, living organisms could not be sure of successful reproduction, societies would fragment and personal life would be intolerable.

What is shown by this catalogue of possible disasters, however, is the universal requirement for a modicum of stability rather than the objective existence of an ordered world. Chaos may not be a practical *modus vivendi*, but its persistence as the single alternative to order witnesses to human fear that any individual order, no matter how well established or personally important, may be overthrown or superseded at any point. The forms of order (physical, biological, social, personal order and so forth) with which we are acquainted and which therefore give our world stability and security are not themselves secure, but are always vulnerable to changing circumstances or reinterpretation. Such threats are encountered at every level from small personal disturbances to a settled way of life, through the extinction of species from change or slaughter, to the danger that Earth itself may not continue to exist if vital conditions alter significantly.

Modern awareness of accelerating change and the fragility of any existing order may have contributed to the current decline in metaphysical thinking. Certainly the practice came under recent philosophical strictures from those who found it too speculative and imprecise. Yet that itself is a metaphysical observation, since it implies belief in a commonsense world. A more fundamental objection to past metaphysics, however, would be that when a metaphysician has decided that the world is orderly, he endeavours to express that order in too tidy, closed and rigid a fashion, in a structure which is soon overtaken by the next change or by further complexity. Hegel's declaration that nineteenth-century Prussia embodied the consummation of the progress of the World Spirit is the most notorious instance of such misplaced concreteness in the desire to capture everything within a system. 'At the root of most metaphysical speculations lies the ancient insight of Parmenides, flowering in Hegel and Spinoza, and supporting the strong Idealist tradition: the double conviction that nature is a unity, and that the function of mind is to embrace it in its totality.'[2] But our enforced acquaintance with contingency, diversity and change during this headlong century has left it far from clear whether nature might be a unity, and even if it were, whether 'mind' might know this, since in the process of contemplation, which will in any case be from a point of view, change would probably go on taking place so that no fixed pattern could emerge.

Objections on the basis of this-worldly diversity and movement cannot be raised in the same way against metaphysicians of a transcendent order like Plato, for whom such phenomena as change clearly indicated imperfection and led him to locate his 'reality' outside the world of experience.[3] Yet if it is the nature of the world we know which concerns us, so that the metaphysic is immanent rather than transcendent, then a place must be found not only for order, but for change, diversity and polyvalence as well. These last three aspects resist any neat classification of existence into one architectonic structure or movement. The varieties of different ordering to be found, for instance, in the various species in nature, the different forms of social organization or different traditions in, say, epistemology may at points be inter-related, but they are also competing, changing at different rates and in unexpected ways, and are patient of differing interpretations. Yet order remains a necessity: every interpretation is an imposition of order; the variety we are aware of is composed of different orders; change is the movement from one configuration of order to another.

This suggests that the original option between order and chaos is inadequate, since neither describes fully the world of experience. Order *per se* is insufficient for the continuing process of irregular change going on in the world. Chaos, strictly speaking, is as inconceivable as nothingness, and is a term we use imprecisely for alien orders we dislike or cannot understand, which appear to us disorderly. There must be a third proposal which will encompass both the necessity of order for any kind of being or becoming, and the actual existence of diverse and fluid orders which may be variously understood. A *tertium quid* which fulfils these conditions is that the world we experience is not so much ordered as *orderable*, capable of being ordered by the action of any agent upon it, for ever plastic to new or modified shaping by its components or its inhabitants. In that case the world is seen to change because it is being acted upon at different times and places and in different degrees; it is diverse because each item in it represents an order differently achieved; it is polyvalent because human beings can always order it in different ways by their understanding and interpretation. Order exists, or more exactly, orders exist, as we know by experience, but they exist diversely and changefully because they are the result of various agencies in cooperation or competition acting upon the orderable world.

To say that the world is orderable is to give a characteristic of it found in experience, but not to posit some primal matter which may be differently ordered, nor some noumenal realm of being beyond our various phenomenal orderings. What is orderable at any point is the world as it is understood, or rather that part of the world with which we have to do. Our only experience is of the variety of orderings which currently obtain, and we have knowledge of past difference through memory, history and so forth. After the limited certainties of childhood the world is never 'given' as an ordered unity. Order which has been brought about by others may be inherited passively, and thus may appear to be objective and given in the nature of things. Yet such assurance is continually upset by further experience of variety and change. Order, whether biological, social, personal, institutional or whatever, is always something devised, happened upon or achieved by action upon the orderability of the world. By the same token it is always something fragile, for if the world we know demonstrates continual plasticity to alterations in circumstance and interpretation, then the order which gives anything its coherence may be challenged or overthrown by rival or new orderings which produce change.

The 'world', which is a shorthand term for a conception of its components, inhabitants and cultures, and stands indeed for the less particularly known universe, is in principle mutable and malleable and in practice shaped and reshaped. Its character, therefore, is always unfinished and no definitive rendering of it may be given. It is in process, but that word is not to be confused with progress, a term which has connotations of improvement. The world changes, but it does not necessarily advance from everyone's or everything's point of view. The success of one organism, society or mode of thought is generally at the expense of another, so that loss as well as gain is involved, however one may evaluate the change. No overall purposeful teleology is evident in all the processes of change, and we have no extra-terrestrial means of judging improvement or recession among the variety, although from our own point of view some change will be better and some worse.

Ambiguity defined

Commenting on the drive to conceive a metaphysical picture of the world, Dorothy Emmet writes: 'Our minds seem impelled to seek or to create significance in the world as a whole in terms of concepts originally formed to express relations within experience.'[4] The relations chosen here as paramount are open, fluctuating and various, indicating neither static closed orders, nor a smoothly teleological movement; or at least nothing teleological for the world as a whole, although individual purposes are achieved. Such relations in action give rise to *change, diversity and polyvalence*, the interconnected features of the orderable world which defy all pretensions to finality. They normally coexist with continuity, balance and consensus in irregular, unpredictable ways, but because humanity with its requirement of basic stability already has a deep investment in the order of continuity and consensus, these features do not need to be emphasized as metaphysical conditions to the same extent as diversity, change and polyvalence. I propose to use Ambiguity, capitalized to indicate the whole metaphysical view, as an umbrella term for the three, and for the conditions which they create.

The *Concise Oxford Dictionary* offers for 'ambiguity' only the possibility of double meaning, but for the adjective 'ambiguous' it adds doubt concerning classification and the meaning 'of uncertain issue'. Thus a fight between two evenly-matched boxers would be ambiguous in that its outcome could not be predicted with confidence. *Ambiguity* as I shall use it enlarges 'double meaning' to polyvalence, that is, the way in which anything may be interpreted or evaluated in a variety of ways according to one's point of view, intention, practice or culture. Even a rock in the remotest jungle is ambiguous in this sense, since it may be analysed geologically, mined, climbed, depicted, act as a tribe's totem or a home for plants and animals, and will be seen differently in each case. The dictionary definition 'of uncertain issue' will be intensified in the meaning I give to Ambiguity to cover openness to change and sensitivity to circumstance. Change is less readily seen to be ambiguous in our normal use of that adjective, but because it is the condition which defeats fixedness it renders its subject ambiguous, impossible to define in a final way. It has uncertainty of issue written into it. Change, however, is not always rapid, so interim classification may take on the appearance of finality during long stable periods. But all classifications are subject to amendment and redrafting with reinterpretation, change and the passage of time – including, no doubt, this description of Ambiguity. Change, therefore, is part of Ambiguity and along with polyvalence gives rise to the diversity we encounter in any area of possibility at any time.

It could be argued that diversity and polyvalence are consequences of change and therefore should not be put with it under one term. But they are such intimate and immediate consequences (does change follow or precede a new interpretation?) that they all hang together. Instances of diversity and polyvalence are tokens that change has taken place and may by their existence give rise to more change. The three are different enough to warrant individual specification, yet related enough to justify using one portmanteau word for them all and their consequences. In combination they represent Ambiguity, the condition which arises from diverse action upon the changeable and changing world, continually producing new organizations, complex variety and multiple interpretation – all of which has to integrate with or overthrow what already exists.

Ambiguity in evolution and history

Having defined Ambiguity, I should like to illustrate it in process, but here difficulties abound. To give a proper illustration all the relevant variables must be shown in their changing inter-relationships, and every interpretation ever devised must be included. Interpretations, however, determine what is relevant, so for each there may perhaps be a different set of data. One instance, therefore, properly handled up to date would require a lengthy book on its own and is manifestly impossible here. Yet some illustration may communicate the vision while acres of conceptual analysis may not. I have chosen, therefore, with some temerity, to illustrate the way of the ambiguous world from a very early point in its history, when there are fewer variables to take account of. Even then it has to be simplified narrative which does not encompass all the viewpoints of various biologists, nor all the matters deemed relevant by everyone.

At one stage of the earth's development, when seas were hot

and volcanoes common, the atmosphere has been described as a composite of hydrogen, carbon monoxide, ammonia and methane. If that point (or indeed any other) had become its fixed, immutable character there would have been no further story. But precisely because Earth is ambiguous, open to diverse and changing activity as our understanding interprets them, molecules could interact until DNA was formed. Although the great virtue of DNA was its ability to replicate itself, it was not immutable either, and from the circumstances of its 'mistakes' natural selection could over the ages result in evolutionary change. Each development, however, created a number of new conditions within which any further change had to occur. One such condition was produced, at least in part, by a notable early organism called the cyanophyte. This extracted its necessary hydrogen not from volcanic rocks, like its predecessors, but from water, thus producing oxygen. Over the millenia, that oxygen accumulated to alter the composition of the atmosphere and assist in building the ozone layer which blocks out ultra-violet rays. While the cyanophyte is not responsible for the continuing character of our atmosphere, nevertheless through its action on the orderable world change took place, and the ability to breathe oxygen became a necessary condition in further adaptation. In this kind of way the world was shaped in certain directions for later ages, but not to the point of immutability; otherwise, to continue with the present example, we would not now be concerned with the preservation of the ozone layer. Our oxygen-rich atmosphere illustrates one kind of order, one variable in balance, brought into being because the orderable world admits change. But the world is still ambiguous, still changeful, so that this particular order is a precarious one which can be damaged or overturned by further circumstance, including human folly.

As varieties of life multiplied and the prevailing weather also responded to changing atmospheric conditions, so the requirements for survival and development became ever more complex, demanding not only genes already adapted to novel circumstances, but also the continuous effort of finding and defending habitation and food supply, attracting mates and reproducing. An ambiguous world is not only one open to action but one which requires action, and is therefore likely to be experienced as strenuous. Yet for each most developed life form, supreme in its own field, a relatively secure interlude may have existed until it was threatened by competitors. Thus the first amphibians may have found dry land peaceful until they were challenged by new arrivals. But most species simply failed to survive. Among these are the dinosaurs who had dominated the land for millennia. Various reasons have been suggested for their extinction: it may be that their nervous systems could not cope with the immensity of some forms which they took, or it may be that the weather became cooler while the solar heating of their huge bodies was unable to adapt to that novelty. It is a melancholy conclusion that failure to meet the changing conditions of the world has led to extinction. The example of the dinosaurs emphasizes the untidiness and unpredictability of Ambiguity, characteristics which can be concealed in a term like process. If evolution is evaluated only in terms of advancing process, then dinosaurs become an aberration in that advance, although an aberration which lasted successfully for millions of years.

When the stress is on Ambiguity, however, every form of life in its own day is a kind of achievement, albeit temporary like all achievements, having made use of the plasticity of the world and demonstrated a capacity to respond to previous circumstances. For a greater or shorter time each flourishes, creating its own order, striving for its niche in the system produced by its predecessors and contemporaries, having to preserve what it has won against present competitors and new circumstances.

As in evolution, so in all the diversity of human history the world can be traced as continually malleable to reshaping through change, although each generation receives it already shaped by previous cultural circumstance and interpretation. Such matters as ideologies put into practice, external exigencies, innovations in technology or social organization bring about change and diversity which, short of cataclysmic upheaval, go along with elements of continuity. Change, however, is not so facile or predictable that the world is simply there for humanity's shaping. There is resistance to change on the part of all those who prefer the status quo, while attempts to bring about change may be thwarted by anything from bad weather to bankruptcy. The malleable world is not malleable precisely in accordance with any person's intentions and wishes, for these have to coexist with contemporary conditions and the intentions and wishes of others.

Yet even in periods not known for rapid change, like the Middle Ages, change and diversification gradually took place in, for instance, the growth of the merchant class or the rise of the universities.

To find Ambiguity throughout history is not to erect a pattern for the subject like the organic growth and decay Spengler described in *The Decline of the West*, or the challenge and response of Toynbee's *A Study of History*.[5] Whatever individual insights either of these studies achieved, they also demonstrate the problem with patterns in history in the endeavour to impose a regular form on the untidy, manifold, unique events of the past, 'rejecting whole centuries as uninteresting, forcing it all into a scheme of presumptuous construction', as Geyl wrote indignantly of Toynbee.[6] Ambiguity produces no pattern; rather, it is the condition which gives us history at all. The past is a possible study only because humanity and natural circumstances have acted on the world to change it in various ways; if there had been no changes there would be no subject matter. History continues and will continue to be a possible study because with our polyvalence we keep reinterpreting the past – not *de novo*, but with changed interests and emphases. Economic history, women's history and the history of ordinary people are three quite recent developments. The study of history shows supremely the validity of seeing the world as orderable in its unpredictable plasticity to circumstances and actions which bring about change.

To move attention from the world to the actors in it, one may also describe history as the individual and communal responses of each generation to the diverse conditions which have governed life. For the character of the world as susceptible to change, and therefore to the decisions which bring about such change, may also be described in terms of a world offering continuous possibilities, some of which are always being responded to and realized. Evolution can then be described as a series of responses to possibility, but without attributing consciousness of response to, for instance, the cyanophyte's realization of the potential of drawing hydrogen from water. Ambiguity similarly throws out possibilities in every aspect of human life. Those which have been realized form actual history, and it is part of a historian's skill to discern as far as possible the context of choice within which action is taken.

It is difficult enough to illustrate Ambiguity in evolution, and quite impossible to do it brief justice in the full range of human potential, which includes such aspects as psychology, morality, politics, the arts, religion and so forth. But an exploration of, say, political forms of order would find continuity, balance and consensus continually being rearranged or upset by change, diversity and polyvalence. Much exploration of particular areas of Ambiguity has already taken place. For instance, in the matter of semantics, Jonathan Cohen in *The Diversity of Meaning* has shown the different values 'meaning' has for lexicographers, translators, historians of ideas, psychologists and philosophers. He describes the eighteenth-century discovery that meanings are temporal and mutable, then criticizes recent attempts by philosophers to establish 'meaning' solely in terms of putatively timeless but actually contemporary rules of word use.[7] Similarly ambiguous processes of living and thinking would emerge from investigation in other fields. Ambiguity may show itself, for instance, in a diversity of starting points, as ethical considerations may begin from principles or from situations. It may be seen in changes of conception and practice over time, as in the history of suffrage notions of who was eligible to vote were enlarged. The plasticity of the world to forms of inventiveness shows in abounding innovations of all kinds from technology and art to economics and philosophy. A long historical view or any cross-section of a tradition or personal feature of human possibility would show both a current 'state of the art', that is, how things are currently ordered and established, and the movement generated by polyvalence, diversity and change.

The relation of order and Ambiguity does not appear in a regular pattern, however, nor is Ambiguity evident to the same extent in each case. Artistic change, for example, has probably occurred more often and more suddenly than variation in moral standards: the English language is so malleable that innovations appear almost every year, but change in church order is regularly resisted until the last moment. The range of allowable interpretation in law, while always a matter of learned opinion, is considerably more curtailed than it is in literary criticism. So Ambiguity and order exist in diverse ways and degrees while their relationship is variously apprehended by different people at sundry times. In the last analysis Ambiguity is in principle impossible to encompass because its effects are continuing as the description is written and as different readers relate to that description with personal preconceptions and values from a variety of backgrounds. The phenomenon has to be grasped almost intuitively from the indications given here and personal experience of continuity and change.

Ambiguity and order

A response to the description of Ambiguity, and even more to the encounter with it, is not only intellectual, but will include psychological and emotional aspects as well. Even here there are variations, for some people are more ready than others to welcome change and enjoy diversity, at least in some respects. Generally speaking, adolescents who are less set into patterns of values and behaviour than their elders are more flexible in changing situations: yet in their insecurity about the adult world they may be more rigid. Some adults have learned by experience to live with Ambiguity, but many cling with strong adherence to the continuity in their lives of the order they know, which to them is 'reality'. Reality is popularly perceived as what is sufficiently ordered to be taken on trust; it is the way things are, what we are used to and has proved reliable. Surprises, upsets and innovations are often experienced as unreal until they are assimilated into daily life. The role of the concept of reality in the history of philosophy is not so very different either, for philosophers have invoked different realities according to what they most valued or found most worthy of trust. In stable circumstances during a dominant culture reality is unproblematic. But it is precisely the contemporary malaise that circumstances have long since ceased to be stable and pluralism is rampant. If 'reality' is definable only in terms of stability, endurance and agreement on how things are, it will be experienced as continually frittered away or overturned altogether, to humanity's loss. These features of the world expressed in Ambiguity require recognition as being also part of reality, that is, part of what is to be expected and valued.

The degree to which a familiar order may have a stranglehold on a society facing change has been vividly described by Doris Lessing in her novel *Memoirs of a Survivor*. Here the society is on the verge of final and rapid disintegration. The young are ready to move on, but the older members cannot relinquish that order which has given them their identity.

> While everything, all forms of social organization, broke up, we lived on, adjusting our lives, as if nothing fundamental was happening. It was amazing how determined, how stubborn, how self-renewing were the attempts to lead an ordinary life. When nothing, or very little, was left of what we had been used to, had taken for granted, even ten years before, we went on talking and behaving as if these old forms were still ours . . . Order could also exist in pockets, of space, of time – through periods of weeks or months, or in a particular district. Inside them people would live and talk and even think as if nothing had changed. When something really bad happened, as when an area got devastated, people might move out for days or weeks, to stay with relatives or friends and then move back, perhaps to a looted house, to take up their job, their house-keeping – their order. We can get used to anything at all; this is a commonplace, of course. But perhaps you have to live through such a time to see how horribly true it is. There is nothing people won't try to accommodate into 'ordinary life'.[8]

Psychological resistance to change on a smaller scale than Lessing's apocalyptic picture has been analysed by the anthropologist Mary Douglas in *Purity and Danger*. She compares 'the reaction which condemns any object or idea likely to confuse or contradict cherished classifications' to the offence produced by dirt or personal pollution.[9] She revives the definition of dirt as 'matter out of place' (egg on a plate is food; egg on a dress or tie is dirt). Just as the houseproud are affronted at dirt and disarrangement, yet cannot avoid some contact with them, so those who are accustomed to the existential neatness of settled ideas and a stable way of life are upset by Ambiguity, yet cannot avoid encountering it. 'Dirt' in this sense occurs only when there is already a system with which it is discordant, and Ambiguity may affect people adversely because they have already invested in a particular pattern of life, thought or belief which they are unwilling to change. Yet adaptation will be thrust upon them, for, as Mary Douglas comments: 'Any given scheme of classification must give rise to anomalies and any given culture must confront events which seem to defy its assumptions. It cannot ignore the anomalies which its scheme produces, except at the risk of forfeiting confidence.'[10]

Suzanne Langer has caught the quality found in Ambiguity which can make it seem instinctively frightening or undesirable: 'Man can adapt himself somehow to anything his imagination can cope with; but he cannot deal with chaos. Because his characteristic function and highest asset is conception, his greatest fright is to meet what he cannot construe.'[11] She was referring to 'the uncanny', but the combined effect of change, diversity and polyvalence as massive amounts of unknown quantities is distinctly similar. Chaos, however, by definition cannot be dealt with: it is the end of order. While the onset of Ambiguity may be as unsettling, it is not the end of order but a change in order, and that is how the world goes. The difference in conception has effects on human reaction. It is when an instance of Ambiguity becomes thinkable that it can be faced, even managed. Therefore when variety of experience and change in general become part of people's expectation of how the world is (as they increasingly do), their arrival will be less disturbing, although particular instances still remain to be coped with. When such a change in attitude takes place, the positive possibilities in Ambiguity become apparent, for any *status quo* will have its anomalies and imperfections. Given that the world is ambiguous, change may be liberating and exciting instead of threatening; diversity may confuse or it may enlarge our conceptions of the possible, including the possible for us; the existence of polyvalence means that the worse as well as the better in present values and interpretations no longer have the air of inevitability. In this way acceptance of Ambiguity may free the understanding for growth and development as well as representing a farewell to familiar conditions.

Acceptance of Ambiguity, however, demands of humanity something like a Gestalt switch in metaphysical perception. On a normal day most people see their foreground and middle distance filled by customary order, while Ambiguity is relegated to the periphery as something which may surprise or threaten by its appearance. Instead of this, Ambiguity should be perceived more as the restless, fruitful and destructive sea, powerfully surrounding temporary archipelagoes of orderliness. There is both hazard and promise in this picture. The sea, although not chaotic, is not manageable or predictable; it has to be co-operated with rather than controlled. It is both life-giving and life-destroying. But there is excitement, demand and achievement in sailing on it, or in fending it off from one's land. For along with the sea exists the land on which we are at home in the order devised there. The shoreline, however, is not static, since that represents the point where Ambiguity and current order meet. The land is not always in opposition to the sea, and the main limitation of this metaphor is that it understates the way in which Ambiguity may infiltrate current order without threat or major disturbance. The point of the Gestalt switch is not to destroy or underrate conceptions of order and continuity, but to underline their openness, or from another point of view, their fragility and vulnerability to unknown elements. The model attitude to follow in that case would be that of fishing communities, who have learned to live by and from the sea without certainty but with tempered hope.

I shall continue to write of 'order', since this term is common along with its shadow side, disorder, and has had powerful connotations of how things should be, although recently satiety with order produced a reaction in favour of disorder, visible in the contemporary arts. As violence and disorder increase in the country, however, there is a movement again towards 'law and order'. But the term 'order' is misleading. It implies a mode of thought in fixed ontological categories assigning to everything and everyone a definite place in the order of things. But now that modern thought works in terms of dynamism and relation, the fixity of 'order' had given way to the contingency of 'balance'. Any order is composed of a contemporary stability or balance among a number of variables in relation and is contingent upon there being no great upheaval within or between these variables, and no disruption from outside.

The difference is particularly clear in what was once called the Order of Nature, which in the eighteenth century was held to be regular, dependable and a model to wayward humanity. The popularity at that time of the argument for God's existence from the design displayed in Nature witnesses to this belief. In the twentieth century, however, conceptions of the Order of Nature have given way to those of ecological balance among an open group of species in relation, whose continuance depends on equilibrium being maintained among its component variables. In a similar way, notions of personal balance in our psychological disposition have superseded the conception of an ordered character with a fixed list of virtues. Indeed in this case Ambiguity has already entered deeply into modern thinking to the point where the ancient ideal of an ordered character seems too rigid and *parti pris* to be open to experience and life.

Individually and communally, however, people require some order for the integration of balanced lives and coherent thought. For its own benefit, therefore, humanity has repeatedly established forms of order through such apparently fixed points as custom, law, religion, morality, philosophy or science. Yet when these are seen in historical perspective it is clear that each of them, like nature, has also been a balance among mutable variables in relation. Moreover, all such oases of stability (which may alternatively be experienced as deserts called peace) occur within the continuing complexity and manifold of the world at large, so that they are constantly challenged from without; and if they cannot adapt, they collapse or atrophy. Expressed in the starkest terms, any human attempt at order is a locally agreed cluster of values and interpretations involving a temporary simplification of complexity and the transient arrest of some aspects of change. On the other hand chaos does not exist, continuity and consensus are common experiences and Ambiguity is not simply disorder, although it may appear in that light when one is threatened or uncomprehending. It represents the forces of change, the multiplicity of possible interpretation and co-operating or competing difference which are the conditions of growth as well as of disruption. Ambiguity is itself ambiguous in its potentiality and its impact.

Ambiguity and action

'Vanity of vanities,' says Ecclesiastes in the Old Testament, 'all is vanity.' He has seen change, inequality and injustice in this life and has no hope after death, so he recommends that people should enjoy their work and recreation under God as they can. Anything more is emptiness and the chasing of wind. A similarly disillusioned conclusion could emerge from the recognition of Ambiguity in every aspect of human and natural possibility. If change is going to occur unpredictably, and if any estimation of how things should be is only one out of many possible, what is the point of taking thought or action? In the end that will be another emptiness and chasing after wind. Any endeavour will be superseded or will change its character ambiguously with the passage of time and interpretations. Many actions which have seemed categorically demanded in one age or culture have no such positive evaluation in another. In this manner the flux within which 'our little systems have their day' makes them relative to their time and place, and even then there are usually alternative ways of doing and thinking. The effect of such relativism upon thought and knowledge will be considered in the next chapter, but for the moment I wish to argue that in an ambiguous world some action is unavoidable and even desirable, and that although it is finite it can be worthwhile.

The kind of action which is required to go on living in a society is unavoidable: even among those 'drop outs' who are parasitic upon the system, some action for survival is required. Ambiguity is not a metaphysic which allows uninvolved contemplation of variety or the disinterested collection of examples, as leisured eighteenth-century divines amassed instances of species in their enthusiasm for nature. Ambiguity is the character of a process in which everyone is caught up, a process of change, polyvalence and diversity, all of which make demands. Change demands adaptation to the new; diversity and polyvalence require choice among possibilities. People must act, individually or communally, in co-operation or conflict, in relation to some at least of the changes continually taking place in society or the world at large. Moreover, it is part of the process of becoming a person to choose certain things and not others from the range of the possible. Rarely, if ever, in any aspect of life, can people have all the things they want, all the time, simultaneously. Choice can be a delight or a frustration, but it is continually required. The most thorough-going relativists, who refuse to commit themselves to a style of thought since all varieties of knowledge are relative to incommensurable presuppositions, still commit themselves to a style of life (as they must) through choice among even greater variety with even less justifiability.

Action is unavoidable, then, as response to the exigencies of life in a mutable and malleable world. It can also be argued that this is a desirable state of affairs. That contention gains its force from the contemplation of one animal scarcely affected by Ambiguity, the three-toed sloth. Change and diversity have passed it by for many generations, while it has lived securely in South America without fear of predators and with no competitors for its abundant and accessible food supply.

Lulled by this security it has sunk into an existence that is only just short of complete torpor. It spends eighteen out of twenty-four hours soundly asleep. It pays such little attention to its personal hygiene that green algae grow on its coarse hair and communities of a parasitic moth live in the depths of its coat producing caterpillars which graze on its mouldy hair. Its muscles are such that it is quite incapable of moving at a speed of over a kilometre an hour even over the shortest distances, and the swiftest movement it can make is a sweep of its hooked arm. It is virtually dumb and its hearing is so poor that you can let off a gun within inches of it and its only response will be to turn slowly and blink. Even its sense of smell, though it is better than ours, is very much less than that of most mammals. And it sleeps and feeds entirely alone.[12]

The sloth's life is not unambiguously bad. Yet since most humans prize society and the use of the senses, and are now very conscious of hygiene, his picture may well lack appeal. What registers as the apathy of the sloth's life has come about precisely because it has had no need to adapt, to choose, to encompass the new or different. No more action takes place than is necessary to survive in his comfortable unchanging circumstances, and so the capacity to respond is diminished. For some people a similar outcome among humans might represent a welcome tranquillity, but for many it would seem an intolerable impoverishment. If the negative view is taken, it is possible to conclude that fluctuating states of affairs which demand alertness and action are preferable to static conditions which diminish or curb responsiveness, even though Ambiguity may sometimes distress and unsettle, or present more complexity than can readily be integrated.

Although our immersion in the changes and chances of this mortal life demands action, that demand is rarely total or continuous. Much of the force of Ambiguity is suppressed in normal current practice. In ordinary times people do not have to confront change and choice daily with the necessity of shaping from zero their reactions to the world's multifariousness. Everyone is educated into social patterns of perception many of which may continue to be taken on trust even while change in others occurs. Other responses are developed a little at a time as part of who people become or what they learn. Most people most of the time do not have to decide whether or not they will shoplift whenever they go into a department store; whether they still prefer jazz to classical music or pop; whether to start the day with muesli, croissants or steak. When simple decisions like these do not have to be made afresh, the attention is freed for other matters and it is usually in larger, single decisions that the stringencies and possibilities of choice become apparent. Yet temptation, new experiences or travel may serve as reminders in relation to such ordinary choices as those given above that *any* ordered response to the variety of possibility is neither immutable nor universal. Even in the most ordinary conduct of daily life Ambiguity remains latent.

To the extent that the process of living, individually or socially, requires it, then, action is necessary. It becomes more than a mere response to circumstances, however, at the point where the choices made and lived with embody values. It is from the point of view of one's values, for instance, that the sloth's life may seem inadequate. Values such as those found in a professional or skilled tradition, in a political party or a religious faith, involve more than survival, for they affect the experienced quality of life. Moreover values create priorities among the varieties of possibility and these guide action, a matter to which I shall return in the next chapter. They make action worthwhile to participants because the values themselves are esteemed. It is worthwhile to someone imbued with the ideal of the redistribution of wealth, or a Christian belief that God is love, to endeavour to bring about a state of affairs where these values obtain, however mixed the result in practice may be. When the value counts for enough, even a mixed result is better from the protagonist's point of view than a status quo where it is absent or minimal. Even if the value is only one's own self-importance, that can act equally as an incentive to use the orderability of the world to one's own advantage as far as possible. In the most ordinary choices of life, such choices as the preference for locally-baked brown bread over mass-produced white, values appear which give a tone, an ethos, to society or one of its sub-groups. This ethos with its values, like other traditions, is passed on to the next generation, but that its members are free to respond in their own way and may reject established values or adopt them, since the world remains orderable in each generation.

When something is believed or valued enough to warrant communication or the conversion of others (not solely religious conversion), it is worthwhile to try to shape the world actively, not merely by reaction to circumstances. The value to the agent will then outweigh the difficulty that all action, choice and decision in the midst of a world in process will be *finite*. Everything and everyone is conditioned by an inherited constitution, by past opportunity of development and by the present degree of freedom to act. People are the result of past finite choices and coexist with other agents who curtail their room to manoeuvre. The most usual possibility is the choice of one thing among many, so that the other possibilities are lost while future choices are further conditioned by the effects of the one made earlier. Further, all response to possibilities and all exercise of values occurs without full knowledge of what is involved, or of what the consequences are to be at that time or later. This is evidently the case with natural responses in evolution, but is equally true even when human thought and foresight are involved. The German Communist Party, for instance, could not foresee that by supporting a socialist candidate in the 1932 elections they would split the vote in such a way that the National Socialist Party came to power. Unless subsequent change obliterates all effects of any action, it remains a datum which may figure for good or ill and in many different ways in later contexts of possibility. No one can avoid action to some extent upon the world, even at the most local or familial level. But action is always partial with unimaginable possible consequences, even when it is the best or clearest we are capable of. New circumstances will alter the character of an action, while the interpretations and actions of others will confuse any original simplicity it had. Finitude, then, is not a fancy from the morbidity of Existentialist writers, but another inescapable result of the way the world is.

Freedom and determination

Human experience of freedom and determination corresponds to a sense of the world and its inhabitants as continuously malleable and continually shaped and reshaped. In the first place such a world makes freedom possible. Freedom is usually discussed in terms of an agent who is sufficiently unconstrained to choose among possibilities and implement that choice. But more is required than that. Freedom requires also a set of circumstances plastic enough to interpretation and decision to be acted upon. If the world were not ambiguous in this way, one could not even deliberate on theoretical possibilities, let alone make and pursue choice. The orderable world is thus a necessary condition for freedom.

Yet the world people experience is also shaped by the decisions, actions and valuations of others, and is in this way already determined. Similarly each person inherits physical and psychological characteristics and is educated into local contemporary patterns of speech, thought, behaviour and society. Even though each person will receive this conditioning and respond to it individually, it does represent a determining influence. But as it is only by devising order in the midst of Ambiguity that we can have a coherent world at all, such initial conditioning is necessary to the emergence of a person. It may be judged adversely, however, if its effects curtail the freedom to develop or instil inflexibility. Yet people could not be so conditioned, determined in this manner, unless they, like the rest of the world, were not to some degree malleable so that their inherent orderability allows them to be shaped and to shape themselves.

At the same time people remain ambiguous – open, unfinished – so no one need be determined past all opportunity of change or novel action. Just as the world remains orderable, although it is constantly ordered, so humanity remains *determinable*, although the present state of order in any life is that person's current determination by outside circumstances and personal orientation. To be ambiguous, therefore, is on the one hand to be changeable and variously interpretable, hence able to be worked on, conditioned, determined by one's own choice and by external happening. But on the other hand ambiguous people are still free for further change with fresh circumstances, new interpretations and their response to all these. In this way most people, apart from those suffering psychological disorders or perhaps the rigidities of a totalitarian régime, are recognizable continuing identities, who have arrived at an adequately orderly way of being in the world. They have continuity and balance in their self-understanding as the norm. Yet they are not so determined that their state is fixed and final, so they remain open to be upset, challenged or enhanced by the variety and change of the world, and able to make some response to that change.

In that case people are sufficiently free to observe Ambiguity and to employ the ubiquitous plasticity of the world so that by their decisions, actions and persuasion of others to their point of view it is possible to bring about change. Nevertheless the exercise of this freedom is counterpoised by present achieved order and the contemporaneous freedom of others to shape the world, including ourselves, for their own ends and values. This freedom in some degree will belong to every ambiguous member of an orderable world. Although degrees of freedom will vary from the width of multiple possibility to the stringency of no visible choice, the fact of freedom cannot be denied, for any determinate state is the result of someone's actualization of past freedom to choose and act.

Freedom, in the more limited sense of the capacity finitely to change states of affairs rather than the capacity to choose among options, is not merely a possibility for humans in a world which is entirely orderable. Cancer cells have the freedom to multiply where they are not inhibited or destroyed; aphids have the freedom to attack lucerne where they are not checked by ladybirds or chemical sprays. We have to contend not only with the orderings of other people, but with those of every particle of matter, all of which develops as best it can in its own circumstances. Further, it is the orderability of the world which allows Marxists, for example, to hope and work for change; but the same opportunity is open to realization by capitalists, while each group in its history and present composition gives rise to circumstances which must be taken into account continually by the other. The world's Ambiguity may be used to implement any values. The Marxist/capitalist example involves competition between only two groups, ignoring their sub-divisions, and is therefore relatively simple. When vast numbers of groupings in the world, human and natural, are seen as making use of its orderability, realizing ambiguously their own possibilities, endeavouring to advance their present form of order in interacting competition and conflict as well as in co-operation, the effect is vertiginous to contemplate and bewildering to encounter.

Natural and moral evil

One of the ways in which Ambiguity most makes itself felt is in the moral sphere where an action may be called good or bad from different points of view, even when values are shared, while different values can produce irreconcilable conflict. I shall return to this point. But it is not only among people that Ambiguity of human evaluation is displayed; it shows itself in nature as well. Some of nature seems propitious, readily beneficial to humanity, while other animals and terrain are called hostile. Moreover disruptions of nature which affect humanity adversely, such as earthquakes, tornadoes and droughts, have been called instances of natural evil. The only evil in them, however, is their undesirable effect on humanity or other species, for such occasions are the effect of the finitude in every response to possibility. Earthquakes, for instance, are almost universally agreed to be due to movement at the juncture of tectonic plates, while the plates themselves are complex and still developing responses to the conditions of earth as they were formed. Yet they are finite responses, making some order of their own but imperfect in regard to every contingency, including humanity's arrival and choice of habitation. The earthquakes of Lisbon in the eighteenth century or of San Francisco or southern Italy in the twentieth are dramatic and disastrous manifestations of the finitude inherent in all actualized possibilities in nature.

Every part of nature does what it can for itself at the time in the midst of its own conditions. Often this has been beneficial to humanity, as when rich deposits of soil make farming flourish. Few, however, have expected 'natural good' to require explanation because of humanity's ingrained habit of expecting beneficial order to be fundamental (whether it is seen to come from God or the way things are). But nature has not been teleologically designed for the benefit of humanity, since it is at best the easily disturbed balance among variables in process of change. The developments of nature which are called hostile and the disasters of 'natural evil' are to be explained, like the benefits with which they coexist, as the result of finitely actualized possibilities in nature which happen in the course of time to affect men and women.

Suffering which derives from the action of humans rather than nature has been called moral evil. It has been described largely in terms of excessive self-concern to the point where others are injured, whether it appears positively in self-aggrandisement or negatively in neglect of others; whether it is demonstrated personally, by a group, by an institution, or by a whole society. I shall return to this matter later. But not all the evil which people do to each other can be accounted for in terms of self-centredness. Some results from the same finitude which was exemplified in nature and which Leibniz called 'metaphysical evil', since it arises from the condition of the world. Humanity cannot foresee all the outcome of its decisions and actions. For instance, missionaries who thought of themselves as bringing the gospel to the Pacific Islands did not know that they also carried European diseases which would decimate the indigenous population. Nor were they aware of the diverse and often destructive effects of their culture on a different society. In so far as such harmful effects are the result of the action of one person upon another, they are moral evil of a kind, but as they happened through finitude and the interaction of circumstances which was not foreseen or intended, they have a metaphysical character and have more to do with the Ambiguity of the world. 'Metaphysical good', when an action has unintended beneficial results, is equally a possibility.

Some have seen in the most horrible passages of human history a radical evil, forces of evil unleashed upon the world which are beyond the power of humanity to control or subdue. But what such forces represent is the accumulating momentum of decisions and actions in which both selfishness and finitude are to be found. As natural evil is to be explained naturally, so moral evil, even of the most powerful and established kind, is to be explained humanly. Its existence shows that it is possible to shape the world in ways widely judged to be abhorrent, and in that case it matters which values and interpretations inspire action in the world. Although Ambiguity means that no one can foresee just how an action will develop, it also implies that at the height of oppression, war or brutality the world in all its features is still ambiguous, still open to change through circumstance, struggle or vision.

Conclusion

The world which I have described in this chapter contains a vast diversity of species, cultures and so forth; there have been many interpretations of itself as a whole and of its elements and inhabitants; it has changed and is changing in various ways at different rates. If this is the case, it will be the kind of world where these characteristics are possible, along with instances of balance, continuity and consensus. It will be orderable, plastic to whatever brings about some actual alteration: it will be open to varieties of understanding, patient of many explanations. This is the character whose existence and impact I have called Ambiguity. *Everything we experience* – humanity and its artefacts, animate and inanimate nature – *is ambiguous*.

Without Ambiguity there would be no world, no history, no culture, no freedom and no future. But Ambiguity alone is not responsible for these things, although it is fatally easy to hypostatize it from being the character of the experienced world into some kind of World-Spirit, giving and taking, making some things possible while complicating others. Ambiguity, strictly speaking, does not *do* anything. It is a necessary though not a sufficient condition for the production of the new or the different. It is not sufficient because there must be something for effort, contingency or thought to work on, since the new is not produced out of nothing, nor without agency. But it is necessary because Ambiguity renders what is perceived workable into new or different shapes, whether in further evolutionary development, a change in technology or yet another interpretation of *Hamlet*. That novelty, if it is to endure at all, has to establish itself in relation to the order or balance currently obtaining. It is either integrated, with the balance duly adjusted to take account of it, or it overturns the contemporary received order. The condition of Ambiguity thus coexists with the establishment of order. It is an uneasy coexistence, however, because order is a temporal balance, not an immutable state. It must maintain itself in face of the incessant possibility of Ambiguity arising through contingency or through the efforts and values of others. The stability of any particular balance may endure for a month or for millennia; it may be shared by a family, a tribe or a major civilization, by humans or by insects. But in every case it is mutable or extinguishable by the effects of the Ambiguity.

The very description of Ambiguity does not escape its own consequences. As I have portrayed it, an ambiguous world is strenuous both in the vigilance required to maintain a preferred order and in the struggle to bring in a new one. Rest can take place only when there is stability enough to permit it; or, for that matter, boredom can take place only when there is sufficient stability experienced as vacuity. But conceivably Ambiguity could have been pictured otherwise. A more contemplative and aesthetically orientated interpretation might rejoice in variety without emphasizing competition, appreciate change without regretting loss or the convulsions of new birth, and find polyvalence intriguing as a puzzle picture. That would certainly complement the somewhat arduous reality I have described.

The very conception of isolating change and variety, arguing from them to the metaphysic of an orderable world with consequent Ambiguity, will at every stage meet with a different response. It is an ambiguous exercise. To share this view involves a readiness to feel what Louis MacNeice called 'the drunkenness of things being various' and to depart from notions of an underlying or teleological unity. 'World is crazier and more of it than we think/Incorrigibly plural.'[13] When one considers how strong the drive to unity of thought and practice has been, the acceptance and elevation of diversity may seem to have sold an ancient and valued pass. The question is whether unity still holds that deep intuitive appeal which is the mark of a habitable metaphysic. For myself it is the 'incorrigibly plural' aspect of the world by which I am convinced. In so far as this has become a common contemporary perception the notion of Ambiguity will be persuasive.

What I have described as Ambiguity has been relative to my own perception, understanding and experience. Relativity is an implication of the orderable world, for each kind of order is related to those who share it, while they in turn are largely conditioned by it. Yet relativity of understanding and thought has seemed as threatening as the loss of any other absolute standard. What in that case happens to truth? Can knowledge be described as a temporal and local balance among variables, and if so, what value can it have or what commitment can it elicit? These questions are so large and so demanding that they require separate and detailed examination in the next chapter.

3

Knowledge and Judgment

The endeavour to entertain Ambiguity is vertiginous, for one ambiguous instance has to be explained by something else which is itself ambiguous, unfinished, open to interpretation. So nothing can be finalized. Taken seriously, it leaves no firm rock on which to stand, no perduring order on which to rely. Yet in practice in our lives only some of the untidy, endlessly individual examples can be grasped at any moment, or can impose themselves contingently upon us as an interruption of our current order. This is just as well, for as people require a degree of order to be an integrated self in a comprehensible context, so our understanding seeks some sense of order, coherence or relation with what we already recognize before it can comprehend what it contemplates. This feature of human understanding is the basis of education, so that although students encounter variety in the process of learning, it is introduced in separate streams of orderly progression from basic units and principles which at the earlier stages have the appearance of objectivity and finality. Such orderliness in knowledge, however, is deceptive when it is taken to imply a corresponding tidiness in the world at large which is studied. For if the world can be described appropriately in terms of diversity, polyvalence and change, any knowledge in the sense of a durable, comprehensible pattern of information will be yielded by a process of selection and shaping rather than discovered ready-made.

Epistemic order

How do we come to know? One answer from child psychology is that 'infants scan the environment and extract a representation of what they see, hear, feel, touch or smell. The representation is called a *schema* and is the child's first knowledge. The infant also possesses the capacity to detect a similarity between a new event and a previously acquired schema, and to form a new schema or to alter an old one in a way that preserves the relation between the ongoing perception and the prior knowledge.'[1] There is a rudimentary Kantianism evident here, for Kant argued that knowledge is the outcome of two factors: the intuitions of the senses and the manner in which the human understanding processes these. His specific apparatus of a single set of categories for the activity of the understanding has been criticized from a later point of view as too rigid, uniform and ahistorical, but his basic conception of knowledge as the combination of external suggestion and human ordering would account for the existence of knowledge in the ambiguous world.

Notions of relativity and projection which are implicit in the ordering of sensation may also be elicited from Kant, although for him an unknowable really real 'thing in itself', which is not posited here, stood behind all phenomenal understanding. Consciousness could not exist without some awareness of space and time, without being able to distinguish near and far, before and after, in relation to the self. Space and time, therefore, Kant argued, are the *forms* of experience, brought to the experiencing rather than gained from it, and necessarily present in every conscious moment. His conception of space and time, like our own everyday one, was Newtonian, and hence has not escaped change, but the relativity of space-time to the observer remains even after Einstein's reformulation of the concepts. Moreover Kant took seriously the way in which the understanding projects its categories onto what it perceives. Before him Hume had argued that notions of causality were attributions arrived at from seeing an alleged cause and effect in constant conjunction. Such attributions were a matter of habit and custom inspired by the imagination and could not be proved. Kant on the other hand claimed that causality is part of the framework in which we think, which we then *project* on to cases of constant conjunction, and other occasions when we want to know why. Although Kant's notions of relativity and projection have to be rendered more open to variety to allow for historical and personal differences of which he was not aware, it can still be said that the understanding creates order out of sensation by relating its intuitions together and to what it already knows, thus projecting its categories of comprehension on to them. 'The understanding' refers to human ability to make sense of and arguments from its intuitions, an ability which is flexible and growing and whose scope changes and diversifies. People change in the acquiring of knowledge, for they do not remain static as mere observers of an outside world.

Further, we learn to observe in terms of socially agreed classes. Outside my window as I write is a laburnum tree in flower. I give meaning to that, in one sense of meaning, by calling it a tree and further a laburnum, since I have learned these English botanical classifications and can apply them to my own schemas. *Concepts* of all kinds are produced by the understanding synthesizing, classifying or applying learned classifications which are then related to each other. The concepts we learn are public and shared, the basis of communication, though they may be developed, changed, dropped or used idiosyncratically, while new ones are regularly being produced. These concepts for everything we can name, which result from the understanding shaping its intuitions into classes and relations with current social meaning, are the basic instruments of *epistemic order* in the ambiguous world. A species achieves biological order within the ecological system when it creates a durable niche for itself which allows it to thrive. A society realizes social order when it observes a coherent body of laws and customs in its community life. Similarly, humanity achieves epistemic order within the world and its reactions to the world when it develops durable, coherent families of concepts which may be grammatically expressed to permit communication and knowledge to flourish.

The 'conceiving' in the formation of concepts was originally a metaphor from the biological act of conception and is still in many ways analogous, if genetic exactitude is not pressed too far. Accounts of knowledge other than the one given above may also be expressed by that metaphor. Thus, just as once a woman was thought to be merely the receptacle and nursery of male sperm, so in *naive realism* the mind has been seen as passively receiving and nurturing impressions direct from the 'real' world outside. *Idealism* on this model becomes parthenogenesis, the virgin birth of ideas without external prompting, ideas which alone are held to be 'real'. Although no description of the acquiring of knowledge is amenable to 'proof', both of these versions appear inadequate biologically and epistemologically through their one-sidedness. In practically all species, male and female contributions are each necessary, and they combine to produce a child who is related to both parents but is not a clone of either. In the same kind of way the activity of the human understanding and the sensation from the world which it synthesizes combine in a concept which reproduces neither parent but is relative to both. A difficulty with this metaphor, however, is that we do not know what either parent (understanding/world) is on its own. Our experience is of their union. To think thus of concepts is to hold a form of *critical realism* which acknowledges both an input of sensation and the concomitant processing activity of the understanding.

Concepts, then, are organized selections from whatever is experienced, and do not simply reflect the world. This is made clear by what Max Black has called their 'looseness', the 'penumbra' of imprecision at the boundaries of each concept.[2] Disputable cases occur at their periphery when they are applied in continuing experience. The tidy patterns of any taxonomy have to be rearranged repeatedly to fit the diversity of cases. The duck-billed platypus, for instance, which is intermediate between a mammal and a bird, caused utter disbelief when a specimen was first received in Britain. Historical concepts like 'revolution' are notoriously loose, covering such disparate examples as palace revolts, peasant uprisings and the Bolshevist takeover in Russia. Sociologists have not yet achieved consensus on the precise definition of as common a concept as 'secularization'.[3] Everyday concepts involve the same kind of difficulties. We may know for particular purposes when something is heavy or light, but cannot state exactly at what point heaviness stops or lightness begins. Max Black points to similar difficulties in applying the concept of baldness, and asks if one hair makes a difference. Even the borders of so definite a concept as 'chair' are hard to define.

Qualified concepts do not bring absolute precision either – 'balding' may imply more hair than 'bald', but is still vague. Such qualification elicits the latent relativity of even the most common or the most highly defined concepts. For a concept is relative not only to its parentage, but also to other concepts and to its current user or users. Youth, for instance, gives way to middle age, but there is no consensus now or historically on when this takes place. Decision on borderline cases can only be arbitrary. Often such arbitrary decisions are necessary, as, for instance, in deciding where wealth begins for tax purposes. If one's income is £1 less than that point one is not wealthy. The absurdity of this demonstrates the problem of making concepts precise. There are even some concepts like 'democracy' which W. B. Gallie has called 'essentially contested', 'concepts the proper use of which involves endless disputes about their proper uses on the part of their users'.[4] The concepts of logic and mathematics, which do not have content from sensation and are not directly applied to experience, are not so affected, although logic has to refine the vagueness of language in such concepts as 'all'. Other concepts, however, reflect the diversity and changefulness of the world and its observers in their penumbra of imprecision. The epistemic order which they produce is not exact in practice, but is normally workable when it permits communication to take place. Without that, knowledge would be impossible. Communication can, however, and frequently does break down. I have recently come across an instruction to plant seeds 'edgeways on', which is hardly illuminating.

Concepts are the basic building blocks of epistemic order. They may expand through analogy or metaphor, and may function in models or theories which produce more complex order. The process of synthesis and classification increases the domain of a concept in a way which is itself implicitly metaphorical, for the known features of one object, or the relations of one system, are perceived by intuition and projection in another. But the activity of using metaphor is much more conscious when two different domains are brought together abruptly, involving an exercise of the imagination to see the point of contact and bringing about a new way of understanding. This has always been the case in poetry. When Wordsworth calls England 'a fen of stagnant water', the concept of England with all its connotations is brought into cognitive relationship with that of stagnant water. Wordsworth presumably intended the revulsion caused by stagnant water to be felt towards England as he saw it then, but when metaphors are used in academic study the emotional connotations are thought to be excluded, although, as I shall argue, they can continue to have effects. One instance of an academic metaphor is the use by social scientists of 'role', taken originally from the theatre where it is a public scripted performance relating to others, and applied to express 'the ways of behaving that are expected of any individual who occupies a certain position'.[5] Metaphors, then, illuminate and enlarge epistemic order by overlapping two originally disparate areas. But by that very fact they are suggestive and useful rather than precise. The way in which a theatrical role follows a script, for instance, led many social scientists into too determined a view of social roles.

The function of a model is that of a 'sustained and systematic metaphor' where large ramifications of structure, relationships and implications are involved.[6] While 'role' itself is a metaphor, dramaturgy provides a whole model for social psychology with such extensive and interrelated concepts as 'role', 'performance', 'script', 'improvisation' and 'audience'. Thus the working relationships in one system are used to give comprehension in another. Ian Barbour, from the point of view of a scientist, describes a model as 'a symbolic representation of selected aspects of the behaviour of a complex system for particular purposes. It is an imaginative tool for ordering experience rather than a description of the world.'[7] There are many types of models from the abstract mathematical kind to the theoretical variety which 'is an imagined mechanism or process, postulated by *analogy* with familiar mechanisms or processes and used to construct a *theory* to correlate a set of observations'.[8] Like concepts, therefore, but in a more elaborate way, models select and organize relevant experience to make knowledge possible. The capacity to imagine, to hold pictures together or transfer them from one thing to another, plays a large part in the whole process and underlies even those theories which give point and meaning to the whole organization, deploying models and concepts to order material. The whole subject could be given much more extensive and refined treatment than this, but my purpose here has been simply to indicate the nature of models and theories and their role in making understandable clusters and hierarchies out of aspects of experience.

Epistemic order is something devised or achieved rather than found, because the world is orderable rather than ordered. Both individual concepts and interrelated conceptual schemes produce epistemic order because they are shared among a group of people or a whole society who see things in broadly the same way and can therefore communicate among themselves. Different groups and societies throughout history may arrive at different concepts, for epistemic order is no more singular than biological or social order. Thus the German concept of *Geist* is not rendered exactly by either 'mind' or 'spirit' in English, while the French *esprit* has different connotations again. Differences at the level of isolated concepts are compounded in groupings of concepts, forms of argument or even forms of language. Many of the well-known problems of translation stem from the varieties of epistemic order at its linguistic level, while differing theories and complementary or incompatible models exemplify that variety in its more recondite aspect.

Just as a concept isolates, synthesizes and gives meaning to a feature of experience, so theories and models focus attention on conceptualized information deemed relevant to them which is shaped into significance and endowed with meaning relative to their assumptions. But the process is rarely as self-conscious, neat or exclusive as its description suggests. There is, for instance, no fixed answer to whether the information or the theory comes first. There may be material hitherto unassimilated, or a theory may be expanding into a new domain, or other historically contingent starting points may obtain. But in any case the moment at which significant order is produced is the union of both parties. Moreover, there is no one formula for the role played by information in relation to the meaning given by the theoretical understanding. Some theories of great generality, such as those concerning the origin of the cosmos, are underdetermined by facts and appeal to, among other things, the elegance and economy of the mathematical models involved. Other theories, dealing with more mundane and specific matters of explanation, prediction or control in the environment, are more firmly anchored by empirical evidence as interpreted by that theory. Then there is also a spiralling interpretative interaction between the human understanding with its potential of theories and models and the information it studies – an interaction of contemplation, investigation, checking, extending, pruning, transferring and so forth, whose pattern varies with different people, different subjects and different levels of generality. Therefore the process which produces extended epistemic order may be indicated, but there is no one recipe for its achievement. Even excluding outside hazards, neither the order of the ingredients, nor their amounts, nor their relationship may be specified uniformly, since they are all so varied. In a diverse and polyvalent world, whose inhabitants are themselves mutable and malleable, that is not a surprising conclusion.

The achievement of epistemic order, however it may be brought about, is a necessary condition for knowledge. But Ambiguity has already left its mark in the relativity of conception; the vague borders of concepts when applied to continuing experience so that they are normally workable rather than always precise – and may indeed even fail to communicate; the unspecifiable way in which any order is devised. All of these points raise questions concerning the meaning of truth, but before turning to that I wish to dwell on the way in which models and concepts can have effects on their users, influencing both the shape and the ethos of the knowledge they produce.

The effects of metaphors and concepts

'It is pictures rather than propositions, metaphors rather than statements, which determine most of our philosophical convictions. The picture which holds traditional philosophy captive is that of the mind as a great mirror containing various representations – some accurate, some not – and capable of being studied by pure non-empirical methods. Without the notion of the mind as a mirror the notion of knowledge as accuracy of representation would not have suggested itself.'[9] As Richard Rorty observes here, pictures of how things are can shape and harden the understanding even when they are not consciously entertained. It is easier to see the effects of a dominant image or metaphor which one does not share, and Rorty objects strongly to 'the domination of the mind of the West by ocular metaphors' on the grounds that it has set up a divide between contemplation and action. He could have added the social point that it has been when men were sufficiently unencumbered by action or general chores that they have had the leisure to indulge and value contemplation, thus setting up philosophical schemas. The image of the mind as a mirror has led not only to the divorce of thought from action but to a relationship of confrontation, face to face with the object of perception, rather than what Rorty calls 'conversation' with what is experienced.[10] The metaphor has therefore dictated a whole way of being in relation to experience.

Mirrors are useful only for the sense of sight, so along with the metaphor has come a cluster of related ocular notions. When we understand something we exclaim, 'I see'; contemplation, vision and insight are considered admirable; perception has been fundamental to epistemology in a variety of ways as touch, by comparison, has not. There are nevertheless the expressions 'to grasp' and 'to come to grips with' for close involvement with a subject, as opposed to the distance implicit in 'perspective'. David Edge, who has commented on this phenomenon, suggests that sight is the dominant metaphor for understanding because our perception of things spatially ordered in relation to us (what Kant would call space as the form of our consciousness) makes the world seem tidy. When we enter a room after an absence, a glance around it is enough to establish that its order still obtains. The effect of the metaphor on attitudes to the world is similar. 'Habitual categories harden and simplify. The world appears a tidy place, requiring the merest glance to reestablish confidence – until, that is, things change. When social change crosses a threshold these neat categories no longer "fit", the habitual pattern collapses and confusion results.'[11] A presumption of order and tidiness therefore goes along with the visual metaphor, but Ambiguity keeps breaking in.

Thus people habitually apprehend in terms of seeing. Unobservables may be understood by physicists through mathematical models giving statistical results, or by theoretical models of behaviour posited by analogy with things seen, yet they remain obscure to the general understanding. But no one can see everything from every possible point of view, and that limitation is implicit in finitude. Moreover, even from our limited perspective, we do not simply see things in the naively realistic conception of receiving faithful impressions. The sense we make of what we see is due to the learned concepts, with their connotations and the expectations they involve, which we bring to the seeing. For the most part people see what they expect or have been taught to see. The process is visible in the history of art, where E. H. Gombrich has traced it in various traditions of artistic perception from the timeless potent images of the Egyptians to the Impressionists' success in conveying the fleeting appearance of light in bright patches with dabs of paint.[12] Although the Impressionists were at first scorned as mere daubers, finally they re-educated the Western world in what and how to see. No later movement has had such widespread and durable success, but each represents a new way of seeing – and feeling about what is seen.

Traditions of perception are not confined to the arts, however, and equally affect what is taken as 'knowledge'. In *The Anatomy of Judgement* the biologist M. L. Johnson Abercrombie describes how her students showed little flexibility in thinking.[13] For instance, they saw in their dissections only what they had been taught they *ought* to see. Their adherence to the tradition they had been reared in crippled their responsiveness to what was before them. To counteract this effect Abercrombie devised a discussion course on the process of arriving at judgments, using puzzle pictures and directing attention to the various assumptions and perceptions involved. The reaction of the students ranged from angry incomprehension to delighted openness. Ways of seeing *anything* may become static within a tradition. This is not necessarily a bad thing where the tradition works satisfactorily, but it does reduce present responsiveness. 'Our veneration for what has already been created, however beautiful and valid it may be, petrifies us and deadens our responses.'[14] So Artaud wrote of plays and developed a 'theatre of cruelty' to break out of the mould. As that reaction illustrates, people need not be trapped against their choice in any tradition experienced as constricting, since they and the world they observe are ambiguous, plastic to fresh shaping. Yet what we are open to are new *ways* of seeing, not the transcendence of all viewpoints. Even the display of disorder in surrealism, or of the absurd in the plays of Beckett or Ionesco, is a way of seeing with its own terms of reference as much as the most rigidly classical painting or drama.

The orderliness of a mode or tradition of perception thus gives access to the thing seen, but at the same time has the effect of excluding or at least subordinating other ways of seeing. Again the theatre illustrates this well. Pirandello exploited the expectation set up by traditional plays to give a destabilizing shock in *Six Characters in Search of an Author*, where the cast alternate between being actors, with actors' problems, and characters in a play. The shock comes because the concept of a play as a self-contained dramatic unit excludes the expectation of seeing actors looking for an author on stage. Yet the post-war audience (1921) recognized a dramatized form of their own insecurity. Since Pirandello's time similar shocks have been incorporated into drama so often that the concept of a play has lost its nineteenth-century rigidity. Therefore, although a tradition of seeing sets up expectations which exclude or subordinate others, that tradition itself may be capable of modification.

When a concept selects certain data from the world it must exclude others, and equally, when a model becomes dominant it excludes or subordinates others, to that extent determining not only what we think, but also the appropriate attitude and behaviour. Popular models exemplify this best, and one which has gained great currency is that of the body as a machine. The picture of the brain as a computer, for instance, has both increased and determined our understanding. The machine model has affected our speech and attitudes to the body: we tick over or we rust; we run down and need tuning up; we let off steam; we are on the right tracks or run off the rails; we have psychological or biological mechanisms; on redundancy or retiral we are on the scrap-heap. But if this model were to become completely dominant, determining *the* way our culture conceives the body to the exclusion of all alternatives, that dominance would carry with it a number of undesirable consequences. Among these would be first, that the body/machine model provides no conceptual apparatus to accommodate such things as organic growths, which are absolutely foreign to machines. Second, while it may assist medical detachment to think in terms of repairing machines rather than assisting sick people, that detachment is not always a desirable or even helpful attitude. Third, if we regard our own bodies as machines we have no way of expressing our psycho-somatic unity. We create a machine for a ghost to be in, so that a person who is not a machine struggles inside a body which is. Alternatively, if the entire person is subsumed under the machine model, a gross and stultifying materialism results, as in 'scrap-heap' – exemplified most dramatically by the two old people in dustbins in Beckett's *Endgame*. These criticisms are not neutral, of course; they are made from an alternative point of view from which the shortcomings of the body/machine model for medical theory, social practice and individual self-understanding are evident as they would not be were there no alternative.

So concepts and models exclude and determine, although in an ambiguous world this does not happen absolutely. They are not simply useful, value-free tools since they reflect and influence attitudes well beyond their specific technical application, while their capacity for determining thought is in proportion to their success in academic communities or in society at large. The influence and determination may be extremely fruitful and stabilizing, however, and some determining will always occur, because order is itself current determination. The important point is that concepts carry connotations which mould expectations, attitudes, values and beliefs. A way of seeing is not a neutral point of view. While our understanding imposes meaning upon the world, that meaning has social, psychological and imaginative ramifications which impose themselves on us.

Edge has written of the use of models: 'An uncertain or obscure area is construed in terms of one both familiar and apparently similar. Inappropriate aspects of this transfer may remain unnoticed in the first flush of clarification that the new metaphor appears to bring.'[15] The sting in this quotation could well apply to the body/machine model, and another equally well-known example mentioned briefly by Edge began when Kepler proclaimed that he would no longer regard the world as an organism but as a clock. Even when this metaphor and the numerous machine models which succeeded it were lost sight of, the shift of perception and orientation for which they provided imaginative conceptual incitement continued. In general terms expectations and attitudes changed from passivity and resignation in the face of experience to investigation and control, for a clock is a manageable entity with no mystery, detached from humanity but controllable by it. The confrontation Rorty noted in philosophy was thus transferred to the scientific attitude, at least in theory. Even Hume's scepticism about the philosophical bases of empiricism (a 'mitigated scepticism' which would not interfere with action[16]) could not stem the confidence of the empirical attitude generally because that was eminently successful. It raised issues, provided results, extended its influence and kept Ambiguity so powerfully at bay that the world itself appeared to have the order scientific empiricism supposed it to show. The information processed seemed to lead to final truth, and not to the truth relative to the prediction and control required for an organism in its environment.

There was no serious rival to this mind-set, for more personal or ambiguous accounts of reality were consigned to the unfashionable domains of fiction or continental philosophy, since a successful model excludes or subordinates alternatives. Theological views of the world as God's creation could be disregarded, for in principle they invoked a God who could do anything, and thus did not assist in prediction and control, and in practice they were unproductive of significant empirical results. Therefore at best they could be held only privately, concerning private lives, while scientific empiricism expressed public attitudes to public matters. It appears to have been the crisis of conscience over the atomic bomb which brought some scientists to face a responsibility beyond their engineering capacity and also suggested to a wider group in society that a view of the world as divorced from humanity, whose mission was to manipulate or control it, was not the unalloyed good or simple truth it had appeared. Since then the concatenation of ecological difficulties, population growth, depletion of non-renewable resources and so forth has further undermined humanity's belief in a world set over against itself, of which it is master. This is not to belittle or deny the results of empirical attitudes and theories. No one would wish to return to the primitive medicine of humours and cupping, nor to the attitude which was content to posit the spontaneous generation of rats from piles of dirt, since they were found in constant conjunction. But this account does illustrate the contention that theories, models and concepts, which all produce the order in which alone knowledge is possible, are *ways* of seeing, and that 'inappropriate aspects' may lurk in even the most fruitful models, or in the beliefs and attitudes which accompany them.

Since the late 1950s another line of attack has developed from within the scientific community itself. The empirical method had been so successful and dominant that it appeared to embody the only possible approach and to be free from subjective distortion. Now it is denied that there can be neutral observation language with no theoretical presuppositions.[17] All data are theory-laden: that is, concepts and theories are assumed in all research, so that observations are made in their terms. Choice between theories, therefore, especially those of great generality, is extremely difficult because the only available criteria are themselves dependent on the theories involved with their different individual assumptions. Further, no theory is simply verified, because at any point future findings may conflict with it, and other theories may account for the evidence differently and at least as satisfactorily. This is the discovery that there is no timelessly true epistemic order. Outright falsification, however, is not so likely as modification or abandonment for an alternative, for theories, even in the face of anomalies, provide order for research and elicit commitment until a better way of solving problems persuades people to change. Thus the theory or 'paradigm', which is Kuhn's term for the exemplar of what a particular kind of scientific work involves and the web of assumptions with which it operates, has an influence far greater than was supposed. It imposes its own point of view, its own inter-subjectivity, upon its proponents. Normal research, so far from wresting Nature's secrets from her, as Francis Bacon hoped in the seventeenth century, is 'an attempt to force nature into the preformed and relatively inflexible boxes that the paradigm supplies'.[18] Although the debate continues in the philosophy of science on what brings about change, and what role paradigms play, there is no doubt that another shift in perspective is taking place among an increasing number of professionals, if not yet in society at large.

Metaphors, models or theories, then, are ways of seeing and organizing information which have connotations and involve social consequences. Implicit in them all is a cluster of metaphysical beliefs concerning the nature of the world and humanity's relation to it. One such collateral of empiricism which must be discussed by anyone advocating Ambiguity is the belief in the self-consistency of nature. If experiments are to be repeated, if accounts in documents from the past are to be entertained, if induction is to have any force, and even if the law of contradiction is to apply in the world, nature must be adequately self-consistent. Indeed past, present and future must be comparable in significant ways for the thesis of Ambiguity to apply. Ambiguity is a different matter from chaos. In a chaotic world there would be no order and no ordering could be effected: it is total absence of order. An ambiguous world, on the other hand, is the result of its orderable nature being differently acted upon to produce varieties of order, although any order is vulnerable to new perceptions or changed circumstances. The existence of Ambiguity, therefore, relativizes any particular order, but that order will have its own general self-consistency while it lasts. Any achieved order will obtain for a particular time and in the eyes of a particular group. For as long as it obtains, induction based on it will be possible and comparisons may be made with the past. A historian has to discern which past orders – physical, social, economic and so forth – have remained comparable: where difference must be taken into account and where regularities may be relied on. General theories or assumptions, such as that economic deprivation always produces discontent, have to be tested in the interpretative process with documents from the past.

A simple example of induction at work is the generalization that acorns grow into oak trees, because all hitherto known oak trees have established a biological order which includes their propagation by acorns, and we expect this to continue. But a stress on Ambiguity is a reminder that no order is unchangeable, since the world is unfinished and in constant interaction of circumstances bringing about uneven change. Therefore any particular acorn may be eaten by pigs, rotted by water or starved of earth before it becomes an oak tree; secondly, oak trees as a whole have to maintain their order in the face of competition, disease, possible meteorological change or any other adverse happening; thirdly, in response to new conditions, oak trees themselves may change over a massive amount of time, perhaps evolving ways of propagation other than acorns. In short, part of what Ambiguity stands for and gives importance to is all that makes induction uncertain. Nevertheless, given that the biological order of oak trees is contingent in the ways described – and in this case the ways are trivial for most probable purposes – as long as it endures acorns will (generally) turn into oaks. In like manner, but with much stricter controls, scientific theories which create their own epistemic order permit induction to take place within that order as long as it obtains. Even to call the world 'ambiguous' is to introduce a kind of replicable perception which embraces diversity, polyvalence and change. The expectation that the world will continue to be ambiguous is based on the assumption that the characteristics of diversity and change will continue in the future as they have in the past. What would upset that is not, in this case, further Ambiguity, which would only lend support, but the end of Ambiguity in annihilation. With Ambiguity knowledge is not provisional in the sense of being not yet final, but it is provisional bbbecause there is no other kind while the world endures.

The relativity imposed by the world's Ambiguity is visible in the number of conditions which have to be replicated exactly in an experiment for the same results to emerge. Self-consistency is relative to these conditions and is achieved only by excluding the hazards of the world and rigorously imposing order. The same exclusion and ordering is visible in the logician's rubric 'if, and only if . . .'. Logic itself provides formulae and processes which ensure the validity of the form of an argument but have no bearing on the empirical state of the premisses. 'If p, then q: p, therefore q' is a valid form whether p stands for 'it is raining' and q for 'I shall stay in', or p stands for 'my cow is sick' and q for 'some witch has cast a spell on it'. In so far as logic as a set of laws deals with what must be the case if an argument is to have validity, it is 'topic-neutral', an ordering without content, and is exempt from the ambiguity of input. Anthony Quinton argues that the concepts of logic, such as 'not', 'all', 'or', are *a priori* and syntactic, for 'their function is not to describe the world of experience but to arrange and articulate the descriptions we can give of it'.[19] Yet logic does not escape polyvalence of thought, for there exist alternative logics, many-valued logics in which, for instance, there is no place for the law of excluded middle (that is, that something must be either A or not-A). This is one of the grounds on which Quinton allows that even the laws of logic are 'conventions', while Nicholas Rescher from a Kantian perspective calls their status 'regulative', useful for thought rather than constitutive of how things are.[20] This definition applies even to the most fundamental law of contradiction, namely, that nothing can be both A and not-A, or that proposition p and its negation not-p cannot both be true together. Nevertheless, as Quinton and Rescher agree, however conventional or regulative the law of contradiction may be, it is required if communication or thought is to have a viable mode of negation. It is a fundamental piece of ordering.

In this section I have been concerned to show that in the use of concepts and models it is always possible for accompanying connotations, attitudes, beliefs and values to make themselves felt in varying degrees. As the dominance of scientific empiricism has been the most influential, that in particular has been discussed, together with its belief in the self-consistency of nature. The conclusion is that knowledge, even of the most fruitful and durable kind, has ambiguous features in the way it determines thought and attitudes to the world.

Truth

'At what a dusty answer gets the soul
When hot for certainties in this our life!'

What Meredith expressed poetically in *Modern Love* has been more soberly put in recent philosophical discussions of truth, or the application of 'true'. These reflect a diminution of claims to certainty and an appeal to public agreement quite unlike the optimistic quest for truth in earlier epistemologies.

Of traditional accounts of truth, one which has commanded widespread allegiance in this country is the Correspondence Theory. 'To say that what is said is true is to say that what is said corresponds to a fact; to discover whether what is said is true is to discover whether there is such a corresponding fact.'[21] There may on this account be different criteria for truth according to what kind of fact is at issue, but truth itself is correspondence to how things are. On this view, commonsensical though it is, there is no place for the activity of the understanding in its concepts, models and theories, that activity which makes a fact what it is by synthesizing information and endowing it with meaning. Alan White, whose definition I have given above, instances 'the battle of Waterloo was fought in 1815'. But even in regard to this apparently straightforward statement, before a corresponding fact could be established, numerous concepts would have to be agreed on, of which 'battle' is only the most obvious. There are other difficulties with this theory, such as what correspondence consists of, whether it is only basic propositions which correspond, and what these might be. But from the point of view out of which this chapter is written its principal defects are its assumption that 'how things are' is uniform, and its denial to the human understanding of any process but checking to arrive at truth.

The Coherence Theory is very different. It has been invoked for the truth of a metaphysical system, such as Hegel's, and derived from systems of pure mathematics and theoretical physics by Neurath. In either case it is the comprehensive system in its coherence which is held to be true. All parts mutually corroborate one another, and at their most secure are bound by ties of logical implication. While a number of criticisms have been made of the Coherence Theory, to which I shall return, its chief shortcoming is that *as a theory of truth* it lacks the continuing input from, and modification by, experience of the ambiguous world. This relationship I have described as a component of epistemic order, and of the process of interpretation to and fro between conceptualizing humanity and the world it studies and describes. Coherence itself, however, remains important.

A third theory is the Pragmatic: the true is what works. On this account scientific hypotheses or ordinary beliefs and opinions are instruments which are true if they work in practice and fulfil whatever function they are seen to have. It is an important matter in an ambiguous world that a theory or concept should work, but it seems to me rather a justification of a claim to knowledge than a description of truth, so I shall leave consideration of Pragmatism to a later stage.

In most discussions of truth there appears a strong presumption that it is of one kind and timeless, in that it is not affected by the vagaries of our finite understanding and our mutable world. Truth may have shed its mystical overtones of being the One over against the many, the Unchangeable beyond decay, but unity and objectivity are still commonly regarded as its essential characteristics. Truth has been seen as the ultimate, or at least the correct, order; how things really are. Yet if this world is not primarily ordered, but rather is malleable into many and diverse orders among which there is at best balance and at worst incompatibility, the presumption of timeless, unitary, basic truth is undermined. Whatever one may want to say about God, human truth about the world is relative to the change and diversity perceived in the world, and will therefore be pluriform. It will be relative also to those who use current models and concepts which depend on agreed intersubjectivity rather than on a secure objectivity. Not only conceptions of 'the Truth' are so affected, but 'truth' understood as a property, value, standard or possession of beliefs, theories or statements concerning the world. Truth is relative to the historical conditions in which it obtains, however brief or enduring these may be.

Arguments against such an apparent capitulation to relativity are most commonly found among those who give no determining role to human concept formation, who believe in effect that orderliness is to be found rather than created. J. L. Mackie, for example, makes a modest but firm claim for 'simple truth': that 'for a statement to be true is for things to be as they are stated to be'.[22] He does allow that scientific hypotheses and commonsense claims to truth may be fallible, so 'although it is rather rash to claim simple truth even for such well-confirmed theories as the gene theory of inheritance or special relativity, it is not at all rash to claim simple truth for a careful report, checked by a second observer, about the number of chairs in a room, or for the anti-Berkleian thesis that material things exist independently of minds. In some very obvious areas simple truth is within our power.'[22] But inter-subjective concepts of number, chairs and matter all enter in here, and it is only *given these agreed concepts* that simple truth obtains on an inter-subjective or communal basis. A counter of chairs, for instance, would suppose that the normal counting in tens would apply, and might hesitate over the classification of a bean chair, while Berkeley, who was an immaterialist, would differ so thoroughly and consistently on 'matter' that Mackie would have to appeal to common-sense majority usage much as Hume did.

An account of the criterion of truth which allows for the inter-subjectivity of concepts is given by D. W. Hamlyn in *The Theory of Knowledge*. 'The criterion of objectivity and therefore of truth and fact is public agreement. Normally if people agree on something it is true . . . if people did not agree in judgements there would be no room for the notion of truth; if there were, for example, universal disagreement about every matter, it would be unintelligible to speak of truth, since the notion would not get a purchase.'[23] Inter-personal agreement is thus what Hamlyn calls 'the point of application' of the concept of truth, since this, like all concepts, is social. Further, 'we can raise the question of what is objective and what is not only within the conceptual scheme which we have. It may be that this fact prohibits the possibility of attainment of absolute truth in the sense postulated in traditional epistemology, but that is a wild goose chase in any case.'[24] Hamlyn is not inhibited by this from ascribing truth and discussing its conditions, since he optimistically takes the social conceptual scheme to be normally without difficulties in application.

Awareness of relativity, of having a particular way of seeing things which is neither universal nor timeless, has increased, however unwelcome it may be to those who believe that some form of atemporal objectivity is a necessary condition for truth. Relativity need not be vicious, however. It need not mean that standards are lost, that truth is forfeit, that every man does what is right in his own eyes. But before any distinctions are made which will rescue values and commitment, the primary objection to relativity must be aired. That can be expressed in Copleston's criticism of Nietzsche's conception of relative truth: 'it presupposes the possibility of occupying an absolute standpoint from which the relativity of all truth or its fictional character can be asserted, and . . . this presupposition is at variance with the relativist interpretation of truth. Further, this comment by no means loses its point if Nietzsche is willing to say that his own view of the world, and even of truth, is perspectival.'[25] Copleston is right that there is no absolute point from which one may say that everything is relative. Even the perception that relativity reduces the status of all arguments to proposals and all demonstrations to recommendations does not remove the difficulty. Thus, although I am *recommending* Ambiguity, because I am myself persuaded of it, rather than naively attempting to *prove* its existence and its implication of relativity, nevertheless I am propounding a universal position which makes an exception on its own behalf to the limitations of points of view.

That difficulty, however, as Ernest Gellner points out, is endemic in philosophy: 'making an exception on one's own behalf, having difficulty in accounting for oneself, is the professional ailment of philosophers, and is virtually written into the terms of reference under which they work.'[26] Certainly other influential examples could be given. The Coherence Theory of truth, for instance, which claims that truth lies in coherent systems, refutes itself in a facile manner since it is a theory, not a system, and therefore cannot be true. Wittgenstein in his *Tractatus* argued a number of things which by his own criteria could not be said, then at the end recommended throwing away the ladder which had taken him to where he was. At the very least, then, relativity is in wide philosophical company in failing to account for itself. Moreover, the objection, while logically irrefutable, misses, or avoids, the main point. It endeavours to put the onus of proof on to the relativist, whose position is that there is no proof. *The possibility of proof with its unshakeable foundations and universal import is precisely the matter at issue.* 'Each time that an objectivist has come up with what he or she takes to be a firm foundation, an ontological grounding, a fixed categorial scheme, someone has challenged such claims and has argued that what is supposed to be fixed, eternal, ultimate, necessary or indubitable is open to doubt or questioning. The relativist accuses the objectivist of mistaking what is at best historically or culturally stable for the eternal or permanent.'[27] For the relativist in that case there exists incorrigible plurality rather than a series of mistakes which are corrected en route to truth, while 'proof' is relative to whatever part of that plurality is espoused. Whether or not Kuhn may properly be called a relativist, his argument concerning the effect of paradigms on scientific inquiry, so that research is conducted in their terms, is typical of the comparative historical reasoning which produces this outlook. His conclusions have been summarized thus: paradigms are 'logically *incompatible* (and, therefore, really in conflict with each other); *incommensurable* (and, therefore, they cannot always be measured against each other point by point); and *comparable* (capable of being compared with each other in multiple ways without requiring the assumption that there is or must always be a common, fixed grid by which we measure progress).'[28]

Variations of the opposition between 'objectivists' and 'relativists' are common today in every field of knowledge. Richard Bernstein notes this and asks: 'Why have relativists been unconvinced when objectivists argue, as they almost invariably do, that relativism is self-referentially inconsistent, self-defeating and incoherent? Why have objectivists been unmoved when time and time again it is shown that they have failed to make the case for the objective foundations for philosophy, knowledge or language, and that the history of attempts to reveal such foundations must

be judged thus far to be a history of failures?'[29] His tentative
answer is that, 'Perhaps, despite the self-understanding of many
philosophers that they are the defenders of rational argument,
the positions they take are influenced more by social practices,
metaphors, matters of temperament and other non-rational
factors than the arguments upon which they place so much
emphasis. Perhaps, despite grand claims about clear and distinct
ideas, transcendental proofs, conceptual necessities, philosophy
never has been and never will be more than a shifting battleground
of competing opinions.' I have sympathy with this answer,
although I find the conclusion too bleakly put in that Bernstein
does not allow here for success and satisfaction, two matters to
which I shall return. But I believe that there is more to the division
than is often the case with different points of view, for the move
from 'objectivism' to 'relativism' is as great and as fundamental
to thought as the Copernican revolution was to science. It is
therefore not lightly undertaken: as with the Copernican revolution there are arguments on both sides, but there are also more
fundamentally two different ways of experiencing the world
involved. One sees the world progressing towards or falling from
'unity' and 'truth'; the other finds variety and change to be part
of its continuing character. In the sixteenth century there were
philosophers and theologians who had great satisfaction from,
and had given a lifetime's work to, the geocentric conception of
the universe, and now there are philosophers, scientists and
theologians who adhere equally strongly to objectivism. I recognize that this way of putting it sets relativity in the role of the
unwelcome newcomer who will yet succeed in spite of initial
opposition.

One reason for the resistance to relativity may be that it leaves
humanity making its own orders with no final validation and no
security of objective order to relate to, at a time, moreover, when
the West has lost most of the confidence it showed in the
nineteenth century. Relativity certainly evokes a greater modesty
in human pretensions. Another reason may be that it appears to
give no handle for rational decision, action or advance. But this
is the case only if the response to relativity is the paralysed
contemplation of variety. Another dangerous response is
described by H. S. Hughes in his study of European consciousness
from 1890–1930 when intellectuals began to take seriously the

relativity of a point of view: 'from an awareness of the subjective character of social thought it was an easy step to denying the validity of all such thought – or, alternatively, to a desperate resolve to "think with the blood".'[30] Yet neither irrationalism nor disengagement is a necessary consequence of relativity. Both seem like over-reaction to a loss of absolutes. At this point a distinction can be made between *relativism*, which throws in the epistemological sponge at the the onset of diversity, and *relativity*, a stance which sees variety and change as a call to judgment among possibilities and the justifying of one's option. For relativism things may be described, but they must be left where they are: since no absolute judgment is possible, no judgment among the variety is to be made. I shall argue, however, that contingent judgments are made all the time, and that justification of these choices has some force, even if it is not absolute.

Gellner has noted that when *relativism* becomes normative ('*cuius regio eius veritas*'[31]) no distinctions may be made between better and worse in perceptions, morals, cultures and so forth, and therefore no action is possible. He argues that the real refutation of relativism which 'takes what others regard as a problem and uses it as a solution' is that it is empty.[32] 'Given that our problem arose precisely from the collisions, total disintegrations, erosions and fissures of these alleged units, the advice to return to them not only quite misses the point of our predicament but also corresponds to no available course of conduct or thought.'[33] He is well aware of the formal difficulties in justifying one's decisions, choices and actions at a time when traditional norms have lost all authority. Yet the practical problem is inescapable, so 'we can but make do with the best solution available, whether or not it satisfies the strictest formal criteria'.[34] His solution is what he calls '*critical* monism', 'the attempt to restore intellectual order by the sustained application of simple, delimited, lucid principles, principles designed to isolate and use the marks of genuine knowledge, an attempt which is mandatory in conditions of intellectual chaos such as in fact often obtain – such monism is absolutely essential for our life'.[35] What Gellner calls critical monism has some similarity to what I have called relativity. Both demand that one choose the best one knows (intellectually, morally and so forth), although there is no absolute justification for any one choice.

The way in which relativity can work, although riddled with contingency, is best illustrated in that area where it has been acknowledged longest, that is, in the study of history and among historians. It is interesting to note that it was when the philosophy of science began to be conscious of its *historical* development that the question of relativity arose there too. The sense that everything is related to its time and possibilities arose from historical consciousness of the variety of thought, belief and social organization within and between different past epochs, and between past and present. Gibbon wrote his *Decline and Fall of the Roman Empire* in 1776 without any great consciousness of difference. He judged the Romans as if they were his contemporaries, so that where they failed to hold some enlightened eighteenth-century view he regarded them as deficient. But two years earlier Herder had already conceived the relative propriety of everything in its historical context: 'everywhere on our earth, whatever could be has been, according to the situation and wants of the place, the circumstances and occasions of the times and the nature and general character of the people.'[36] From this emphasis the sympathetic sensitivity of historians to the past has been developed.

With the increase of its ability to investigate and explain the varieties of the past, historical study in the nineteenth century adopted the confident posture of science then and in the twentieth. It expected, in Ranke's words, by 'the strict presentation of the facts' to show 'how things really were' and even to rise to 'a knowledge of the objectively existing relatedness'.[37] Historical positivism flourised with Comte, Taine and Buckle. Taine's maxim '*après la collection des faits, la recherche des causes*' is analogous to recently past scientific views on the straightforward collection of observations leading to the erection of a theory. That positivism, however, was challenged by the perception of what happened in practice, and historians had in general decided that their study showed aspects of both an art and a science long before the social sciences had any doubt that they were correctly named.

The Rankean and positivist emphasis on facts, for instance, was questioned. 'The nineteenth century was, for the intellectuals of Western Europe, a comfortable period exuding confidence and optimism. The facts were on the whole satisfactory, and the inclination to ask and answer awkward questions about them was correspondingly weak.'[38] Perceptions like this indicate a consciousness not only of the variety of the past, but also of the influence which the present exercises on a historian's attitudes, an influence which can persist through the interpretative process with the sources, and may indeed even direct that. In the writings of the Victorian Roman Catholic Lord Acton, for instance, 'moral judgments appeared in their most trenchant and uncompromising form'.[39] Again, E. H. Carr quotes Burckhardt on the Thirty Years' War: 'It is scandalous for a creed, no matter whether it is Catholic or Protestant, to place its salvation above the integrity of a nation', and comments: 'It was extremely difficult for a nineteenth-century historian, brought up to believe it is right and praiseworthy to kill in defence of one's country, but wicked and wrong-headed to kill in defence of one's religion, to enter into the state of mind of those who fought the Thirty Years War.'[40]

Examples could be multiplied of assumptions, theories and the absolute presuppositions of an age influencing historical interpretation in subtle ways, although blatant examples receive short shrift from colleagues. Further, historical 'facts' are not simple, fixed and indisputably objective. In Collingwood's moderate description which I shall take as a paradigm of what a 'fact' is: 'All that a historian means when he describes certain facts as his data is that for the purpose of a particular piece of work there are certain historical problems relevant to that work which for the moment he proposes to treat as settled: though if they are settled, it is only because historical thinking has settled them in the past, and they remain settled only until he or someone else decides to open them.'[41] This puts the establishment of the fact corresponding to 'the battle of Waterloo was fought in 1815' into its contingent perspective.

Nevertheless historians are not blind guides in a welter of relativism. It has not been thought useless to continue the study of history, nor to distinguish between better and worse accounts of the past, although facts are what is for the moment settled while the selection and ordering of historical data goes hand in hand with conceptual interpretation influenced by the present. In the first place, the Ambiguity of the world, as so often, cuts in two ways: it produces the variety and polyvalence of the past, but it also means that historians, malleable like everyone else, are open not only to present ordering and priorities, but also to those of the past. Because people are ambiguous they can transcend their present, either into their own future developments, or into imaginative connection with the past. Indeed the very difference between past and present can give the historian an advantage in seeing what is taken for granted by his or her contemporaries, while an acquaintance with past historians in their strengths and weaknesses may increase self-awareness. Moreover, the case of historical study illustrates the importance of justification, the discussion of which may be anticipated here. A historical account has to be justified by its cogency in accounting for relevant evidence; by its fairness to all participants; by the validity of its argument (here usually in terms of the humanly rather than the logically possible); by its persuasive powers in giving a credible narrative of the past in relation to what is already known, whether it reinforces, questions or overturns previous interpretations; and by its ability to endure through further research and explanation. These are stringent standards, and while historians no longer claim to tell us how things really were, an account which fulfils them may claim to be the truth relative to the conditions in which it was produced. As Marwick has written: 'History is a dialogue. Each age must reinterpret its own past. Nonetheless with advances in technique, with advances in self-awareness, and with the powerful shoulders of our predecessors bowed for us to stand on, there is also absolute advance in the quality, the "truthfulness" of history.'[42]

Throughout this discussion of relativity in historical study I have made comparisons with the attitudes and methods of science in general, although the content of the two disciplines is very different. The pattern of empiricist success followed by doubt about the pureness of objectivity is visible in both. It has simply been longer the case with science that 'the facts were on the whole satisfactory and the inclination to ask and answer awkward questions about them was correspondingly weak', as Carr wrote of positivist history. The loss of confidence in historical study was not seriously regarded outside the discipline, since history dealt with the past, always less sure than the present, and with evidently mutable humanity. Its knowledge, although important in its own field, did not constitute a criterion of what knowledge is. Science, on the other hand, has provided such a criterion, but now even the scientific citadels of objectivity have imploded, if it is the case that there are no neutral observation statements, since all data are theory-laden. Presumably scientific accounts will now have to be justified in the same manner as historical renderings. Cogency, validity and durability are likely to be common criteria, though there will also be different standards since, for example, economy and simplicity, prized by scientists, are not necessarily virtues in historical accounts. *The conclusion is that relativity has in no way diminished the success and usefulness of historical study, so there is no reason to fear that the effects of recognizing it will be catastrophic elsewhere.*

In that case objectivity in its most stringent traditional conception, independent of human construction with its frailty and finitude, gives place to the inter-subjectivity achieved either by a group of highly-trained professionals or by society at large. The experience and intelligence of the former, and the sheer size of the latter, underwrite the viability of their inter-subjective concepts. To deny the possibility of objectivity is not to deny the existence of the world independent of our conceptions of it. The only implication we can properly draw is personal, namely that we can order and hence understand the world we intuit through sensation only by means of our concepts with their content of human, social meaning. We arrive at the truism that humans understand the world humanly: 'reality' for humans is some particular form that understanding happens to take. When Ambiguity becomes part of such understanding it is part of reality. The relativity inherent in the condition introduces a degree of humility into human thought concerning its powers, its objects and its truth. But these powers, objects and truth remain. Objectivity is to be reinterpreted as the current inter-subjectivity of a dominant group or society;[43] facts are best expressed as what may be taken as settled for the time being. What, then, is truth?

Concepts and their elaborations may be challenged at two points – in their formation and in their application to a certain state of affairs perceived in the world. They may be inadequately formed, either in content of information, which may be insufficient or partly irrelevant, or in the meaning given to that information. *Vis dormitiva* (sleep-inducing power), a concept once invoked to explain the soporific properties of opium, is inadequate in both content and meaning, for it explains nothing. Again, a concept may be adequately formed but inappropriately applied, as early anthropologists applied their own society's concepts of, for instance, religion, to the cultures they studied. Concepts may thus be seen and agreed to be inadequate or inappropriate, and this in Hamlyn's turn of phrase, is the 'point of application' of the concept of falsity for those who do not share that viewpoint and therefore also the arguments by which it is defended. Truth is the converse of such falsity. When a concept is agreed to be adequate and its application is seen to be appropriate, it is true. A statement embodying a group of such concepts in logically valid form is therefore true.

This account gives logical and historical priority to the concept, since any statement presupposes acquaintance with the concepts it contains. It therefore emphasizes the applicability of the concept, rather than a fact to which it corresponds. The application is appropriate rather than correct because a concept may expand metaphorically, and at any point its use is that deemed suitable. In face of the Ambiguity of the world the clear-cut precision of 'fact', 'correct' and 'correspondence' has given way to the more supple, arguable but no less demanding notions of conceptual 'adequacy', 'appropriateness' and 'applicability'. A defence of the adequacy and appropriateness of any particular concept in any specific situation is an instance of the justification of knowledge to be discussed in the next section.

One formal condition of adequacy, however, relevant to a discussion of truth, is the coherence of a concept, and *a fortiori* the coherence of clusters and hierarchies of concepts in models and theories. A concept is the smallest unit of coherence in any epistemic order. Hamlyn describes the criteria for a concept thus: 'To have the concept of x, to know what it is for something to be an x, we need to know not only the formal defining conditions for an x, but also what counts as an x.'[44] To have a concept of 'bed', for example, we need to know what makes a bed a bed, that is, to know what conditions have to be fulfilled for something to be a bed; and be able to recognize instances of beds when they occur, applying the concept correctly. In the process of acquiring a concept the two go hand in hand as interpretation and experience interact. It is the coherence produced by defining conditions which permits continuing and novel application. This coherence shows in the internal relation of these conditions – for example between the shape and purpose of a bed, and in the completeness of the sum of these conditions, so that a chair, for instance, will not be mistaken for a bed. Such coherence is necessary for adequacy and thus truth.

Yet precision in the formation and application of a concept is not entirely possible. Concepts represent a making rather than a finding of order; they are the social organization and application of information from a world experienced as changing, polyvalent and diverse. I have already described the penumbra of disputable cases which lie on their borders, fulfilling only some of the defining conditions (for 'bed' these might include chaise-longue or lilo). Then there are 'essentially contested' concepts like 'work of art', where there is no settled agreement on the definition. It is important to acknowledge and be aware of this infiltration of Ambiguity into the bases of knowledge, though most communication within a society is not vitiated by it. For however vague the borders or varied the use, there must be a sufficiently consistent core for a concept to be formed at all, and from that core defining conditions may be inferred. Thus there is an agreed cultural concept of red, although it shades off into purple or orange. Further, a concept may be subdivided into more precise units where these are required, as fashion designers, for instance, have numerous colour concepts from wine to apricot to cover their nuances in the reddish part of the spectrum. Academic concepts may also use subdivision to decrease the penumbra of imprecision; yet the tighter a concept is drawn, the less it applies to, and the less it can accommodate new developments. The proliferation of small, precise concepts inhibits the imagination and could lead to a rigid scholasticism. A degree of flexibility is required even in law, where the need to draw defining lines is more acute than in most subjects. The coherence of a concept in practice, therefore, will not always display sharp-edged precision, yet sufficient coherence is necessary if we are to know what we are talking and thinking about. 'Sufficient' is a deliberately vague word, for the standard of precision required will vary according to the context of use. But any concept which is a candidate for truthful application must be sufficiently coherent for communication and thought to proceed, and for arguments and theories to be built up without intolerable ambiguity. Most concepts in ordinary use are indeed so coherent that they are taken for granted.

Concepts do not stand on their own. The understanding of any single concept involves understanding a whole cluster of related ones. To understand the concept 'bath', for instance, as a modern article of bathroom furniture, one has to understand at least the concepts of taps, water and plugs as well, even if plumbing remains a mystery. Similarly, to understand academic subjects, or theories and schools within subjects, one must understand complexes of internally related concepts. The nature of that internal relation will vary according to the level of generality and the types of subject matter involved, but outside mathematics it is unlikely to be as rigid as logical implication. Yet again the coherence must be defensible as sufficient to give definition and applicability to a method, an area of study or a hypothesis. Barbour describes coherence for a scientist as 'the comprehensive unification of separate laws, the systematic inter-relation of theories, the portrayal of underlying similarities in apparently diverse phenomena'.[45] A historian, on the other hand, might well be suspicious of a grand scheme of unified historical laws, and fear that seeking underlying similarities would preclude understanding each phenomenon in its own set of relations. Yet historians themselves must not only produce an individually coherent final narrative; as a profession they require consistency and inter-relationship in the concepts by which they compare and understand their sources.

Coherence thus plays an important role in the adequacy of concepts and their groupings for which truth is claimed. The objections to the Coherence Theory of truth in its traditional style, which claimed truth for one comprehensive system within which statements corroborate one another, do not affect this more modest use. For instance, the principal objection is that 'there can be a plurality of internally coherent systems or statements, each of which has members that are incompatible with some members of the others'.[46] From the metaphysic I have outlined, the plurality of systems is the result of ambiguous reality being moulded into different orderings and it is to be expected that incompatibilities among them will occur. The Coherence Theory of truth could not justify the use of evidence in the comparison and evaluation of systems, because it claimed that truth lay entirely in coherence. But I have argued that truth lies in adequate and appropriate concepts which contain information synthesized from the world and thus may appeal to evidence, although that evidence will relate to the system it supports, and a judgment on it is far from straightforward. The possibility, however, does exist.

Knowledge and its justification

A word which is not 'given' as ordered and uniform, but rather as plastic to diverse, changeful and polyvalent orderings, is rendered intelligible by means of social and intellectual constructions which produce epistemic order. To know something, then, is to understand and be able to use suitably the concepts and their elaborations to which we are currently, communally and justifiably committed by a prevailing epistemic order. The first requirement is that concepts be understood individually and in their relations. Obviously people cannot know anything significant about gases, novels or accounting procedures until they have understood current conceptions of them and their concomitants. Mastery of such knowledge is demonstrated by using the concepts in appropriate situations beyond the paradigm one in which they were learned: for instance, by building arguments out of them. What is discovered by a lone wolf or a small pack on the frontiers of investigation becomes knowledge in the full social sense of the term when it wins support and enters the general pool of available concepts or hypotheses. It is legitimated by public or influential approval.

Knowledge is relative to the epistemic order which begets it; endures, although it may undergo changes, while that order endures; and is overturned when the order is superseded. Thus, from the intuition of their senses and their synthesizing understanding, people formerly concluded that the earth was flat. New information and allied concepts brought about a new order cancelling the old knowledge. But it was knowledge while its order obtained, although from our point of view the previous concept of earth was inadequately based and therefore falsely asserted. The present existence of flat-earth believers may have more to do with nostalgia than knowledge, but may also illustrate that there can be utter resistance to what others find to be incontrovertibly established.

A.J. Ayer, in *The Problem of Knowledge*, concluded that 'the necessary and sufficient conditions for knowing that something

is the case are first, that what one is said to know be true, secondly
that one be sure of it, and thirdly that one should have the right
to be sure'.[47] His middle condition, that one be sure of the matter,
means nothing stronger in Ayer than 'not being disposed to
doubt' and has no overtones of mental states of conviction. Even
that explanation, however, might not satisfy A.D. Woozley, who
criticized 'a tendency to psychologize knowing', while he argued
that 'if being sure is necessary to knowing, then many candidates
at *viva voce* examinations have been credited with knowledge
which they haven't got'.[48] Since knowing is a public and social
activity it can hardly be totally divorced from psychology, for
what sureness as a condition of knowing appears to reflect is the
personal backing implied in claiming something as knowledge.
The judgment and commitment involved in such personal
endorsement will be the subject of the next section. When all
psychological overtones are removed by Woozley he finds that
being sure is not a condition of knowing, but a condition of
justifying a claim to knowledge. The same may be said of having
the right to be sure. What remain of Ayer's conditions, therefore,
are the truth of the matter involved, and the justifiable nature of
the claim.

I have described truth as relative to what is currently seen as
the appropriate application of adequate concepts. Many and
diverse truths have been asserted in history which have arisen
from varieties of judgments and epistemic ordering in our
ambiguous and unfinished world. When the variety is taken with
full seriousness, no single essence of truth can be distilled and no
one type of ordering exalted to be guarantor of timeless truth.
Either practice is an attempt to force austere classicism on a world
which may be baroque, and whose descriptions have certainly
varied, even within the Western intellectual tradition alone. But
if truth is relative to concepts and theories and how they are used,
the justification of claims to knowledge assumes an even greater
importance than before. Awareness of relativity makes one aware
that one is arguing for one's point of view, so justification
accumulates and shapes the evidence like a barrister in court
desiring a favourable verdict. Undoubtedly the justification will
be in accordance with the epistemic order which defines the
knowledge, but its appeal, especially when reinforced by pragmatic success, can transcend these limits. There is no human

criterion outwith all forms of human knowledge by which each may be judged in some final manner. Yet I shall argue that this does not leave us stranded in a state of relativism, where no judgments, choices, changes or distinctions between better and worse are possible.

Internal logical consistency is a formal requirement in any justification of claims to knowledge. A justification is an assembling of evidence designed largely to answer the question 'how do you know?', and cannot infringe the forms of valid reasoning (by, for instance, introducing *non-sequiturs*) while it leads to the conclusion at issue. Beyond this formal point, however, little that is general may be said. A justification will defend the concepts and models involved in their adequacy of content, scope and coherence, and the appropriateness of their application in relation to the (already conceptualized) evidence. Yet what counts as adequacy will be very different in, say, opto-electronics and social anthropology. Every study has developed a tradition or series of traditions with its own standards in assessing the relevant evidence, deciding what qualities will count as criterial standards, and what degree of precision or suggestiveness is to be expected in their application. Although any tradition may become rigid, it does provide a framework for thought. The standards demanded in justification change as the subject itself changes, though rarely so completely as the seventeenth-century move away from authorities like Aristotle and Galen to the primacy of empirical evidence. That no one code of standards can be laid down to justify all knowledge is evident from an example mentioned earlier, concerning the different values simplicity and economy have in history and science. In history they mean little more than that accumulated detail in the text should not swamp the coherence of the narrative. A simple account of even relatively contained events like the Highland Clearances in Scotland is likely to be over-simplified, while an elegant economy in dealing with the French Revolution will do no justice to the complexity of historical sources, and will end in an account badly distorted by omissions and reduction. Yet the simplicity and economy of assumptions, concepts and above all of mathematical formulae make a strong aesthetic appeal in scientific theories. One reason for preferring the 'big bang' theory of cosmogenesis, for example, is the elegance of the mathematics involved. 'Accounting for the evidence' may be a common justificatory ideal in both disciplines, but there is a belief in science that simplicity best achieves that account, and an equally forcible belief in history that matters are much more complicated. Both beliefs, and the academic standards which embody them, appear to derive from what gives each success and satisfaction in dealing with the different subject-matters involved.

Justification thus has to do with the standards by which adequacy and appropriateness may be defined in any particular case, but further it concerns itself with the practical methods by which the concepts and theories are put to use. Methods are justified pragmatically by their effectiveness in achieving the purpose for which they are designed.[49] The appeal to methods does not remove all circularity from apologia because methods and criterial standards are interlinked, as in the pure physicist's appreciation of elegance finding expression in mathematical models. Yet that second-order pragmatic justification enhances the defence of a claim to knowledge because it becomes irrational to ignore palpably efficient action or regularly dependable results, and hence to dissent completely from what gave rise to them. Indeed in conversations with physicists it often seems that their entire rationale for their subject is that 'it works'. More strictly expressed, the claim is that the methods work, thereby showing that the particular ordering proposed by a hypothesis is fruitful.

The basic argument against the Pragmatic Theory of *Truth* (the true is what works) is that something may be useful, fulfil its function or provide a strategy for success, but need not on that account be true. A false belief may be as useful in practice as a true one. But the pragmatism here linked to methods along with beliefs does not have to do with truth as the one true order, but is rather a reason for or against committing oneself to, or at least considering, an order of knowledge. Justification by results is not infallible; for one thing, methods may produce results for reasons other than those believed responsible. But then justification is not once for all, and has to be continued through all the changes a subject demonstrates. Where results are satisfactory and the method therefore deemed trustworthy, the theory which directed the process becomes more plausible and the criteria it invoked more worthy of acceptance. Universal water-tight demonstration is impossible in an ambiguous world, but a persuasion to accept something as knowledge which can appeal to such interlocking justification has force. Thus an intricate historical account and an economic scientific hypothesis may both be justified by their standards and methods.

There is a sense, too, in which a powerful claim to knowledge is justified by the success with which it holds off Ambiguity. At the most basic level people create order physically, psychologically, socially and epistemologically to survive. Although each kind of order may grow flaccid if it goes too long unchallenged by change and diversity, an order which gives security and the chance to develop is justified by the extent of its sway, for it must then have afforded a very comprehensive, attractive and trustworthy way through diverse phenomena. Thus the capacity to survive through further research and changing circumstances provides a strong justifying argument. An ideal kind of justification may thus plead the practical case of methods producing results it is irrational to ignore, or the theoretical case of suitable and rigorous standards being met, but most often a combination of both. It may also point to the continuing success with which a school of thought has brought order and significance into some aspect of knowledge. In actual experience justification may rarely be as straightforward as this account implies, since people and things are so various, yet the possibility of carrying conviction manifestly occurs.

The possibility of effective justification across differing points of view is regularly denied when relativism, the sheer acceptance of diversity, becomes normative, rather than relativity which demands choice among possibilities. In relativism it is held that there is no justifiable recommendation or criticism to be made of different stances so each has to be left as it is where it is. But this again appears to be an intellectual over-reaction to the loss of the quest for a single universally applicable criterion of validity. In practice, contingent local and temporal assessments of validity occur continuously as people are persuaded to 'change their minds'. So the choice is not simply between the advocacy of the elusive timelessly true and the tolerance of anomie in relativism. Justification has become contingent but not pointless. What is lost is the notion that there is *one* test which *all* intelligent humans can apply to candidates for knowledge at any time: it is replaced by the observation that there are *various* tests which humans do in fact contingently apply by which they are sometimes persuaded. Results, standards and durability among other values may be appreciated by those of differing presuppositions. That recognition may then lead to the modification of other viewpoints or to downright conversion.

Contingent justification is effective because people are not locked for ever into their present points of view. They are ambiguous, unfinished and continuously capable of change. While men and women require some order in which to flourish, their capacity to diversify and change prevents encapsulation in any one order from being a necessity. Transcendence of particular orders is limited by what is contingently possible or thinkable, but such transcendence is a human possibility. Transcendence of one order, however, leads to the adoption of another; the capacity is to change points of view, not to transcend them all. Absence of order or a point of view is simply disorientation. Frequent change on the other hand appears to indicate lack of commitment to any epistemic framework and the entertainment rather than the acceptance of claims to knowledge. It is not necessarily easy to change; I am arguing only that it is possible, and that such possibility is an indication of relativity rather than relativism.

Judgment

If justifying knowledge is like pleading a case, judgment is like giving a verdict, though not necessarily a verdict in response to justification as such. It is the decision to espouse, entertain or reject a proposal, and all arguments in their relativity are proposals. Such persuasions invoke evidence and reason, but these are presented from a particular point of view and set of assumptions which are ultimately metaphysical in character and form what Collingwood called 'the absolute presuppositions' of those who share them. These beliefs about the world and humanity are absolute in the sense of unquestionable, fundamental, all-embracing and behaviour-directing, for everything is construed in their light.[50] A judgment in favour of an argument, and the knowledge it contains or leads to, is also an acceptance, conscious or unconscious, of the point of view from which it is propounded, and an alignment with the metaphysical assumptions it contains. On the other hand one may find oneself out of harmony with a proposal because one does not share its presuppositions, and for that reason render a negative judgment. Between these two definite responses lies the area of indecision in which one is not prepared to commit oneself (and the verb is important) by either judgment. In that case there can be no action, although the proposal may be intellectually entertained.

The metaphysical assumptions of political parties make a good example where judgment may be exercised at elections – even if it is the judgment to abstain. Although any party will be constrained by current circumstances in the actual content of its policies, one type may be guided by a belief that the world is a cornucopia to be shared as fairly as possible in return for work, the capacity or the right to work being the principal defining character of all humanity. Assistance is to be given, then, to those who cannot so define themselves. Another party may consider the world a quarry for which the adventurous, intelligent and businesslike compete, although some go to the wall, for only in the wake of the successful is there profit for others. Humanity is defined by financial acumen and derring-do. What these metaphysics have in common is a market-place view of the world measured in economic terms – very unlike an ecology party, for instance. Where they differ is on how the market should be run. To give a favourable judgment to either party is to endorse an entrepreneurial or a socialist metaphysic. Argument, evidence and reason may be produced to support either view, but it is the vision of how the world is or should be which underlies these and gives them direction. Values are also provided by the metaphysic, for it plays up some qualities and subordinates others. Competitiveness, for instance, is a value to the entrepreneur, but has no such immediately positive estimation from a socialist. Any individual businessman may be moved by concern for the well-being of others, but for him *qua* entrepreneur competitiveness comes first and social concern is subordinated to the needs of competition or kept to private life.

The metaphysical assumptions in the attitude of the natural sciences may in general be said to be (or to have been until recently) a view of human beings as capable problem-solvers, engineers on a large scale, who can confront, comprehend and control a world which may be rendered self-consistent and patient of scrutiny and management. This again implies the adoption of certain values and the subordination of others, since any metaphysic in action has that effect. Empirical curiosity, for example, became a novel social value with the advent of such an attitude, and the values scientists attribute to theories, such as scope of explanation, the opening up of new fields, degrees of predictiveness, are clearly consonant with it. To be a scientist is, among other things, to adopt some form of the metaphysic and the values it implies, for they become the general background to one's professional judgments. Metaphysical values are not always *consciously* adopted, however, for they may harmonize with beliefs acquired earlier or with personal psychological preferences. Thus the scientific attitude or the socialist ideal may be an extension or intensification of how one judges the world already, so that either seems 'instinctively' right. Just as a church has members through life-long custom, or because a style of service suits them, as well as those who enter from changed convictions, so a metaphysic may have been imbibed from childhood, found personally congenial, or adopted by conscious choice.

As Kuhn has emphasized, scientists work in groups or communities, and it is characteristic of any community that its members share to a significant degree those values held to be important. While individuals contribute to groups, groups frequently impose certain constraints upon their members, as W.J.H. Sprott notes: '(Individuals) are, as it were, pulled into the value system of the group, made less extreme in their judgments and anxious to avoid deviating so far from the group standards that they run the risk of ostracism.'[51] The companionship of like-minded people is a stabilizing influence which provides 'a collectively accepted frame of reference for their judgments and their perception of the world outside them'. Thus while rugged individualism or absolute conviction may incline some people on occasions towards personal judgments different from their professional or social group, it is quite common to make a judgment on the basis of a shared metaphysic and values. This social aspect of judgment is morally ambiguous, for although it may deter foolish idiosyncrasy, it may also mean the suppression of independent thought deviating from accepted norms. There is a conservative tendency in an achieved and successful order such that conformism and unthinking acceptance of the *status quo* are its dangers as well as its stabilizing strength. For there is a sense of security, rightness and trustworthiness given by the sharing of values and assumptions with others, especially with those one esteems. Therefore, although the Existentialists had reason to emphasize lonely individual decisions embodying an independent self-conception, most judgments most of the time come from commitment to a group, community or society with their way of seeing, behaving and allocating priorities.

Yet values, even when shared by a group, may be held with differing priorities. Kuhn has noted this among scientists whose values,

> can thus be differently applied, individually and collectively, by men who concur in honouring them. If two men disagree, for example, about the relative fruitfulness of their theories, or if they agree about that but disagree about the relative importance of fruitfulness and, say, scope in reaching a choice, neither can be convicted of a mistake. Nor is either being unscientific. There is no neutral algorithm for theory-choice, no systematic decision procedure which, properly applied, must lead each individual in the group to the same decision.[52]

Although these scientists have more in common with each other than with, say, an acupuncturist of oriental theory, they yet differ among themselves in assigning priorities to their values, and such disagreements affect the work done. In any group such variety is perceptible. Personal preferences and the impact of past experience do have an effect on how matters are judged, and short of utter conditioning, groups do not produce uniformity among their members, whatever the pressures to conform. In the actual process of living, working and thinking, considerable personal diversity occurs even among like-minded people. The image of the scientist until the recent past has presumed that such idiosyncrasies were set aside in the process of research which was conducted in a value-free zone. But this is just what has been called into question with the thesis that data are assessed by the assumptions of the theory and Kuhn's comments on the degree to which scientists proceed according to their own priorities, even while being scientific. Because the scientific method has been the criterion of all knowing in the West it is important to emphasize that it too has its roots in judgment, which arises in part from personal character and is further influenced by a group ethos.

Earlier I quoted the philosopher A.D. Woozley regretting 'the tendency to psychologize knowing'. Yet Ayer's condition of knowing, that one be sure, even when interpreted as not being disposed to doubt, does indicate the importance of disposition. The implication is that one backs a proposal not only for its reasoned exposition, but because the kind of reasoning it represents harmonizes with one's disposition. Dissonance as well as harmony has had its effects in the history of philosophy. Hegel, for instance, who elaborated an all-embracing scheme of Spirit advancing to self-realization through nature and history, pronounced his acute dislike of *raisonnement*, the cool deductive type of reasoning for which the French have been famous since Descartes. On the other hand G.E. Moore abandoned the abstractions of Idealism in favour of a more congenial philosophy of ordinary language. Disposition or temperament played its part in what each found valuable, although, of course, each could give his own kind of reasons for the preference. William James has observed the same phenomenon: 'Of whatever temperament a professional philosopher is, he tries, when philosophizing, to sink the fact of his temperament. Yet his temperament really gives him a stronger bias than any of his more strictly objective premises. It loads the evidence for him one way or the other, making for a more sentimental or a more hard-hearted view of the universe . . . He *trusts* his temperament. Wanting a universe that suits it, he believes in any representation of the universe that does suit it.'[53]

Carl Rogers, the psychotherapist, concluded quite independently of Kuhn that the same kind of personal input was present among scientists. He had to reconcile for himself his role as scientist, which demanded objectivity, and his role as therapist, in which subjective relationships are of prime importance.[54] 'Science,' he argued, 'exists only in people. Each scientific process has its creative inception, its process and its tentative conclusion, in a person or persons.' That inception occurs 'in a particular person who is pursuing aims, values, purposes which have personal and subjective meaning for him'; the methodology 'checks the hunch' and the final hypothesis is 'a statement of tentative, personal, subjective faith'. The degree to which shared assumptions operate is underlined when he declares that 'knowledge – even scientific knowledge – is that which is subjectively acceptable. Scientific knowledge can be communicated only to those who are subjectively ready to receive its communication. The utilization of science also occurs only through people who are in pursuit of values which have meaning for them.'[55] It is the case, then, with scientists as with philosophers and other contributors to knowledge, that although the vagaries of disposition are disciplined by the needs of rational elucidation and communication, and will be contained by some relationship to the traditions and community of the study, within these confines varieties of personality will produce varieties of judgment.

If personality contributes to judgment, then psychological, social, aesthetic and moral considerations take on importance, for all these aspects go to the making of a person. Psychological, and perhaps aesthetic, preferences appear in, for instance, the option for small tidy patterns or great rolling themes, confidence or insecurity in following imaginative guesses, satisfaction in demonstrating relationships or the insistence on individual uniqueness. Such preferences play their part in all study. In the matter of social preference it has to be realized that knowledge is largely the domain of the educated middle class, and its values in general reflect the interest of that class and hitherto of the men of that class. Some change is being effected here, however, in such matters as the history of working-class groups, neighbourhood law offices and feminist scholarship. Morality affects knowledge in the integrity and honesty of the researcher who will not fudge results, or who will not work on projects which may be used destructively. It appears in the conviction that this is the right way to pursue the right thing, or in the belief that it is good, not merely beneficial, for mankind to have knowledge.

Fundamentally, therefore, one may rephrase Rogers to the effect that knowledge takes place in persons, and that in the pursuit of knowledge they do not cease to be the persons they are with their diverse and ambiguous make-up. This accounts for pluralism even in one field of study with shared concepts, theories, values and metaphysic. But the discipline of study and research within an ordered tradition which has its own standards and methods prevents that pluralism from dwindling into an accumulation of idiosyncrasy. Ideally the amount shared makes for stability and continuity, while the degree to which people differ allows for choice and flexibility of approach. Again, however, actual practice is rarely as tension-free as that description suggests.

With this we come to the basis of knowledge, and the whole process may be described in reverse. Fundamentally there are people with their own genetic endowment and social experience. These people are both individuals and members of a society as well as various sub-groups of that society. As individuals they have their own identity, preferences and proclivities, but as members of various groups they share in the order, ethos and outlook of these groups. Some find their personality consonant with or successfully shaped by the group, others sit more lightly to it and retain a more individual viewpoint. But for everyone there is some blending and some tension between personal values and attitudes and those of the groups and society to which they belong. From this background some things are going to appear more worthy of credence than others: much will seem self-evidently right because there are no valued alternatives and the *status quo* appears to work adequately; other matters involve choice among possibilities or the quest for a better understanding. Thus unconscious and conscious judgments are arrived at. A judgment is not simply an intellectual assent because it has consequences which commit one to the viewpoint and reasoning proposed, that is, to the metaphysic and its values as well as argument based on them. But the individual will still embody all these things individually. When a significant group agrees in its favourable judgment on a hypothesis with its concepts, models, theories, methods and reasoning, the results are called knowledge. It is truth for its time, adequate in scope, appropriate in application, which is accepted on trust by those who are not expert, and justified both by the standards it has met and by its practical and durable success.

Ambiguity is present throughout this process both in the sense that things are open to more than one interpretation, and in that they are unfinished and hence incapable of final interpretation. There is first of all the personal Ambiguity of the people in whom knowledge takes place. People are not fixed entities but humanity in process, open to new influences and capable of change. Further, no one is all of a homogeneous piece, predictable and consistent in all moods, attitudes and judgments. Novelists know the difficulty of reducing the diversity and complexity of a living person to what may be contained coherently in a book without leaving the character two-dimensional. It is a complex character in process who as an infant makes schemas from sensed intuition, who later learns to apply current concepts to these and absorbs, modifies or rejects the orderly way of seeing, behaving and knowing in which he or she is brought up.

Ambiguity of knowledge comes also from the continuing order-ability of the sensed world. Because people can change and see things differently, knowledge is not fixed for ever, but obtains as long as its premises are on the whole acceptable and its justification apparent. Diversity of knowledge exists, not only diachronically in the whole course of history, but synchronically between different specialist subjects and even within them (although it is usually only the more successful varieties which achieve the status of 'knowledge', a term of approval). The very concepts through which we know anything are imprecise in their borders and open to change; precision can be achieved only by the artificial imposition of order to the exclusion of chance or outside development. Finally, knowledge is ambiguous because it has unlooked-for effects. In prescribing how things are to be seen it highlights certain aspects of experience, leaving others in shadow; its metaphorical descriptions take on solidity such that the impli-cations of the metaphor come to be seen as implications of the object of knowledge. Moreover, in spite of the individuality and capacity to change in humans, we are most at home in a situation which is more ordered than not, and tend therefore to identify with the order which has defined us. There is therefore a psycho-logical investment in maintaining it, and a sense of bereavement in losing it. Knowledge has a hold on us as much as we have a hold on it.

While this completes the discussion of knowledge, more remains to be said on the subject of judgment, for decisions are made in many areas which are not academically epistemic. We make a host of trivial judgments daily, and on important matters quite regularly. To opt for bread and cheese at lunch rather than paté is to make a judgment of sorts in which experience, long-standing preferences and present opportunities all come into play. Applying for a certain post, moving house or emigrating are personal decisions of greater magnitude with reasoned judgment.

And the point is that it is usually possible to decide otherwise; matters are rarely so clear that only one course is conceivable. Is it better to have a small, charming but rather inconvenient house at some distance from work, involving early rising and coping with commuter traffic, or to have a larger, more ordinary flat in town without the views, but without the inconvenience? The question admits of no absolute answer, and one's judgment of preferences and priorities decides. As the perfect fulfilment of all our changing preferences is unlikely in this world, some compromise has to be reached which, in our judgment, meets the greatest number of our most important desires at the time.

This decision-making can be difficult enough to cope with at a personal level, but the problems are exacerbated when judgments of the same relative nature have to be made by committees, or by local and national government. Several sets of preferences, interests and values are then in competition and no decision will please, or do the best for, everyone. Only the most single-minded committee with a limited remit can avoid the give-and-take of compromise decisions in which no one's judgment is fully satisfied. Differences within and between political parties, quite apart from the pressure of external circumstances, make politics not only the art of the possible, but the art of the best possible compromise, probably closest to the preferences and strategy of the dominant group.

There is, moreover, no single right answer or course of action for the questions which arise. To take a small example: should the government allow open-cast mining to be developed in a valley of great natural beauty and valuable ecology? The answer is clear to those whose interests are at stake one way or the other, but the government's weighing up of the best thing to do in the short or long term involves assessing and assigning priorities to these interests, together with consideration of 'the public good' now and in the future, and the political acceptability of a proposed course. No solution will be obviously and incontestably right. Although reason and evidence will be adduced in its favour, the chosen solution will still be a matter of judgment and could have been otherwise.

Political interviewers on radio and television exploit to the full the intricacies of judgment by suggesting undesirable consequences of the particular decision made and demanding its justification in view of the alternatives. Indeed the famous media principle of balance would not be possible if there were not at least two ways of judging every question, with each way relative to a point of view with its own values. At the same time it is notoriously difficult to agree on whether balance has been achieved because assessment of priorities varies so widely. Even the most bland collocation of possibilities may appear to some to have an inbuilt bias, if only on account of its order, and it will have to have some order.

Individual, social, political and professional judgments are all similarly relative. The most coolly logical economist, for instance, works also with metaphysical principles concerning the world and humanity in terms of commodities, exchange, labour and so forth. Among other things he or she will have made a judgment on whether labour alone gives value to a commodity, as Marx believed. Not only is the starting point relative to a particular perception of how things are, but the entire programme has to be worked out in a world which is partly predictable, but includes also incalculable contingency and competing judgments. Generally speaking the public has less faith in economists than in scientists because differences among the former are much better known than the more esoteric scientific disagreements. Most people have heard of Keynesians and monetarists now, but few are aware of the differences of approach between, say, Bohr and Einstein. Moreover the shortcomings of any economic policy are usually more widely and painfully felt than the results of an unsatisfactory scientific hypothesis, although investigation into early atomic bomb testing in Australia provides a counter-example. On the whole it is the success of science which is publically known and trusted, although judgments there, like those of an economist, are relative to a perspective and values. Broad agreement in judgments among the best qualified is the strongest basis we have for knowledge or any decision-making. Every judgment acted on gives definition to a public self- or group-concept. We are seen to be the people we are, or the kind of community we are, by what gains priority in our judgments, and the kind of values we implement. Further, every judgment affects the context of future judgments since they have to be arrived at in the light of its effects. As individuals and as society we live with the results of past relative judgments, while all present decisions influence the future. The quality and style of our social lives, individually and communally, are governed by a proliferation of imprecise, partial, compromise judgments, at best well-meant and well-informed, at worst selfish and short-sighted, whose accumulated consequences are unforeseeable. The misery this has caused cannot be underrated. Yet humanity often displays a capacity to adapt to circumstances, and to adapt circumstances to its ends which enable it to survive and even flourish in such an imperfect situation.

Conclusion

This study of knowledge and judgment reinforces the metaphysical picture of Ambiguity given in the previous chapter. While ordered knowledge exists, as all our educational institutions testify, it is not a single, objectively-given quantum to be discovered by any properly qualified, right-thinking, value-free individual. Order in knowledge is created, not found. It is achieved by the understanding schematizing its intuitions, building these up into social concepts, hypotheses, arguments. But because it is achieved by humans who are diverse, and whose circumstances alter, knowledge has the same multiplicity, competition and vulnerability as, for instance, biological order. The full force of this situation has not been felt because science has held unquestioned sway in defining what knowledge is: it has been the standard against which other studies could measure their declension into partiality. Now, however, pluralism and relativity are acknowledged everywhere, for we do our own ordering even in scientific subjects. Standards are not lost by this admission, and the usefulness of knowledge is not diminished. But its contingency is emphasized. It depends on the approval of human judgment, on the social context, on available concepts, on success over alternative views. Since it is a balance among these variables it may be overturned or rearranged at any time. The pretensions of humanity to aspire to final truth are shaken, and we are left with the workable truth, the arguably adequate and appropriate, the truth which is deemed more satisfactory than anything else available. For there is no absolute truth in an ambiguous, unfinished world whose chief discernible characteristic is its plasticity to various orderings.

Matters could be left there. Knowledge depends on the judgment of mutable, malleable, diverse humanity, while the world is capable of all manner of ordering. But because this conclusion may give rise to disorientation and insecurity I wish to emphasize again that it need not result in the disengagement of relativism, from whose point of view the impossibility of final truth and the partial, changing nature of judgment and knowledge leave us without fixed points, without direction or incentive in a morass of possibilities. An implication of that point of view is that without the goal of final truth there is no stimulus to advance understanding, for relative knowledge is scarcely better than opinion, and one perspective is as good or bad as any other since there is no absolute criterion of validity. Relativism could also lead to the judgment that if morality is dependent on relative perception of the good, then all is permitted and anarchy is loosed upon the world. With relativism, if absolutes are lost, everything except description is lost or the way is open to irrationality. The understandable reaction to this is to cling to the notion of absolutes, even when that becomes difficult to justify, for the ideals, security, simplicity and motivation they offer, and for their centre of gravity outside fallible humanity.

But the choice is not simply between elusive absolute truth and the impotence of relativism. There also exists what I have called relativity, which accepts that judgment, knowledge, morality, religion, aesthetics and all our other activities are dependent on our personal and social space- and time-bound conceptions, but yet demands that we choose and follow the best we know. If our thinking and doing is relative to our understanding, then that understanding becomes important, because it matters for ourselves, our society and the future what and how we choose. Choice is a reality because in a pluralist world we are aware of how we differ from others in beliefs, attitudes and methods, so that there is a basis for comparison and contrast. It becomes important to be clear what kind of view of the world one has, what values are preferred and implemented in it, and what priorities govern our limited resources. Judgment is so fundamental that an awareness of its components in general and our own disposition in particular is a precondition of responsible decision-making.

Relativity is a view of affairs which demands responsibility in spite of the perception that our thoughts and actions are ambiguous. We already accept this responsibility socially by, for instance, voting at elections among our variously imperfect parties; we accept it individually by marrying ambiguous others, or by choosing any course which seems to have the fewest defects or the greatest satisfaction. Although the world will continue to be ambiguous whatever we do, its religious, social, moral and epistemological conditions will reflect the kind of judgment exercised and endorsed within its societies. Ambiguity need not then be a reason for paralysis; it may serve instead as a stimulus to see to the kind of ordering which embodies our values.

4

Theological Order

A story is told about a nineteenth-century Scottish divine who retired to St Andrews to write *the* definitive theological treatise which would settle all questions for ever and leave no problem unsolved. His study was built at the bottom of the garden and each day he could be seen walking thoughtfully down to it in the morning, and back at night. Then a maid would remove a basketful of that day's discarded attempts. When the old minister finally died, only one sentence of the great project was found to have been written. It read: 'Theology is everything and everything is theology.'

No one who finds the world ambiguous will aim at definitive, timeless pronouncements, yet that same belief in the equivalence of 'everything' and 'theology', daunting though it is, underlies this book. It may seem tardy, therefore, to arrive at theology explicitly only in the fourth chapter, while God becomes the subject of the fifth. Yet it is precisely because theology *is* everything that everything must be considered and not taken for granted. To master 'everything' in terms of all aspects of life and knowledge is manifestly impossible. But it is a different and more accessible aim to propose metaphysical first principles for everything with their epistemological implications, which picture in general the world we know in particular and shape our expectations of how things are and of where we are in relation to them. Ambiguity does not present a regular pattern, but the recognition of its uneven and shifting nature will still yield a background against which our varieties of life and knowledge may be understood both in their particularity and as aspects of the one orderable world.

There are two good reasons for leaving theology to this point. The first is that a metaphysic can and should stand on its own as a credible picture of how things are to anyone whose experience is illuminated by it. This includes those for whom the universe is a 'brute fact', adequately self-explanatory on its own. Belief in God gives new point and fresh orientation to the whole, but cannot cancel out the basic this-worldly perceptions of how things are if it is going to connect with and give perspective to such experience. Otherwise Christians would have to commute between two worlds, one of which involves that everyday perception in which we are all caught up, the other a special theistic orientation for particular places and times away from the everyday. To avoid this kind of schizophrenia, which neither glorifies God nor integrates humanity, the relation of God to the metaphysic of Ambiguity has to be the placing of the whole orderable world in a larger divine context, rather than the move to an alternative picture. No immanent metaphysic can account on its own terms for the origin, value or purpose of the world it describes. If these questions are raised, their answer has to be sought in something other than the metaphysical world itself, and Christians find it in God. The more exact nature of this larger context and of God's relation with the world will be explored in the next chapter, but I wish to emphasize one implication now. I have described Ambiguity as arising from the action upon the orderable world of its components, inhabitants and cultures. This creaturely agency remains when the metaphysic is enlarged to include God, who is not to be seen as an explanatory principle of why things are *just as they are* (as opposed to his being the reason there is anything there at all). I shall be arguing later that although God's presence and influence permeate the world, God in his freedom has left creation free to achieve its own orderings, and is not the designer of the particular ambiguities which we encounter. God will be described as responsible for the possibility of the world, but not for the diversity and change which the contingent realization of that possibility brings about.

This introduces the second reason that theological appraisals were not brought in at an earlier point, even though I argued that all perception of the world is from a particular point of view, and

one such point is the theological one. In general, if the theological
stance is coherent, adequate and justifiable, in the manner
described in Chapter 3, there is no problem in starting from there.
But it seems at the moment that many theological models of the
world are incoherent, inadequate and hard to justify. This is partly
a matter of the most obvious recurrent pluralism in theology,
whereby opposed optimistic and pessimistic viewpoints find the
world either basically good or thoroughly vitiated by the fall. The
evidence which supports one of these views is simultaneously
anomalous for the other, and each by its partial nature in relation
to experience is inadequate. More serious, however, is the
traditional association of God with one given order in the world
which continues to be assumed, asserted or bypassed without
revision at a time when the recognition of pluralism and relativity
is being forced on to theologians on all sides – to the point, for
instance, where David Jenkins acknowledges the 'tribalism' of his
'experiment in white, bourgeois, English theology'.[1] The first two
chapters, then, which have faced that recognition and made it
basic, come under the rubric of *reculer pour mieux sauter*. What we
say of God, order and the world has to be said in their light.

I am not here concerned with the pluralism and relativity of
different religions, although these represent different orderings
in belief and life of the sense of transcendence, as Wilfred Cantwell
Smith has described it, or the sense of 'something' transcending
human experience.[2] Building on this understanding John Hick
has urged that we ought 'to think of the religious life of mankind
as a continuum within which the faith-life of individuals is
conditioned by one or other of the different streams of cumulative
tradition'.[3] I have been conditioned by the Christian stream. It is
the only one which I know from within and therefore the only
one whose capacity to mediate God I have experienced, and
whose concepts have moulded my understanding. It is with that
experience and these concepts I am concerned here, particularly
at the moment with the question whether concepts of God's
ordering of the world are appropriate and applicable in contemporary Christian 'faith-life'.

Theology and divine order

The frontiers of what God is said to have ordered have been pushed back piecemeal as the understanding and capacities of humanity have increased. God is no longer held to be efficiently responsible for rain or harvests or victory in war. Yet the belief in God's ordering has only become more abstract; it has not been removed. One theological habit over the last two centuries has been to take over an order discovered in history or science on the understanding of 'thinking God's thoughts after him'. Historians arrived at an awareness of their own finitude some time ago and no longer claimed to tell how things really were; theologians likewise have surrendered history at large as the theatre of the perceptible ordering of God, although debates still take place over the history of Jesus of Nazareth. But until recently scientists continued confidently to believe that they were describing the world as it really was, and their conclusions have regularly been identified with how God acted. For instance, when the worst convulsions of belief in the face of evolutionary theory were past, that process was frequently adopted as the way God continually created order of ever-increasing complexity in the world. But there is a cluster of problems in this, as in all particularizing of God's ordering. On the one hand the identification of God's action with any form of evolutionary theory cannot be too closely made, since on the scientific side emphases in that theory change. On the other hand there are theological problems as well. The results of God's creating activity have always been called 'good', since it is held to be inconsistent with his character that he should create evil. There has indeed always been some difficulty in accounting for the origin of evil. But in pre-evolutionary accounts of creation-followed-by-fall there was no difficulty in accounting for the mixed, ambiguous character of the experienced world, since that represented the persistence of some echoes of primordial goodness and much that had been more or less corrupted by the fall. Created goodness and experienced Ambiguity were thus both accommodated. But if creation is seen as continuing down an evolutionary time-line, original goodness drops out of the picture, for everything that comes into being is ambiguous from the moment of its conception, not least on account of the Ambiguity already existing. God would then be directly responsible for both the good and bad aspects of evolution. (Goodness and evil are not simple notions, but they are the terms in which creation is usually discussed.) That would include his responsibility for sports, weaklings, the circumstances which wiped out species, unsuccessful mutations and so forth. The creation of 'evil' in these senses is utterly contrary to the character of God in the Christian tradition and makes this conception of God's ordering of evolution highly dubious.

The only way in which a notion of 'goodness' can be preserved in a religious rendering of evolution as God's devising is in the triumphalism of the species which survived, particularly humanity which is currently at the top of the evolutionary tree. But over ninety per cent of all species which have existed have not survived. If God is indeed ordering onwards and upwards, this argues at least for tremendous waste. If theology ignores this in doctrines of creation it becomes as dismissive of spent species as the double decree of predestination is of the reprobate. Only the manner of election is different. Unless people are prepared to discount the disappearance of species as a by-product of God's ordering, and equate his goodness with survival, these ambiguities of the development of the world tell against the identification of a process of evolution with God's ordering.

Another version of science which cuts both ways is that associated with Newton. At first this was exciting, for nature was observed to be obeying divine laws with an exactitude lacking in humanity. But finally theologians were thankful to depart from that mechanistic world of primary qualities and determinism. Some have started to explore the possibilities of Einstein and particle physics – but these again may turn out to have unwelcome theological implications. The danger is that God may be harnessed to whatever paradigm of scientifically discerned order obtains at the moment, with the negative features played down and the vulnerability to further change ignored. Theology has learned painfully the implausibility of identifying God with any particular historical order, and no residual confidence among scientists concerning the status of their findings should blind us to the effects of change and contingency there also.

At present great weight is being given to the constants of the world, such matters as the speed of light, the gravitational constant, the mass of the proton and so on, which determine the

physical world and form the foundation of physicists' calcu-
lations. The combination of exactly the right conditions required
to produce finally a universe and world hospitable to humanity
is statistically highly improbable and very striking, to the point
where even some scientists are entertaining the possibility of an
'anthropic principle'. Nevertheless this present state of understanding is far from making it secure that God is responsible for
that degree of ordering. For one thing, in the midst of a world full
of evil as well as good, one may wonder why God stopped at
ordering the constants. Further, science continues to change and
develop, so it is dangerous to assume 'that the constants of nature
have values that are accidental and forever inexplicable' from
its own point of view. 'Science advances by explaining what
previously was thought to be accidental and irreducible, and it is
possible that the constants of nature will not be regarded as
inexplicable within our universe.'[4] This caveat should be taken
seriously. Time and again a conception of God has gone the
familiar way of the gaps to the periphery and final oblivion, or it
has been so tied to a perceived intra-mundane order that it is
overturned with that order to the bereavement of believers.

The current tendency is to look for intelligibility in some part
of the structure of the world as a guarantee that Christianity is
right to claim God's existence and provision. But earlier that belief
in his providence was the guarantee of an expected intelligibility
in the world. It was faith in the rationality of the world as the
handiwork of God which supported confidence for scientific
exploration, although before that again it had been reason enough
to let the world alone. E.L. Mascall has expressed the connection
thus: 'A world which is created by the Christian God will be both
contingent and orderly. It will embody both regularities and
patterns, since its Maker is rational, but the particular regularities
and patterns which it will embody cannot be predicted *a priori*
since he is free; they can be discovered only by examination.'[5] He
concludes that the world is then eminently suited to scientific
exploration.

But as Hume pointed out to the Deists long ago, *anything* which
cohered enough to be a world would have some kind of order in
it. If the process of scientific investigation were as simple as
Mascall makes it sound, there would not have been these revolutions in scientific thought to which Kuhn refers (albeit in a work

later than Mascall's), nor would hypotheses have to cope with anomalies. The rational clarity which Mascall envisages given by one designing hand would suit an interlocking jigsaw puzzle of a world, where one part would fit in with another and each have its place when all have been understood. But it is hardly appropriate for the shifting agglomerations of orders to be found in the world, each one a fragile balance among variables, regularly changing as new conditions arise. George Hendry makes a further theological criticism of this viewpoint in his *Theology of Nature:* 'If the rationality in the ordering of the world is wholly concealed within the will of God and can be discovered only by scientific investigation, that rationality is, in the last analysis, a judgment of the scientist, and the invocation of God adds nothing to it.'[6] To that it could be added that the point of Ambiguity is that the judgments of scientists change.

Theological insistence on God having in some sense ordered the world comes from the twin beliefs in God's initiative and action, and in his careful provision for and preservation of the world, God's initiative is not at issue here, since the world cannot provide its own *raison d'être*. But his action may be interpreted in other ways than the design of a structure or a process for the universe. It has already emerged from the discussion of evolution that such action raises in its most acute form the problem of evil. If God is responsible in even the most abstract *Deus faber* fashion, what kind of careful provision is it which allows natural disasters to occur, or power to fall into cruel hands? While belief in God's ordering intensifies the problems, however, no form of belief in God as infinite is going to escape them entirely, for at least one must allow that God lets be a world in which pain and sorrow commingle with well-being and joy. It is not wound up on account of its Ambiguity. Although the answer which evolves in later chapters is that God may value creaturely response and responsibility enough to permit the kind of world which elicits these to continue, the tension is still there. But to give God a more active role in the way the world goes is to assign evil as well as good to the divine intention.

The presence of evil in the world is often defended as producing 'a vale of soul-making' (Keats). Certainly suffering can on occasions produce nobility of character, while both the better and worse in our lives go to making us who we are. Possibilities of

growth and happiness can be as 'soul-making' as disaster and
suffering. But if the world is envisaged as an obstacle course
devised or even permitted by God for the production of better
souls, then it is as inefficient a method as evolution. It is not
that God is to be reprimanded like some inefficient middle-
management executive, but that the cost in each case is so
tremendous that it is incompatible with the primary affirmation
of Christianity that God is love. The waste with evolution is the
nullification of many for the survival of a few, and the waste with
soul-making is that many are crippled and undone by suffering
while some few are enriched by it. Again notions of God's ordering
bristle with problems in an ambiguous world.

The other counter to the problem of evil, the 'free-will defence',
allows that humans are not puppets but have freedom to choose
and thus may choose evil. This requires that God circumscribe
his control of the world to allow for individual freedom, and thus
whittles away at the degree of orderliness explicitly originating
from God. This move opens up possibilities of natural evil being
natural and moral evil being human, but its effects of curtailing
divine ordering needs to be recognized. Moreover, humanity is
not the only free agent in the world, so the notion has to be
extended to freedom for all creation to bring about its precarious
orders in which good and evil will be inextricably mixed. At that
point there is nothing left to call God's *ordering*, a matter which
does not remove God's relationship with the world, but requires
that it be conceived differently.

The force of the creation stories in Genesis 1 and 2 continues to
endure in the most general and fundamental affirmation that
everything is ultimately dependent of God for its being. The world
cannot explain itself on its own terms. Yet Genesis continues to
exert a pressure of interpretation which becomes steadily less
defensible. The picture of God calling creation into being where
before there was formless void has been interpreted to mean that
creation is a mode of producing order and will itself be orderly.
Goodness and order tend to be identified, so on this view there
is basically the one good order of God which diversity would
only obscure, while change would debase it. God, moreover, is
identified with order, and order with God. This view reached its
apogee in the mediaeval synthesis described in Chapter 1, but its
power lingers on. Yet as difficulties in the practical association of

God with any particular order in the world at large increase, the form of that belief becomes more and more abstract, and not only in the remoter regions of scientific exploration. It often stops short of *any* identification from our relative standpoint and is asserted simply as a matter of faith. The picture drawn is of the making of a carpet or tapestry which from the back (our view) is a muddle of colours, but from the front (God's view) exhibits order and pattern.

There are dubious features in this. There is first the question whether a matter of faith about the condition of the world may really be sustained without empirical fit, in terms of the sense we make of experience. It has to be a defiant, if not a schizophrenic belief that the totality of diversity and polyvalence as it multiplies in the world makes *one patterned* sense to God. There seems to be no reason why God should not enjoy them as diverse and unpatterned. Moreover, the complexity of Ambiguity as well as the simplicity of order would have to be understood by him, or he could not enter into our condition and comprehend the effects of finitude and sin. Further, if our actions are conforming to a divine pattern which we are too minutely local to see, our freedom is only apparent, not real. When people think they are making choices and decisions, they are only working out the divine purpose laid down beforehand. Teleological justification of the carpet image, that present muddle will be final pattern, is equally damaging to the reality of human and natural freedom. I shall be taking issue with all unitary teleological perspectives later, since they can distort the importance of the present. Equally I do not believe that the part is justified by the finished whole, as that does not do justice to the part itself.

There is a more refined version of the carpet model which allows for human freedom, but argues that God takes the product of all these free choices and orders his purpose through them. Again I have some sympathy with this, as with the free-will defence, and would like to see that freedom being acknowledged for all creation. But if such freedom of choice and action, though finite, is real freedom, in what sense does God *order* creation? He may be otherwise active, otherwise distilling his purpose, but he is not controlling the becoming of the universe. One fear among Christians may be that if creation's free activity is recognized, God's action, his 'ordering', will be proportionately reduced to the point where it is superfluous. But, as I shall argue later, action is not a quantum of activity such that the more creation does, the less there is for God to do.

Probably the most basic reason for asserting God's ordering of the world is the psychological support and comfort the belief brings. Faith in God's order has acted as a protector against cosmic terror and the threat of meaninglessness. The feeling is that otherwise we should be alone in a pointless universe, vainly trying to impose some temporary fictional order upon recalcitrant chaos, much as Nietzsche described the state of the world after the death of God. William Pollard expresses this vividly: 'The Christian sees the chances and accidents of history as the very warp and woof of the fabric of providence which God is ever weaving. Seen in this way they can be gladly and joyously acknowledged and accepted. But apart from this revelation chance and accident mean anarchy, sheer meaningless random incoherence, and utter chaos from which the soul recoils in horror.'[7] Here the belief in God's ordering is pushed back to bare assertion, fortified by the horror attributed to the only permitted alternative. But as the 'chances and accidents of history' include war and destruction, and these are claimed as part of God's providence, it is a choice between horrors. The comfort in this case is much too dearly bought. Moreover, Pollard's division is too stark, although it is implicit in belief in one divine order which has no place for plurality or creaturely independence.

But we do not have to define what appears to us chance and accident as either God's doing or anarchy. Rather, it is the result of a clash among the contingent and varied orders which arise, fall and coexist. When these do not conflict, but remain in a balance favourable to us, a smooth and unremarkable history results. No one, however, raises questions when things are going well, and this all-too-human tendency has led to the equation of our satisfactory order with God's intention, which is surely hubris. There are better ways of connecting God in love with the world than that, or than Pollard's amoral deity manipulating events.

The traditional model conceives the comfort of God's given order somewhat as a school-child finds it in the given structure of classes in the timetable. All the variables of subjects, classes, classrooms and teachers have been worked into a plan of order before the pupil arrives, and his or her ideal duty is to fit in, contribute and benefit from the wisdom of it all. No pupil will understand all the planning, or why things sometimes happen as they do, but he or she presumes an intention on the part of the staff. An upset to that kind of order certainly leaves the pupil disorientated and unable to make sense of the experience, yet the staff can usually overcome the contingency, the 'chance and accident', or adapt it to their purposes. But that order in its givenness and control does not tally with experience of the world, as pupils regularly discover when they leave the cloistered routine.

A more credible picture of the orderability of the world, although few have to cope with it quite so fundamentally, is that of a number of people setting up in different businesses. Each has to achieve and maintain order within his or her own concern in everything from the division of labour to financial viability and market research. In a *laissez-faire* economy these individual orders of business have to find their place in the market in competition with others; a new one has to fit in with or overthrow the existing balance, and it is always possible that one may fail, though on the other hand one may flourish as the green bay tree. Not only do the individual businesses have to coexist, they have to live with such other current contingencies as the state of the commodity market, the strength of the currency, the political stability of relevant countries and so forth. The complexity, uncertainty and fluctuation of the market-place, as well as the need for cooperation and interaction in the midst of competition, much more reflect experience of life than the regularities and received wisdom of the schoolroom. And it is God's relationship to that kind of world which has to be discerned.

It may seem disturbing to liken the world of which God is creator to a *laissez-faire* economy. It is the complexity rather than the ethos of the market, however, which makes it a suitable model. But even the ethos is an implication of creaturely freedom, for freedom is an ambiguous capacity. One is as free to aggrandize the self as to be concerned with one's neighbour. But that same freedom leaves us responsible. 'The market' cannot be hypostatized into an inhuman monster to be fed with one's children like Moloch; it is the result of innumerable human decisions and reactions to circumstances. If it appears inhuman, that is because humanity in its freedom has elected that its criteria be economic rather than social in the name of profit and efficiency.

We can never take refuge in complaint against 'the system', for all systems are of human devising and could be otherwise, since the world remains orderable.

But this is not enough. Responsibility in a world of bewildering complexity and competing orders may have to suffice for an atheistic or agnostic view of how things are, but it scarcely satisfies Christian claims that God relates in love to all that is. An orderable world, however, with responsible creatures contingently achieving order, involves God far more intimately than the conception of prior ordering. The Deists had a coolly efficient machine-maker God who ordered the world and then retired to transcendence. Although they are an extreme case, they only take to its logical limits on the machine model what is involved in any such belief. A God who has already given the original and true order connects with the world like a monitor (the 'governor' of traditional doctrines of providence) to supervise the playing out of that order. But a God who let creation be free to achieve its own orders or balance would be at every point intensely concerned with how things were going. He might be recognized or unrecognized, his influence might be felt and followed, or unknown, or ignored, but his caring concern, his 'loving-kindness' for these fragile, finite and sinful creatures wrestling with life in the unfinished world would go on moment by moment. What this understanding means for his nature and his omnipotence will be explored in the next chapter, where again his presence in the world will be insisted on. I have been removing conceptions of God's ordering of the world not only because they are incoherent and hard to justify, but also to make way for his presence as a vivid reality and value in all changes and chances. There is no single order ordained by God to be a blanket comforter for Christians against chaos like the framework of school life or the rules of a game. Instead, they have to cope as adults with diversity and change, taking responsibility for the way the world is, but always in the presence of God whose influence and patient goodness are available to them.

Theology and change

Such a view of God caring for and companioning creation as it brings about its varieties of finite order will allow religion in general and theology in particular to be much more hospitable than it has traditionally been to notions of *change and diversity*. These features have been noticed, but they have rarely been accorded theological value in the total scheme of things outside process theology. 'Heresy' means choice, and as diversity is the ground of choice, its existence was once hotly denied, even when different schools of doctrine were competing. There could be only one true order in theological thought, just as there was one divine order for the world. The one true order was the one each protagonist espoused, from whose point of view the rest were heresy. Change, moreover, has almost without exception been seen as a threat to current established religious order. Change, of course, is never the whole picture. There are always elements of continuity blended in with the most thorough-going upheaval. Yet change is what needs to be assessed as a theological category, because stability and continuity have for so long been taken as desiderata, echoing the divine order. Change, on the other hand, has traditionally been regarded as an aspect of fallenness, a regrettable feature of the human condition, whose effect upon the sacred must be denied, minimized or circumvented.

Change is denied when infallibility is asserted of anything held to be sacred, such that privileged order or information is considered immune from the forces of Ambiguity – a difficult thesis to maintain. It is minimized when change and diversity are neutralized into a smooth inner development from the nucleus of the faith. The history of doctrine would scarcely support such a view, and moreover it implies that no two beliefs have ever been incompatible.[8] The tenet of pure organic development, however, overlooks not only the diversity of Scripture itself, but also the effect upon church and theology of all the local and contemporary cultures in which they have flourished, and in whose totality many incompatible things have been believed. Some of these have been assimilated into doctrine in a way which adds novelty to, or contradicts, and does not merely develop, what has gone before. In the Scots Confession of 1560, for instance, the Roman Catholic Church is taken to task for allowing women to baptize, when they should not even be allowed to speak in the congregation. A little over four hundred years later women were ordained ministers and elders in the Church of Scotland. Again, liberation theology is a notable recent example of addition to, and the rearrangement of priorities in, theological analysis. Gutierrez, for instance, adds the definition of theology as 'critical reflection on praxis' to previous definitions of 'sacred wisdom' and 'rational knowledge'.[9] This definition and its background cannot be assimilated to organic development, although he can find support in parts of tradition. The change with which theology and the church must reckon, therefore, is real difference and not simply development. What Kuhn discerned in the variety of scientific paradigms applies here also: theologies may be logically incompatible, conflicting in their basic metaphors or structures as process theology conflicts with Thomism; they are incommensurable, incapable of measurement against each other *at every point* because their emphases and the problems they were designed to meet vary; but they are comparable in different ways at different points without positing one absolute standard of expression which can be equated with God's true order.

The appearance of real change and diversity may be circumvented consciously or unconsciously in a variety of ways. For one thing, the endurance of a word may disguise multiple and incompatible contents of meaning given to it at different times. Abstract nouns like 'salvation' are particularly prone to change of content without advertisement, but continuing societal roles like 'father' are equally affected. When we project on to God the best of fatherhood as we discern it today, we are not always aware of the difference between that and the Victorian conception of the strict, just father. Today's version could be expressed as, 'God is my loving father, so he will desire that I develop my personhood to its fullest extent', while the Victorian version might be rendered as 'God is my loving father, so he will chastise me if I transgress my place'. A different view of divinity is implied in each. Further, current emphases act as filters to block out contrary perceptions. Thus it comes to some today as a surprise that the loving, forgiving father of the prodigal son was also a patriarch, able to send his servants skipping in all directions to fulfil his commands on his son's return.

Another form of unacknowledged change comes when the tradition has to be sifted, or carefully treated, as opposed to being simply referred to, to produce a more or less tenuous precedent. The church fathers with their mystical/allegorical/symbolic senses of Scripture in addition to the literal could generally find a biblical toe-hold for what would otherwise have been innovation. The Reformers could find no adequate 'scriptural warrant' for infant baptism in the New Testament, but could link it with circumcision in the Old (although that, of course, was for boys only). By today the repertoire of tradition has become so large and varied that it is often possible to find a traditional peg on which to hang a novel idea, or, more properly, a traditional starting-point which is capable of transformation. This is not necessarily a culpable move, for continuity will accompany change, and all changes will stand in some relation to the Christian tradition. But it does allow the fact of change to be by-passed even while novelty is being introduced.

Another means of dealing with change which is probably more instinctive than orchestrated is made possible by the wealth of paradox in Christian doctrine. It is impossible to maintain full justice to both sides of a paradox in any extended discussion or lived faith, since that simply multiplies paradoxes and becomes increasingly gnomic. The tendency, therefore, has been to affirm both parts, but in practice to give priority to whichever one is currently more credible. The implications of this for the paradox of God's simultaneous immanence and transcendence will be discussed in the next chapter, but the process of switching ends of a paradox can be as clearly seen in the matter of the humanity and divinity of Christ. The affirmations of the Chalcedonian formula strike a careful paradoxical balance, but in practice humanity and divinity became more like alternating or even competing models of understanding. Prior to the rise of historical consciousness Christ was for the most part emphatically divine and peripherally human. Today he has become much more obviously human and putatively divine. By swinging from one end of a paradox to the other, then, without giving up the paradox *per se*, theologians may change to emphasizing what coheres with current viewpoints without actually disrupting doctrine or having to justify innovation.

In such ways as these, change has infiltrated theology rather than been acknowledged for what it is. It is not the case that there has been no change, no polyvalence in understanding and judgment. Moreover, these ambiguous effects cannot be avoided by the intention to adhere to an unchanged faith, as creationists and other fundamentalists attempt. Apart from the assessment of any actual argument they adduce, the very fact that this adherence takes place in altered circumstances changes its nature. It now has to be faith 'in spite of' other prevalent conceptions of science or the Bible, which have to be 'answered' in such a way that the superiority of biblicist views are demonstrated. That is a different case from the days when attitudes to the Bible and the world were commonly shared and could be presumed undefensively. It shows that change cannot be avoided by reiterating traditional responses while the world moves on, for at best the traditional becomes an option which has to compete with others, and justify itself in the face of, and in the terms of, novel circumstances and beliefs.

The recognition of change forced upon the church may be painful, but that has been its fate for the last century or more. The debates about creation in the nineteenth century set up a pattern for what happens in such a case: initial denial is followed by minimal yielding. When the evidence for evolution became intellectually unanswerable, after a protracted rearguard action, a small portion of Genesis was surrendered to the category of myth, while the rest of the Bible was adhered to in traditional fashion with the expectation of literal, historical truth. The yielding of literal understanding in the creation stories did not undermine faith once the pain of transition had passed, and was in many ways liberating. It took Christianity off the defensive, allowed it to speak to its time and taught it appreciation of imaginative theological thought within the Bible. But in so far as this lesson in the potentially positive value of change was not learned, so each new discovery of biblical criticism had to be fought over afresh. For many, even among those who accepted the findings of the critics, there was a continued sense of loss, of holy ground crumbling beneath their feet. Their conception was of a static solidity of truth, which each new wave of discovery eroded, rather than a dynamic process of continuity and change in relative finite expression of the fundamentally inexpressible. Change will continue to be experienced as loss rather than as possible liberation or a challenge to fresh engagement until the contingency and Ambiguity of all ways of believing, and all expressions of belief, are not only recognized but internalized. I acknowledge, however, that there will always be times when change feels like loss, not just because we are used to our beliefs, but because one does not simply entertain a religious belief; one is committed to it. There is so much of ourselves and our values, then, in our beliefs, that we may well mourn when some seem no longer feasible for new reasons.

Change, of course, is ambiguous, and cannot always be given a positive value. Even when we are prepared for there to be change, any particular instance may strike us as for the worse rather than the better. Change may appear lateral or up a *cul-de-sac* rather than advancing, and it will coexist with elements of continuity and previous orderliness. But unless Christians aspire to the condition of the sloth, deaf, near-blind and inactive because his comfortable order is unchallenged, we will value change in spite of its Ambiguity for the stimulus of its possibilities. It cannot be seen as a declension from a mythical timeless expression of revelation, and hence as something to be resisted *à l'outrance*. Such defensiveness is appropriate only within the nostalgia of those agnostics for whom the numinous is dissolved without remainder in the antique. For those with present faith, the changeableness, the orderability of the world is rather to be seen as the gift of possibility, immediately deriving from contingent circumstances, but ultimately from God. This does not mean an unqualified acceptance of every novelty, of course, but it does deny the policy of rejecting as much as possible for as long as possible.

But in all this discussion of change in the world, in theology and in religion, is there anything unaffected? The first and most important affirmation in answer to that is that there is no change in the nature and quality of God's relationship with the world. If that is not the case, all religious belief and its expression in theology is pointless. I have not said that God himself is unchanging, because as I shall argue in the next chapter, it is part of his nature to change as a result of his relationship with creation. What is unchanging in him, analytic within the conception of God, is his relating nature with its qualities of sensitivity and care. That is the one constant around which variables of human reception and expression seek their balance. Moreover, some metaphors, concepts and organization, whose purpose is to mediate that relationship and make it effective in our lives, will withhold Ambiguity better than others, offering a trustworthy way through diversity, eliciting commitment and continuing through change. In beliefs, and in experience of church and theology, there will be continuity as well as change, consensus as well as divergence of opinion, and shared values, although these may be differently held.

A consequence of the acceptance of change not only as something which will happen anyway, but as the gift of possibility from God, is that the response to change becomes important. It requires a degree of wisdom and maturity to assess the potential in the new, to discern the direction it is taking, estimate its consequences and arrive at the best available decision. It becomes our human responsibility to do this, although we are not Nietzschean supermen, are rarely in possession of all the relevant information, will diverge in opinion and can never know the full reverberations of our decisions. If change, outside and inside the church, is seen as deriving ultimately from God, and coping with change requires maturity, then we may conclude that God's desire for humanity is the achievement of such responsibility, wisdom and maturity as we are finitely capable of, with our limited ability to transcend our own time and place, and our egotistical preoccupation with our own comfort. All of this responsibility, however, occurs with the presence and strength of God available to us. The description of this relationship and how it works in practice will occupy the remaining chapters of this book.

To sum up the argument thus far: belief in the one true ordering by God of how the world is in its components and history has become incoherent since the recognition of the effects of change, and unjustifiable when pluralism and relativism make themselves felt. The alternative is not the abandonment of the world to chaos, but the observation of a multiplicity of finite and temporal orderings permitted by God in giving creation freedom and the possibility of achieving order and value. Change in general, and specifically change which affects belief, is not then to be seen immediately as a threat to a divine *status quo*, but rather as another contingent ordering which is to be assessed and used as best we know to fashion our world according to our values.

Theological method

Theological method as well as doctrine is profoundly and materially affected by relinquishing belief in one divine order and accepting both the contingency of actual orderings and the potential value of change. In general terms, theological method derives its character either from a premise of revelation, which is the belief that God has communicated himself, primarily through Scripture, or from the practice of natural theology which argues from a state of affairs perceived in the world to some affirmations concerning God. Revelation and natural theology are usually thought of as opposite and competing modes of the knowledge of God, the one requiring primarily the receptivity of faith, the other the activity of reason. Yet formally they are remarkably similar because both have assumed a God-given order which, faithfully discerned and reasonably followed, will lead us to him and tell us what we need to know of him. Materially, one seeks its order in the Bible, the other in the world at large. But each expects that there will be only one order and has to deal with disharmony in its chosen sphere, for as Bishop Butler argued in the eighteenth century, the book of nature is as obscure, or ambiguous, as the book of revelation.[10] His conclusions have been well documented since then. The desire to arrive at one order in each, therefore, has led to some fairly rigorous selectivity.

Each method, moreover, starts with a judgment of faith. This is evident in those who invoke revelation, but is equally the case with proponents of natural theology who have rightly been accused of presupposing their own conclusion (the existence and nature of God) in the selection of material for evidence and the direction of the argument. This criticism holds whether the argument takes the form of an *a priori* analysis of the concept of God, or of an examination of the world to find *a posteriori* pointers to his being. It can be argued that what Anselm's argument in the *Proslogion* shows, for instance, is not the necessary existence of God, but that *if* God exists, a matter not in doubt for Anselm, his existence is necessary, or he would not be 'that than which nothing greater can be conceived'.[11] Again Hume, in his *Dialogues on Natural Religion*, can point to the tendentiousness of selecting design as the striking metaphor for the world since that implies a designer. He proposes in its place an organic model, which has no such implications.[12]

Yet as a matter of *formal* procedure, this judgment of faith which predisposes believers to select experience which they find significant, and order it so that it points to God, can be found culpable only if it is believed that any neutral, value-free stance is possible. But from the arguments of Kuhn and others in the philosophy of science and the findings of the sociology of knowledge, it has emerged that such a utopian point is impossible. We start from where we are and how we see and judge things, so that our perceptions and arguments are coloured by our disposition and interest, and lead to selection and organization of what is deemed relevant in accord with it. If natural theologians are not to be criticized on this formal point, however, neither are those who begin from revelation. Their intention may be to be obedient to the whole Bible, but in practice they select certain passages as fundamental, organizing and harmonizing as much of the rest as possible around these.[13] Whatever the intention, no scheme can embrace the entire Bible, just as none can encompass every experience. The Bible itself is a repertoire of experience selected and organized from viewpoints which differ in significant ways. This became clear when biblical theologians, with their model of the mighty acts of God, could do no justice to the wisdom literature of the Old Testament. Moreover, the differences in the New Testament between, say, Mark and the author of Hebrews, despite their common orientation on Jesus Christ, make the practice of selection and organization unavoidable if beliefs are going to be derived from the Bible. The *formal method*, as such, is not to be condemned. Indeed it is the only one we have if we are to go beyond the relativistic description of difference. But that does not mean that its *material practice* is beyond comment; it simply removes the crunch to another part of the wood.

The methods of natural and revealed theology are therefore the same in form and manner. Further, after suffering decades of criticism for their apparent partiality, they are now seen to conform to the general understanding of how arguments are created in dependence on interest, which gives the perspective. That statement can then be stood on its head to declare that there is no special, privileged theological method or epistemology. Theological order is achieved like any other, and knowledge within it is like knowledge elsewhere, so it has to conform to requirements for truth and justification if it is to gain credibility. That is where the crunch lies, although other matters must be considered first.

'The crunch' applies to the quality of the arguments adduced, but not to the complex background of temperament and orientation in individuals which predisposes towards certain judgments. Because that predisposition includes psychologically and aesthetically based preferences as these have developed in a particular social milieu, it comprehends more than the rationality of any epistemic or theological order. Experience and argument in that case do not have straightforward predictable effects on our judgments. An argument with evidence has the status of a demonstration only when we are disposed to endorse it because we are convinced. Yet because the disposition is not rigid and impermeable, although it is resistant to change, the impact of criticism, like all other individual and social experience, may change the constituents of judgment and thus particular judgments themselves. What is evidence in one argument may work obliquely and unpredictably, if at all, for others with a different point of view; but unless people are utterly unimaginative, totally closed and self-contained, some news from elsewhere does percolate through.

The feeling of rightness and satisfaction, not only in an epistemic order, but also in a metaphysic, is at home in the predisposition. This is also where William James locates what he calls 'total reactions upon life'. 'To get at them you must go behind the foreground of existence and reach down to that curious sense of the whole residual cosmos as an everlasting presence, intimate or alien, terrible or amusing, lovable or odious, which in some degree everyone possesses.'[14] A theistic metaphysic is a particular case of such 'total reactions upon life', and neither theology nor Christian living is possible without some metaphysic (at least presupposed) concerning what the world and God are about. Theists themselves may find the world 'intimate or alien, terrible or amusing, lovable or odious', for there is no one theistic disposition. But the whole working view of the world and God in relation gives the feeling of rightness and satisfaction, as well as making sense of experience, which is characteristic of the harmony of disposition and belief. This does not render belief in the metaphysic inviolable, but places it in the area where contrary argument comes indirectly and where the whole person, not only the rationality, is involved. Belief in the relationship between God and the world, coloured by the feeling-tone of our disposition, seems in the first place intuitively right rather than obviously reasonable. It is not the result of an evidential process, as the criticisms of natural theology indicate. Arguments flow from the belief, rather than lead to it on their own – a matter particularly clear to those not disposed to countenance them. The other well-known argument against natural theology, therefore, also has force, namely that the leap from pattern, cause or state of affairs discerned within the world to a patterner or cause beyond it, goes beyond any possibility of evidence. The move, indeed, is not based on evidence, because belief in God's connection with the world is prior to anything counting as evidence.

Equally, however, to isolate the question whether God exists, and treat that as a purely rational matter, is to misunderstand, for the question has no meaning apart from the whole metaphysical ensemble of his relationship with creation. There is a formal similarity here with human understanding of the world: although we have only the success of social epistemic ordering of the world to go on, as it were, it is still quite possible that there is a world to be so ordered. The varieties of epistemic ordering do not make nonsense of that possibility. In the same kind of way, although we have only the effect of the metaphysic and the tradition of religious experience and theological ordering to go on, it is still possible that there is a God. Again variety does not remove that possibility. Critical theism, like critical realism, is a possible stance. What is needed at the moment, however, is a viable metaphysic which can encompass the sense of Ambiguity, for without it the instinctive assent of humanity to the attractiveness of religion becomes less likely, while those of us who still believe, and ponder our belief, have as many areas of difficulty as the Ptolemaic system had epicycles. The immediate point, however, is that although belief in God's relationship with the world may be argued about, and all manner of evidence proposed for or against the notion, it is not simply a matter of rationality, so that issues of truth and justification apply to the metaphysical orientation indirectly, and may indeed have more effect on the way the belief is held than on the belief itself.

Belief in relationship with God will not issue in a single type of theology or church, partly because the elements involved in judgment are a different 'mix' in different individuals, and partly because the circumstances and categories of the societies in which it functions will be different. It is no criticism to say that religious beliefs satisfy psychological, aesthetic or social needs, for that is what such beliefs should do. Religion, like knowledge, takes place in people. Yet that does not mean that the varieties may be described and left where they are. That is relativism, the uncritical, paralysed acceptance of diversity. Relativity, on the other hand, while accepting that its point of view is limited, resists determinism on account of its belief that things and people can change, that reasons can be given for what is better or worse which, although framed from a perspective, can carry suggestiveness beyond that. Pluralism then becomes the state in which one is conscious of what one believes because others think differently. That may lead to a conclusion that one's own beliefs are in some way better, but it may also mean that the ideas of others challenge, enlarge or modify one's own outlook for reasons accepted as cogent.

On this view even some differences which reflect deep-seated variation in taste and ingrained preferences (that is, which come from the disposition and are not directly amenable to evidence) may be understood, even if they are not overcome. Thus even a convinced 'typical' Presbyterian may to some extent comprehend the sense of being caught up in an offering of praise, beauty and order which seems to characterize, say, an Anglo-Catholic service of worship: as opposed to being nauseated at the incense, scornful of the vestments and bereft of a sermon. Equally, it is not impossible for a 'typical' Anglo-Catholic by sympathetic imagination to catch some sense of the spiritual exhilaration which comes from wrestling with a good sermon, for which an undemanding background makes the best context: as opposed to finding the congregation passive while it is talked at interminably in a bare church. Differences at this level are not likely to be overcome, but they may at least be understood. Even more might be hoped for, since the understanding could lead to some modification. 'Typical' Presbyterians could learn that beauty and richness are not necessarily incompatible with divine worship, and 'typical' Anglo-

Catholics that intellectual stimulation is as real an involvement of
the congregation as aesthetic appeal.

The personal element in knowing, which inclines judgment
one way or the other, escapes the area of disposal by argument,
but there is still the possibility that the psychological orientation,
for instance, may be seen to be deficient in some way. That
religion should meet psychological needs is one thing; that it
should cloak, or be used to encourage, psychological weakness
is something else. Theologies obsessed with power and control,
for example, might not only be criticized for their content, but
would also come under suspicion of psychological insecurity.
Certainly we are indebted to current notions of mental health for
the perception of sickness. But even these are open to evaluation.
There may, for instance, be a religious preference for discontent
with how society is over an integration with it which raises no
questions. Even concerning the personal element in knowing,
therefore, as it issues in theological statement, criticism is possible,
although it is another question whether that will be understood
by the one criticized.

Personal, moral and aesthetic predispositions issue in judgments which express belief, taste and our feeling of the world.
But it is not until these judgments are taken further into making
order in the world by the elaboration of concepts, hypotheses,
models and metaphors that assessment can be brought to bear.
This does not mean that there are two stages: first belief, then
articulation; rather it means that the articulation of belief is the
locus of the need for rigour and the meeting of arguments. Every
theology in its selection and organization is an achieved order like
any other intellectual or artistic work. Like them it will depend
on current categories and past tradition, whether it endorses,
modifies or repudiates those in the process of arriving at its own
coherence. Unlike a communal scientific venture, theology is
usually written alone, although like-minded 'schools' exist. But
unless a theology is sufficiently persuasive to win the approval of
others, it will pass rapidly out of sight and its findings will not
count as theological knowledge. The individuality of expression
thus submits to group control of possibilities – a social feature
of all knowledge which may both suppress oddities and miss
promising innovation. Theological orders are various, and each
one is precarious in a changing world, for there may be an

enduring core to the theological agenda, but its expression will change with circumstances.

Theological truth

Once questions of evidence and assessment arise, they are directed to the perceived *adequacy* and *coherence* of the concepts and models employed, their *appropriateness* to their function, and *applicability* to what they order. A theology is justified by how it meets these standards, but also in its pragmatic achievement of expressing a faith which may be believed and lived. 'Theology,' Martin Thornton insists, 'cannot claim to be practical unless it changes, or develops, or improves a complete human being, together with his total environment.'[15] Although all theologies will be concerned in different ways with the relation between God and creation, there is no one timeless version of truth in the subject which may be ever more closely approximated or fallen from. Instead, there are contingent expressions of the faith which may be found better or worse on any of these criteria. In practice, however, assessments of 'better or worse' are likely to differ.

Adequacy involves the scope of material deemed relevant to a concept or model with its explanatory power, and links up with notions of applicability. A concept which covers too much loses its definition and becomes impossible to apply, while one which is too precise and small in scope becomes rigid and unyielding to change. Theology tends to both extremes. When I began theological study it was popular to say that the Christian aim was to achieve full humanity in the light of Jesus Christ. The concept of 'full humanity' is staggeringly undefinable if taken seriously as an empirical possibility without Platonic overtones, but in practice could be represented by the aspirations of Western, male, twenti-eth-century bourgeoisie. Theological concepts are likely to have a larger penumbra of imprecision than most: partly because so many of them have a long history through many cultures; partly because God is not a subject to be nailed down precisely; and partly because the intention is to speak in universal terms. It is this last reason which has led theology to be expressed in wide and generous abstracts so that it can include every possible circumstance within its scope. By doing so it may inspire unspecific ideals, like 'full humanity', but for that ideal to become applicable, a possibility to be aimed at and not mere rhetoric, it will have to be translated down into local categories and possibilities around the world, and will finish up meaning a multiplicity of things some of which may be incompatible. Another way of understanding abstracts which include great sweeps of possible meaning is that they will sketch a symbolic universe, such as that across which God marches in judgment and mercy. This again, however, relinquishes the everyday applicability of its terms. The world is too ambiguous, too diverse, polyvalent and changing for such abstracts to have any force: any event or state is such a mixture of good and bad in different ways to different people that the general identification of God's judgment and mercy is impossible; if, indeed, 'good' may be equated with mercy and 'bad' with judgment. There does, then, come a time when theological concepts lose meaning rather than gain universality by the intended width of their reference.

On the other hand, small precise concepts have their limitations too. Scholastic Calvinist arguments, for instance, concerning the exact meanings and moments of such concepts as justification, adoption and sanctification, betrayed a desire to have the measure of the Holy Spirit, whose works these were in humanity, and to tie God down to a system which was rigid in conception and application. Instead of having one voluminous concept which is intended to cover everything, this way of proceeding tries to cover every contingency by having concepts for everything carefully delineated from each other. But apart from anything one may wish to say about hesitation over prescribing God's action minutely and without remainder, the Ambiguity of the world usually defeats the attempt because the classification cannot change with changing circumstances. Between those concepts which are palpably too wide and those which unduly circumscribe meaning lie those whose adequacy has to be decided individually, assessing whether they make communication and applicability to present life and action workable, and whether it is the God of the Christian tradition who is so communicated.

Another source of inadequacy in theological concepts which renders them inapplicable in practice is a selection of material which ignores too many contradictions, or against which change has brought in too many contradictions, rather like the growth of anomalies in a scientific paradigm. It is not at issue that evidence will have to be selected and organized, but the result also has to be justified. From this point of view the whole description of Ambiguity in the opening chapters is an amassing of evidence against the conception of a single order in the world whose author is God. Further, in this chapter I have argued that the effect of such modifications as the 'free-will defence' in the problem of evil render 'order' a hollow and inapplicable term. There is no prescription for the amount of contrary evidence needed to tell against a traditional model, for its accumulation will become persuasive at different points for different people. A consensus may arise, or a theological feud may result as the new viewpoint competes with the old in acquiring a standing.

If adequacy is one requirement for a theological concept or model, another is coherence, both in the matter of central defining conditions and in relationships with other beliefs. That coherence will not necessarily have the tightness of logical implication, but it does require that doctrine hold together and make consistent sense. An analysis of a positive example in practice would be too long and too much of a digression here. Instead I wish to indicate briefly a potential area of current incoherence. It has become increasingly clear to a number of theologians that the picture of God as a remote sovereign is not communicating his presence to people today. From the time when Bonhoeffer described God as 'pushed out of the world on to the cross'[16] the notion has grown of a God who suffers, who in weakness, vulnerability and woundedness knows our condition from within. There is a great deal which is attractive in this picture. Yet, because this state is attributed to *God*, it creates a problem, not only for the humanity and divinity of Christ, when his suffering is taken as paradigmatic, but also a remarkably similar one in the concept of God. On all accounts God must have power as a central defining condition, or nonsense is made of *any* ascription to him of creation and salvation. To attribute weakness to him, therefore, requires that his power be redefined in its nature or use. Otherwise, some account of his relinquishing of it must be given, in which case the same kind of difficulties will emerge as were pressed against kenotic christology; or his weakness must be admitted in the last resort to be apparent rather than real, like the docetism of Alexandrian christology. Therefore, unless the case concerning God's omnipotence is carefully argued, there is an incoherence in the assertion both of God's power and his weakness which cannot be written off as yet another theological paradox, nor allowed simply to stand in its inconsistency. In a service which I recently attended, every hymn and prayer celebrated God's glory and power, while the sermon pictured him with great pathos as the wounded healer. There was, I have to admit, the further irony that when I pointed this out to members of the congregation, none of them had noticed.

Some people believe that too much logic is bad for theology; that the intimations of the religious consciousness may become over-regulated to the point of theological nonsense by an excess of clarity, consistency and the rules of inference. What is valid in this objection is the fear of tying God down to a QED in either his nature or his relationships, and hence, secondarily, of circum-scribing our conceptions of him. The theological appeal to mystery need not be sheer mystification, but the reminder that every statement made of God is made by a finite human about the strictly inconceivable God on the basis of what to divinity must be a little local relationship. 'Acknowledgment of the mystery, however, ought not to be a simple way out of conceptual difficulties. We ought to be clear about what we mean by mystery, what it is about the concept of God which gives it the character of mystery, and what sort of meaning we consider to be compatible with this mystery.'[17] Such description will come in the next chapter. The assertion of mystery, therefore, does not turn theology into a catch-all for any conglomeration of descriptions to which coherence is irrelevant.

There is no doubt a personal element in the degree of argued consistency felt to be desirable. But if theology is the achievement of reflective order among the religious intuitions and expressions of the past and present, it can scarcely forgo the requirements of coherence. Much theological argument takes the form of pictures (images, metaphors) with reasons, and will certainly require imagination. It is important also to insist on the metaphoricalness of the language, so that pictures and models do not harden too fixedly into concepts set in concrete. Nevertheless, even the best-exercised imagination will falter at entertaining inconsistencies (which would be something like the attempt to see a puzzle picture both ways simultaneously), and the reasons have to make sense. Moreover, the whole inter-relationship of doctrine has to 'work' in Christian life and devotion without rendering the Christian schizophrenic.

On the other hand, absolute coherence is impossible in an ambiguous world. If absolute internal coherence in interlocking and interdependent conceptions were ever achieved, that system would probably become moribund immediately through change, and it would have disregarded the fact of change in its composition. Concepts have vague edges at the best of times, and the values given to terms by one person may not be those another finds there. A theological lecturer once asked a group of twenty students to write down what they understood by 'God exists' and received thirteen significantly different replies.[18] Whatever the coherence of a theology lecture to the one giving it, then, it is being received in a number of different ways. Yet lectures and student essays are more or less understood, and workable communication for the most part takes place.

Theological building blocks, therefore, have to be adequate, applicable and coherent within the limitations of finitude and their subject matter. They must also be appropriate. Notions of appropriateness apply both to the tradition out of which knowledge comes and the complex of present conditions of which it is to make sense. Correlation, then, with all its tensions, is endemic in a theology which wishes to be both faithful and understood. Correlation, indeed, may be too smooth and clear-cut a term for the balance among variables of differing priorities which any theology represents. Components which have been found appropriate in the construction of a theology have included worship, scripture, church and theological tradition, philosophy, culture: many of these overlap (philosophy, for instance, is part of the cultural milieu in which theology takes place), while two further components, experience and imagination, can be found in all of them. Evidently the kind of use made of these, and the manner of interrelationship, will vary from one theologian to another, but each will have some relation to all of them. There are no settled criteria for the use of the components, for in practice whichever is dominant itself becomes the criterion for the rest.

Much of the balance among these variables being sought in this book will already have become clear. Patently I find present experience and contemporary culture the matters which in the first instance are to be brought to bear on traditional expressions of faith rather than the other way round, although finally both interact. I believe this to be the dynamic in every matter, not just theology: what is new requires that the old be defined in relation to it. Both continuity and change emerge consciously from the dialectic which begins from the new. The dangers of the other starting point, namely that already existing theological categories are primary in all consideration of the new, are threefold: first, it presumes that all theological categories have already been drawn up and there is nothing new under the theological sun – a dangerous assumption in any study and particularly in one which has to do with God. Second, from this point of view what is new may not be seen in its full impact, as has been the case with secularization, since theology continues to use its old terms of power and dominion. Third, these theological categories may be stretched to cover new eventualities in ways which do justice neither to the new nor to the category: the minimal redefinition of creation to cover evolution illustrates that danger. Along with that difficulty goes the possibility that by increasing the scope of a category its actual applicability will be reduced.

Further, in my use of theological components, I do not see theology or the church standing apart from the rest of life, although their perspective is not that of society at large. This means not only that cultural concepts and thought-forms will be those which make God a present, lively reality, but also that theology concerns *all* life, public and private, industrial, national, political, in relationship to God. I hold very strongly that the centre of gravity in a theology is God's relationship to the present time and place of believing, so that past and future play their part in relation to that. In all of this the character of the world as ambiguous has to be taken into account, but because that can lead to relativity rather than relativism I may endeavour to persuade others to my point of view.

There will be reference to the theological components of worship and scripture scattered throughout what follows, but I wish to discuss them both at greater length here. I take worship to be the core of religion. Salvation is certainly of great importance also. But it concerns ourselves with the help of God, and for all the emphasis on God's initiative to save our weak sinfulness it is anthropocentric, since it is our state which is at issue. Worship on the other hand is theocentric: it is an end in itself and not the means to anything else, although it has effects. Its primary characteristic, as I understand it, is that worship takes attention off oneself and fastens it on God. Perhaps there may be degrees of worship when both God and ourselves occupy our attention, but the core experience is when one forgets oneself in being drawn to God. Worship differs from mystical experience in which God and the believer are experienced as united (or darkly separated): in worship distinctness remains, but is not a matter of concern.[19]

Such experience is notoriously difficult to describe, but may be approached through illustration. As one may be arrested on a fine May evening by the delicacy of a tree in blossom which is just there, making no demands and requiring no conclusions, but drawing one to itself by its natural beauty, just so, in wonder, attraction and self-forgetfulness, may one enjoy the Godness of God in worship. This aesthetic and natural illustration is not neutral, however, for it reflects, and indeed the original experience defined, my understanding of worship. I would not find the self-advertisement and power of an electric storm appropriate, although some people no doubt lose themselves in exhilaration there. The sight of mountain ranges can also have this liberating effect, although that can also be caught up with a feeling of personal insignificance. In the heart of worship the attraction of God so occupies the attention that one forgets oneself, and this is not possible if comparisons between might and powerlessness are being made, nor if God seems to be imposing himself on me in such a way as to curve my attention back in on myself.

The illustration did not have to be aesthetic or natural; it could have been social, moral or liturgical so long as the stimulus takes us out of ourselves in simple admiration and enjoyment. The experience of worship can happen in church or out of church, alone or in a crowd, through a medium such as nature or with no obvious trigger. Such worship is often thought of as a rare experience, but that may have more to do with harrassed lives and preoccupation with the proximate so that people have to be shaken free of their daily concerns to be open to what is other and attractively there. When one becomes sensitive to the possibility of this still experience it may become less rare.

At the centre of worship even words interfere, since they define, limit and carry connotations, while worship just *is*. Yet this silent and theocentric nucleus is surrounded by the words of devotion, the forms of church services, the concepts of theology, the acts of Christian living. The effect it has on these is that the God addressed, described and illustrated by them will be such as to evoke the free, spontaneous response of attraction. We do God no service in making him unattractive. It is again anthropocentric to speak as if God's chief *raison d'être* were to deal with our sins. The fact of sin is not disputed; the pity of concentrating on it is that we never get past ourselves, and so believe that sin cuts us off decisively from God. The core of worship is not concerned with the state of the worshipper, but with the presence of God. Yet since God does not repel us in either of the senses of that word, that is, he is not found distasteful nor does he fend us off, but is instead attractive and approachable, it is reasonable to conclude that he is fundamentally *pro nobis* in relationship. It is true that theology will also have to describe God as judging our wrongdoing, since he does not passively endorse whatever we may do. But that is a secondary and circumstantial (though none the less serious) occurrence which at no point removes either his attraction or his approachability.

Thomas Fawcett has written: 'In describing the moment of insight, a subject of religious experience is often at a loss to know whether to speak of it as a revelation or a perception. Within the experience both appear as one.'[20] Scripture is the record of such experience with God, together with its implications for life and thought, although none of its writers would be aware of the distinction Fawcett makes. It is important to recognize the original unity of revelation and perception because approaches to Scripture today have often, for good historical reasons, bifurcated into emphasizing one or the other. Revelation is possible because God relates to humanity; the initiative, or rather the steady state of relationship, is his, while humanity may waver, ignore or forget him. The perception of that relationship, however, which is itself revelatory, is by a person of a certain time and place, who has psychological and social conditioning and uses contemporary categories of understanding. The mind is no more a mirror for God's word than it is for an external world. What revelation does is to give a perception of people, things, events, society, morality and so forth *in relation to God*, and God in relation to all these. That relation is both positive, so that contemporary models and images are used to describe him, and he is seen to be 'pleased' at certain things; and negative, in that some practices and attitudes are seen to stand condemned in his sight. It is not surprising that such perception is felt to be a message from God, for in a way it is: it makes no sense at all unless there is a relationship with God which affects the world. But at the same time its contents are a human perception of human and natural things in a new way. Revelation, then, as a matter of content rather than experience (although it is both), is a record of that perception.

This would present few problems if the world had always exhibited one order given by God, even one order more or less upset by sin. But since the world is at any moment a temporary congeries of natural and human contingent orders patient of different interpretations and in the process of change, the closure of revelation into concrete expression is vulnerable both to a change of interpretation in line with changed circumstances, and to its insufficiency for meeting a new contemporary situation. This is not merely a post-biblical difficulty, for it can be traced within Scripture itself. The Bible records a diverse history of God's relationship with his people, full of fresh insights and reinterpretation of the past. That can be seen in the Old Testament, for example, in the work of the Deuteronomic editors, but most strikingly in the New, where the coming of Jesus engages the evangelists, Paul, the author of Hebrews and others in various forms of interpretation and reinterpretation. In the Bible changed perceptions accompany such novelties as the exile, the adoption of wisdom, the future hope of apocalyptic, the death and resurrection of Jesus, the extension of the gospel to the Gentiles, the developing organization of the church. The history of addition and reinterpretation did not end 'when the last apostle laid down his pen'. Because the relationship with God goes on in the midst of a changing and polyvalent world, so does the history of novelty and reinterpretation. To treat the Bible as static and revelation as closed is to misunderstand entirely what it means for the relationship with God to have continued and to be a reality demanding vision and expression now. Gabriel Moran has written: 'Revelation is not a thing, an object that can be placed somewhere and kept intact. Revelation is what happens between persons and exists only as a personal reality. If there is revelation anywhere in the church today, it can only be in the conscious experience of people.'[21]

What is constant is God's relationship with creation. The continuing importance of the Bible in Christianity is justified quite pragmatically by the way it makes known: first, the fact of that relationship; second, what it is like to have such a relationship; third, categories in which the relationship and its implications are to be expressed. Of these, the third gives most difficulty today and the second has received insufficient attention. The three, moreover, are always to be distinguished. If any category now appears remote or undesirable, that does not nullify the Bible's importance on the first two counts.

The second reason for the Bible's importance, its demonstration of 'what it is like to have such a relationship', refers to the effects the relationship produced: such matters as the whole-hearted dedication of which Abraham was capable, or the courage of Amos in confronting a comfortable and unwilling generation with the demands of responsibility. It refers also to the way in which a present relationship drove prophets and others to find contemporary images and actions to express it. In the same way New Testament writers described Jesus in an explosion of images and metaphors which rendered his importance to other people. It is the *doing* quite as much as the final account which is important, so to emphasize the content of Scripture while omitting the activity which gave rise to that is to omit a vital part. The Bible is a record of relationship in process in which generation after generation were moved by it to action and reflection. Relationship has this effect and the Bible demonstrates it, so that we in our relationship with God may see what it does to and for people with no greater advantages than ourselves.

Traditionally, theology has been more ontological than functional. This has meant that it has concentrated primarily on the categories in which the relation has been expressed and has drawn ontological conclusions from them. Many such categories carry over into the present day and we may use them gladly to give expression to our faith. But the traditional understanding of ontology was that it fixed categories of being timelessly – another aspect of God's ordering. Neither timelessness nor fixed essences of being, however, may be predicated of a divine-human relationship which endures through time. 'Language itself is continually changing, and if revelation is to be intelligible for all men, then the language of living men must constantly be taken into account.'[22] Since the relationship continues while the world changes, the categories found eminently suitable in Jerusalem in the fourth century BC or Rome in the first century AD will not all express a comprehensible relationship in living terms and in different societies. To be faithful to the Bible as showing what it is to have such a relationship, therefore, one may have to depart from some of the actual terms the Bible uses. A relationship expressed in foreign categories from the days of kings and shepherds, which are discrepant with modern experience, cripples itself in the matter of present revelation, that is, of how this industrial democracy here and now appears in relation to God, and God in relation to it. The history of novelty and reinterpretation within the Christian tradition goes on and is justified by the effectiveness with which the attractiveness of God is conveyed to the contemporary world.

5

The Presence of God

He, she, it, thou

It will have already become apparent to those who notice such things that from time to time I use male pronouns in reference to God. When I began writing this book I used them without concern, for the matter was not at issue for me. It is entirely consonant with the thesis of Ambiguity that I have since become more sensitive to the argument that male pronouns shape the understanding subtly towards a male God, even when there is nothing else in the text to suggest this. Nevertheless it is not clear what the alternatives are: to replace 'he' with 'she' is equally partial, while to alternate them is confusing; 'she/he' or even s/he is clumsy, especially when a sentence also requires 'her/him', 'hers/his'. I am not at the moment at the point where self-advertising clumsiness is preferable to the comparatively insignificant single male usage for God. I entertained the possibility of 'it', but this has reifying, impersonal connotations and has had such a bad press from Buber who saw I-it as a relationship of instrumentality and convenience only, that it will require redemption before being used of God.[1] The dictum that God cannot be expressed but only addressed has some point, and is a valuable reminder to anyone who has the temerity to discuss the subject. Like Anselm in the *Proslogion*, then, I might have made the whole discussion a prayer for understanding, addressing God as 'Thou' or 'You'. In practice, however, that seems artificial and awkward.

'He, she it, thou' – all of these would have to be used together to approximate what is appropriate for God. To avoid them all by reiterating 'God' in every instance may also make for an awkward sentence while it avoids rather than solves the problem. Nor can that practice assist in self-reflexive sentences. I am about to make the point that 'God is aware of potential within himself' – to say 'God is aware of potential within God' seems to make God a split personality. I have therefore used this device sparingly. Since no single appropriate pronoun is available, the least obtrusive one serves, so that the attention is directed to the argument and not the expression. In my estimation this pronoun for most people in Britain at least is still 'he'. I use it not because it is important or accurate but because it has the least significance – although, admittedly, as feminists draw attention to it, it ironically acquires more. This is a far from perfect solution and my only consolation is that no alternative which I have encountered thus far seems to me any more satisfactory.

God – relative and absolute

The unanimous witness of theistic affirmation is that God has a relationship with the world. God connects with it, cares for it, judges it, works for its betterment and suffers with it. The same kind of picture will emerge here. God is one who lets possibilities arise for all creation to make use of them; who is present as grace in the world while life is lived; who is concerned for good in the world, and the weaving of possibility into the best available actuality; a God grieved by sin and desirous of fulfilment in creation. Such a God is eminently related to everything, affects it and is affected by it.

On the other hand, however, men who have reflected philo-sophically on what God must be to be God, have found notions of perfection, absoluteness and timelessness to be analytic within the conception. They have concluded that God is 'infinite, self-existent, incorporeal, eternal, immutable, impassible, simple, perfect, omniscient and omnipotent'.[2] These attributes are not merely the esoteric conceptions of certain Greeks and their followers, but are requirements in the idea of God of which the most earthbound theologian must take account. Every religious affirmation concerns God's power or his knowledge, and it has always been presupposed that these are not limited. To deny or

ignore God's aseity, his independence of anything else for being
or meaning, is to posit a finite God, less than ultimate, a God who
has to contend with what is not-God. A finite, struggling God
might win our respect and admiration, but would hardly engage
our unqualified worship. For religious as well as philosophical
reasons, therefore, the perfection of God has to be affirmed.

This raises a difficulty because God's perfection is absolute
(*absolutum*, absolved of relationships). Perfection is complete and
total in itself: if it were to relate to anything else less than perfect
it would lose its own perfection. It is therefore paradoxical to
believe simultaneously in God's unrelatable perfection and in his
loving, vulnerable relationship with creation. Yet neither can be
given up. Nor will it do to invoke Christ as the solution to a
problem in the concept of God. This paradox cannot be resolved
by dividing up the Godhead, with God remaining the distant,
changeless perfect one, while Christ shows us divinity with a
human face. The God who was in Christ was the relating,
concerned God, and the problem remains. The simple assertion
of both aspects of God without any endeavour to link them is a
last and weakest resort which renounces the effort to make God
conceivable. Of course there is mystery in God to our eyes, and
our explanations are tentative pictures. But they are drawn up to
help us make sense of the experience which mediates him, so that
the expression of that experience is adequate, is applicable to *all*
we wish to say of him in the most appropriate form we can find.
Therefore, if the paradox is to be resolved at all in a unified
conception, some picture is necessary which will accommodate
God as absolute, and hence independent, and God in relationship,
open to affect and be affected by the world.

The way in which a theology falls apart unless absoluteness
and relativity are unified is demonstrated by Gerhard Spiegler in
an analysis of Schleiermacher's *Dialektik*.[3] He argues that the
weakness of Schleiermacher's theology lies in his failure to bring
together the 'principle of relativity' (that is, the relative difference
and identity of actual things) and an absoluteness exempt from
relativity in his conception of God. If God is absolute he is a formal
transcendental presupposition which cannot become the 'living
conception' Schleiermacher desires for his premise of relationship
between God and the world. Spiegler argues that the lack of
connection between God and relativity gives substance to the

neo-orthodox criticism that his theology becomes anthropology: 'If God, however, is absoluteness, he is beyond actuality, beyond experience and beyond description. And in this case religion or piety as an actuality must be regarded as a-theistic, and theology simply as a form of cosmology and anthropology.'[4] Similar undesirable conclusions are drawn by Nelson Pike in a study of God's timelessness, on which Schleiermacher, like other theologians, had insisted as part of his absoluteness. Pike applauds Schleiermacher's removal of creativity from the absolute omnipotence of God, for he argues strongly that 'a timeless individual could not *produce, create* or *bring about* an object, circumstance or state of affairs . . . A timeless being could not only not be omnipotent on the traditional interpretation of "omnipotent", such a being could have no *creative* ability whatsoever.'[5] Pike's comment points beyond the individual case of Schleiermacher to the necessity of rethinking timelessness, creativity and relationship. The conclusion Spiegler arrives at is: 'No matter by what method, symbolic or hermeneutical, one attempts to bridge the gap between God's absoluteness and man's relativity, without postulating God's participation in relativity it seems unlikely that the God-world relationship can be securely anchored.'[6]

A notable endeavour to hold together absoluteness and relativity in God has come from process theology. In this school God is described as having two poles, one representing a primordial, abstract, potential character as absolute, the other a consequent, concrete, actual character as related. There are, however, difficulties in this picture of a di-polar God. The image of poles is presumably used because it is the function of poles to hold apart and yet hold in relation such opposites as absoluteness and relatedness. But although it is one God who is di-polar, his *di*-polarity is at least confusing in connection with his unity since it suggests something two-fold. It is in any case questionable whether absoluteness and relativity have to be held poles apart: absoluteness by definition cannot be affected by relativity, while divine relativity, as I shall argue, relates to absoluteness without affecting it. Further, Whitehead describes God as both primordial and consequent, with the primordial having logical and genetic precedence over the consequent, thereby building a succession into the picture which is a further stumbling block to unity. By its names and terms the model of the di-polar God emphasises duality at the expense of unity and succession at the expense of concurrence. Therefore, in spite of my debt, particularly to Hartshorne's constructions in *The Divine Relativity*,[7] I wish to echo in relation to process theology's di-polar God what Barth wrote of Schleiermacher's christology: 'What he wanted to say might perhaps have been said better, more lucidly and concisely, if he had been able to say it in the form of a circle with one centre, instead of an ellipse with two foci.'[8]

A circle with one centre will therefore be the picture by which I shall endeavour to make intelligible that God is both absolute and related to creation. This picture will be compatible with experienced ambiguity, but in the process of making a case for it I have set aside the tensions of that condition and argued as if it were simple description in order (I hope) to carry conviction. Both centre and circle are notional and heuristic, for no finite shape may apply to God. Yet it is evident from my criticism of the di-polar God that notional, heuristic pictures have consequences for understanding. It is therefore important to be more concrete than the mystics who said that God is a circle whose centre is everywhere and whose circumference is nowhere. But the same omnipresence and unshapeableness are understood. In the centre of the circle is God's absoluteness, the location of his simplicity, self-existence, omnipotence and other perfections traditionally given *positive* content. Around them comes the circle of God's relatedness, and within that circle is creation. God is related, therefore, both to his perfections and to creation. The understanding of this picture for which I am about to argue is cumulative and no single simple line of exposition is possible.

Traditionally the perfections of God have been described in bleached and extrapolated terms, loaded with unspecifiable content, like self-existence and omniscience. What has given them content at all has been the neo-Platonic tradition in theology and the analogy of being. But I do not understand 'being' as a thing one may have more or less of in quantity and quality, which humanity has in its degree and which God has completely. Rather, with process thought, I find the human terms used of God's perfections to be *abstract*. No instances of them can be given, and any attempted instance could be shown to be ambiguous. Moreover, none of these perfections as such is actualized in relationship, so they are *potential*, they do not exist in time and space. What God relates to, then, is the abstract potential of existence, power, wisdom, goodness and so forth within himself. His perfections are absolute and have no relations outside themselves or they would lose their perfection. Impassibility and immutability, the qualities of imperviousness to influence or change traditionally ascribed to God, are the *forms* of his absoluteness rather than their content, so that they are not part of the centre but indicate its nature. The centre of God cannot be acted upon or changed. It cannot even be located, for centre, like circle, is notional. We cannot give any content to the perfections of God, nor are they the objects of our thought. We do not comprehend what the abstract potential within God may be, although that potential is necessary for God to be God. Therein lies the mystery of God.

Nevertheless, although the perfections of God have no relations of their own, God can be understood to relate to them. Relating is a matter of being sensitively aware of another, and it can happen even among people that one person is sensitively aware of another who is oblivious of the fact. Not all relationships are mutual. It is this kind of one-way relationship which obtains between the circle and its centre, between the sensitively aware relating of God and his own absoluteness. God in all his relating is sensitively aware of the abstract potential resources within him, although these have no such relationship in return. They exist independently within God, being influenced by nothing – if, in fact, what is potential may properly be said to exist. Humans have to relate with critical realism, interpreting experience from their point of view and thus shaping it, but God has no finite point of view and relates with complete realism, a kind of knowing which affects the knower but not the known. His awareness of his perfections, then, does not constitute any change in them. But the God whom we know in relationship is *simultaneously* a God aware of his perfections.

One perfection which I have not yet mentioned is infinity, an attribute which requires some redefinition. In the first place it does not imply absoluteness and the inability to relate. Moreover it has spatial connotations, implying that there is no place where God is not: nothing anywhere exists outside him. It means that God has no boundaries, but it must further mean that God is not bound even by his own boundlessness. Infinity therefore guarantees God's freedom, for he has no boundaries except those which he chooses to observe. This implication of his free infinity becomes important for God's relationship with creation whose boundaries he does observe. Altogether, therefore, infinity is a quality of God's relating, and hence of the encompassing circle rather than an abstract potential of the centre.

Within the circle of God's relating comes creation. (The theological implications of this will be taken up later.) Relationship here, too, is basically a matter of sensitive awareness, but because creation responds as his perfections do not there is also response in God in turn, creating a mutuality of relationship. God is thus to be understood as aware of and open to everything else, while creation responds in a range which runs from its mere being to the enjoyment of his existence and influence. Mutuality, however, is not the same as symmetry. God is eminently related with complete sufficiency of both sensitivity and awareness compared with which the best human relationships are fickle and finite.

'To be aware is to awake to reality,' as Thomas Oden describes it. Awareness covers 'the multiple nuances of keen consciousness, attentiveness, vigilance, sensitivity, care and organismic responsiveness'[9] at all times. This gives some notion of what may be attributed to God at all times, but is found only intermittently and partially in human relationships. Moreover, God's knowledge is not a critical realism based on a point of view, so his realism is unqualified. But this includes God's having all points of view and understanding ours in its finitude and complication. We relate, therefore, to a God whose nature it is to relate, but who is at the same time aware of the potential of power, knowledge, existence within him which are actualized contingently in these relationships. When we respond to God, that response is not to an abstract potency we cannot conceive of, but to the contingent realization of God's power in a particular set of circumstances.

The picture drawn in outline thus far may be given more definition by describing what it means in practice for conceptions of divine omniscience and omnipotence. Omniscience as fullness of being has been traditionally understood as God having before him in timeless eternity all the events of the world as it were simultaneously. From the human point of view this amounts to foreknowledge and implies that we are not truly free in the choices we make, since they have been foreseen by the infallible God. As

Ian Barbour has complained, 'predestination is incompatible with the existence of genuine alternatives in human choice; no subtleties in distinguishing foreknowledge from fore-ordination seem to be able to circumvent this basic contradiction'.[10] Moreover, this static and total omniscience would make nonsense of any mutuality of relationship, if indeed it is compatible with relationship at all. Instead of this, God can be understood as being aware within himself of the continuing potential of all knowledge, such that no situation can arise in which he will not have the knowledge to comprehend it. He is in this sense omniscient. He actualizes this potential of knowledge, however, in specific places and times, so his actual knowing is relative to these. It is knowledge which is necessary and sufficient in these circumstances. One implication of this is that 'knowledge adequate to its objects must be knowledge of the actual as actual and of the possible as possible'.[11] On this view God does not know the future before it happens, but he knows that when it happens he will understand it completely, and he has a totally rounded comprehension of every varied and complex present: what brought it about, what is now happening, and what is possible on these grounds. The creature is then free to respond, to choose, without that freedom diminishing God's omniscience.

Omnipotence likewise changes. No one has fulminated more strongly against traditional views on that subject than John Oman, who saw in them 'the fashion of our own impatient, domineering spirits' and 'our own expectation which is apt to associate absolute power and goodness with instant suppression of wrong and with effectiveness through peremptoriness'.[12] God has been portrayed not only as able to do anything which is logically possible, but as using this power like a potentate to overwhelm sinful humanity and bend the world to his purposes. Power has not been thought to be power unless it is exercised, and the concept of divine power in action has been for the most part modelled on hierarchical structures of dominance because these were the available prototypes. This picture, however, has become steadily less attractive in an age which is acutely aware of those uses of power and authority which deny the personhood of the subject.

There is a sense in which the denial of personhood under omnipotence must always have been recognized, since sin was interpreted as rebellion and the seizing of power for oneself. But that notion of sin is based on the conception that one person can flourish only at the expense of another, and that power is a static amount which can be shared or seized. The understandable, although unfortunate, Christian move with those presuppositions was to attribute all the power to God, leaving humanity unfree, although still somehow responsible for sin. Oman, who took particular exception to Augustine on this score, saw that the reasoning produced 'a conception of grace as the irresistible force of omnipotence directed in an unswerving line by omniscience, which, being mechanical and not spiritual, introduces irreconcilable conflict between moral freedom and the succour of God'.[13] To appeal to God in that case is to betray one's moral independence, and piety becomes 'morality on crutches'.[14] Oman's emphasis on morality can be widened to include everything we mean by 'personhood' today in the way of self-determination, as he himself anticipated. 'Self-determination is determination by the self, by its own character, its own ends and its own motives. This, and nothing else, marks off the frontiers of the person amid the universe and makes them real.'[15] One could not even be a person without some power, the power 'to do, of our own purpose, what we know, of our own insight, we ought'.[16] Faith in God does not annihilate us as persons, nor is it faith if it is second-hand, so 'it is not spiritual unless won by our own insight into truth, received by the consent of our own will and applied to the government of our own lives'.[17]

Oman's sixty-year-old notes strike modern chords, even if self-determination is a more complex and social matter than he allows. Omnipotence in a God who evokes worship cannot be the exercise of power to override creaturely freedom. Instead it can mean that God is for ever conscious within himself of inexhaustible potential power which he continuously brings into action in his relating. God is not timeless because he relates in time, so his power and creativity do not have to be separated as they were in Schleiermacher's theology. God's power may therefore be seen as creative and generative in that it enables others. In his actualizing of potential power, God is first of all creative of possibility. That anything should be at all is due to his gift of possibility: what at any point has existed is a response to that gift as well as to proximate circumstance. Having given the possibility of being (of existence), God then uses his power to establish and maintain relationships with creation in all its various orderings. On this view, God in his relating is social, is sensitively aware of the other (omniscience), but therefore is sensitively aware of the other *as other*. Such awareness precludes the whole model of dominance, and equally the Hegelian model of Spirit with the cunning of reason absorbing the otherness of the other, like a vampire sucking its blood, casting off the used shell and thereby achieving transcendence (*Aufhebung*).[18]

To be sensitively aware of others *as others* is not to have designs upon them, even teleological designs, but to enjoy them and to judge them for what they are, to affect them and to find oneself affected by them. This is the kind of relationship God can be seen as establishing with all creation. Because his power is inexhaustible in its source, he never wearies nor grows cold. His goodness is an aspect of his omnipotence, not something in competition with it, for he exercises the power to draw one to him which is quite different from the power of command over others. Relationship, like possibility, is grace, an unmerited gift we are free to acknowledge and enjoy, or free to ignore. All creation is given this gift, although each can respond only after its own kind and in its own conditions.

This gives a picture of God as omnipotent in that he has a never-failing reservoir of potential power. Whatever power God could ever need, he has when he needs it. But because this power is actualized in relationship it is attractive and empowering rather than coercive. What God does in his omnipotence is to make it possible for all the universe to come into existence, to create and sustain relationship with everything, and to attract human creatures in their freedom to himself, thereby changing their perspective and values and influencing their action.

I have described 'what God does', but to speak of 'acts of God' as if God were an agent analogous to human actors is in my view misleading. I understand God to act through being who he is, for his nature has effects. He consciously makes a difference, but he does not intervene in states of affairs. His 'action' in providing possibility is one such effect. God has a centre well of endless potential existence. Around this is his relativity, which is sensitively aware of that potential, and thereby actualizes it by relating to it. God in his relating is infinite, so his actual existing is not bound by his relationship with his absolute, abstract potential.

From a theistic point of view that actual, relating existence of God, never bound by what already is, generates the conditions for other existence to respond to him by coming into being. That response is, in the first place, one of becoming and being, including all the self-organization, maintenance and evolution that entails. With much of creation that is all the response possible, and a species which becomes extinct has achieved its response in its time. God thus makes a difference simply by being who he is since that elicits response. Because humans have a wider range of possibilities in their existence, they have an equally extended range of potential response. Even when the relationship with God is not acknowledged, their responsiveness and responsibility refer to him. The difference brought about when the relationship is perceived/revealed is that all being and doing is understood in relation to him, so that our proximate concerns are seen to matter in that perspective. The attractiveness, goodness and unoppressive power of God make a difference in what one does in the world, so again God acts in that what he is has effects.

It may nevertheless be an event which precipitates the discovery of that relationship or further illumination from it. As the event has been revelatory it is called an 'act of God'. Since it has brought about revelation, it is seen as a purposive act with that intention. But this identification may be more a function of our normal blindness than a special action by God. We fail to perceive the continuous relation of everything to God, and need to group our perceptions around special moments which define the revelatory for us. Moreover, as G.W.H. Lampe argues, it is not the event which has efficacy, but the interpretation put upon it. (There is no such thing as an uninterpreted 'raw' event, but there are different ways of seeing a meaning in what is happening.) 'It is in fact a particular interpretation placed upon an event which makes it into an "act of God", that is, an event through which a person finds himself confronted by transcendent grace, judgment, claims, demand, calling. There is thus no event, however apparently miraculous, which can itself compel every observer of it, whatever his presuppositions, to acknowledge it to be an act of God; nor is there any event, however apparently ordinary, which may not in certain circumstances be an act of God for someone.'[19] What Lampe describes is the attraction of God having its effect in a specific place and time so that the 'event' as well as the attraction occupies attention, as it must do, since revelation is not abstract and acontextual. Yet when the event is given primacy as something God brought about, all the problems arise of an agency of God in nature or history inserting a happening without antecedents into the reticulation of the world. Gordon Kaufman has argued strongly against the conceivability of such a discrete act: 'An "event" without finite antecedents is no event at all and cannot be clearly conceived; "experience" with tears and breaks destroying its continuity could not even be experience.'[20] Lampe points the way out of this impasse: through any event God may call us and make himself known, with the result that that event appears different in quality. But this is the effect of his constant and omnipresent relationship with the world which we so rarely perceive.

Finally, if God is understood as acting by being who he is and not by taking action in a quasi-human manner, he is not enmeshed in Ambiguity, which itself is the product of the variety and limitations of finite freedom in action. He is constantly taking knowledge of Ambiguity and its effects into himself through his relatedness, and in this sense changes, grows, includes diversity and all the multiplicity of meanings by which order is achieved. He is responsible for Ambiguity only in the sense of leaving creation free to develop this way, and contributes to it only in the sense that his being has effects which are caught up in the whole ambiguous process, since they are open to diverse interpretation and the change time brings. But a God whose nature is to relate to everything cannot abrogate that nature in order to adopt the limited point of view which is required for action in the world, an action, moreover, whose actual results would be unforeseeable, except in possibility. His relationship may be more clearly visible to us in some events and people which appear transparent to his relating, but this must not be interpreted as a diminution of his total relating to the constraint of one place, time, circumstance and world-view.

In my description of God relating to us with eminently sensitive awareness while simultaneously being aware of boundless potential within him, there are many similarities to process theology and as many differences, some of which are worth developing here. It is, for example, an odd fact that process theology, which posits an initial aim given to everything by God, and has much to say of appetition, harmony and the drive to completion, yet holds that process is everlasting. I on the other hand, who find no such aim, but only an indescribable, untidy, interdependent and competing collection of orders contingently achieved, with no completion likely, yet hold that this state need not continue everlastingly. It could end. All known reality is certainly to be seen in process, if not a process as neat as is sometimes envisaged. The question is whether this is everlasting. All we can know is process, so scientific hypotheses are not decisive in this case. There is, however, an important theological point concerning the freedom of God, which appears in the old question whether God needed to create. Philosophically the question becomes whether God's nature entails an everlasting creation. If it is God's nature to relate, must he then always have creation to relate to? That does not seem to be necessary. In his infinity God is not bound except by those limits he chooses to observe. It may be that he chooses to let creation proceed freely for ever, but he himself is also free and not bound to that process. God relates to his own perfections, communes with them, as it were, without needing anything else to exist. That the world does exist makes a difference to God through his relating to it, but if it were to cease he would relate not only to his own perfections, as he always does, but also to his memory of all that has been. His sensitive awareness is thus at all points fulfilled without requiring an everlasting process. Yet since 'who God is' is attractive and generative, and that is how he has effects, he would not end the world himself, and indeed on this understanding would not will destruction.

Another point of difference from process thought is that I posit no teleological thrust given to the world by God. Whitehead found the primordial aspect of God to be his giving of an initial aim to everything. Daniel Day Williams describes this as a 'definite structure of possibility which characterizes every existing reality'. 'It is the order which characterizes the world so that it can be one determinate world, and at the same time be a process in which possibilities are realized and expulsion of incompatibles takes place.'[21] Creation in that case has freedom, but it has to prehend this structure in order to be at all. Such necessity seems to me to circumscribe freedom, and if God expels 'incompatibles' he is back to being director, Whitehead's 'principle of concretion – the principle whereby there is initiated a definite outcome from a situation otherwise riddled with ambiguity'.[22] In my estimation ambiguity remains ambiguous because freedom is unconstrained by God and includes the freedom to fail.

Hartshorne expresses a view similar to Whitehead's: 'Adequate cosmic power is power to set conditions which are maximally favourable to desirable decisions on the part of local agents.'[23] These 'maximally favourable conditions' he outlines as being a scope of possibility neither too narrow to inhibit choice nor so broad that one decision will have disproportionate effects. He acknowledges that creation is free to respond as it will in its limitations and imperfection, and thus may not make full use of these conditions. Whatever response is made, however, God will confront the new situation with another range of 'maximally favourable conditions'. I find this conception difficult to apply. There are many occasions when the scope of possibility is so reduced that none could be called 'maximally favourable', and equally there are examples throughout history of the power to choose being significant enough for the result to have enormous effects. Further, if it is the case in evolution that mutation takes place *before* the circumstances occur which render it beneficial, God as the producer of maximally favourable conditions may be seen to be favouring the surviving species, and dismissing the rest as 'incompatibles'. A similar case could be made concerning successful humans and 'failures'. Freedom again appears to be curtailed in the drive to teleology.

Because God is seen as the lure for 'creative advance into novelty', in Whitehead's phrase, much in the manner of the now discredited Bergsonian creative evolution, and also as the provider of order and disposer of disorder, his direction of the world for his own purposes is only made more subtle, however much emphasis is laid on the freedom of creation to choose.[24] Some choices and states will not only be unacceptable to the ordering God, but will be reversed in the process of the world. This becomes clear when Norman Pittenger, although concerned about the independence of creation, argues that divine power 'both accepts that independence and uses it towards the emergence of novelty, while it also employs a limited coercive pressure to preserve community and prevent orderly advance from degenerating into meaningless anarchy'.[25]

There is much in this with which I would not agree. In the first place 'independence' seems the wrong word for something which is shaped towards novelty and not allowed to degenerate. The emphasis on novelty does not appear in itself bad, but on its own gives no value to maintenance, endurance or the present moment. We are back to the impatient God with omnipotence guided by omniscience to whom Oman took such exception. 'Community' is a conception of considerable value in contemporary use, but like everything else it is ambiguous, for it requires mutually acceptable balance among the variables which produce it. This, Pittenger says, God preserves. There is, however, a good deal of counter-evidence in history and evolution to such a proposal. Moreover the preservation of balance or community is unlikely to produce novelty. Novelty is in the first place deviation from the norm: only when it proves itself or catches on does it become 'advance'. Even then it is a haphazard business. 'Orderly advance' is possible only when notions of orderliness have been established beforehand and the advance conforms to them. So implicit in Pittenger is a much more coercive God than he allows for, while contrary indications in our understanding of the development of nature and history make his claims, like those of Whitehead and Hartshorne, difficult to apply.

The fear of anarchy is used by Pittenger to reinforce the belief in God's governance, as it was in the quotation from Pollard in the last chapter. Charles Birch sounds the same note: 'The purposes of God in creation are not implemented as a series of arbitrary acts, but as a struggle between a disordered state and God's lure to completeness'.[26] 'Disorder', however, as I argued in Chapter 2, is order with which we do not associate ourselves: 'Matter out of place', as Mary Douglas described dirt. Anarchy is extreme disorder, but with hindsight even we can see a clash of orders, or the threads of a new order in historical situations labelled by contemporaries as anarchic. If this were not the case, historical study would break down at irregular intervals. A good example is the appearance of the barbarian hordes to the Romans. Their hostility and difference made them seem anarchic from the point of view of Roman civilization, yet they exhibit their own kind of order to historians today. A God who relates to everything without the limitations of a single point of view is not going to share our perception of disorder, although he will understand it. Everything that is demonstrates some achieved order or it would not be. But this order is not given by God. If God orders the world, creation is not free: if creation is free though finite, God does not order the world. I take the second alternative, which does not remove the freedom of God, but is precisely the result of that freedom.

If the connection with the initial aim or the ideal possibility is broken, I am happy to say with Birch: 'At every stage of creation God confronts what is actual in the world with what is possible for it.'[27] God in his relating knows with realism the actual as actual and the possible as possible. He does then see lying before each part of creation a range of possibilities, some of which will be better than others, though all realizations will have ambiguous features. The new state of affairs will present a new range of possibilities, and so the process goes on. What is important, however, is not the ongoing process, as it is in much process theology, but the kind and quality of decision which is made moment by moment. That will have its effects further on in the process, but its importance is primarily in the present and for present agents. That decision, moreover, may concern maintenance of what already is rather than advance into novelty or greater complexity. For Whitehead, that too is an 'appetition' for self-preservation.[28]

Teleology, as its name implies, directs attention to the end, whether aim or completion, and away from the importance of the moment. In an ambiguous world aims are rarely, if ever, brought about as intended with no other effects, and the only full completion is the end of a life in process. Artists do not believe they have achieved everything when a masterpiece is finished, while a completed piece of intellectual work enters the stream of varied and changing views. Our part-completions, our actions, aims and states have their major importance in the present, although any present embraces some past and future in it. In the same way our response to God is a present matter; we have present responsibility in what we do with the past which impinges on us, and as much future as we can foresee. Relationship with God is always a present one.

One last difference from process theology is important to mention. I find no isomorphism between God and the world or the creatures in it. Whitehead argued that 'God is not to be treated as an exception to all metaphysical principles, invoked to save their collapse. He is their chief exemplification.'[29] All actual entities in his view, of which God is one, are di-polar with primordial and consequent natures: all have the structure of possibility and experience. It is certainly desirable that God should not be a *Deus ex machina* intended to hold an entirely different metaphysical system together, for a Wholly Other cannot explain why things are as they are. But there are two possible ways out of this impasse. One is Whitehead's, which finds God and the things of this world structurally similar, God being the principle (concretion) of what goes on in the world (concrescence). The other direction is not to see God as an explanatory principle of the way things are, and so to have a metaphysic which may from one point of view stand independent of belief in God, but on which a different perspective is cast by such belief, which completes the metaphysic rather than saving it from collapse.

God does not then need to be structurally similar or immanent as a factor (Hartshorne) in all that is. His absoluteness, that is, his endless potential, then becomes his nature alone, although its effects are mediated because God in his relating consciously actualizes them and thereby makes a qualitative difference to what can be experienced by us. Without such a postulate as Whitehead's the analogy between our possibility/actuality and God's is weak, for our possibilities, and those of all creation, do not derive solely from our structure of being (our species being) but from that in interaction with whatever external circumstances surround us. Part of the reason for Ambiguity is the struggle on all sides to realize individual or group possibilities. God, therefore, is not the 'chief exemplification' of the structure of actual entities. But he is the chief example of relationship in sensitivity and awareness. In a particular Christian way of seeing Ambiguity as something which calls forth response and responsible relationship within the world, God's relationship is stimulus, ideal and model. There is no isomorphism between God and humanity, but there is an analogy of relationship to be explored theologically.

God's presence in the world

The primarily philosophical picture of God given thus far has manifold implications for theology. First the conclusion is that creation is in God, for since God is infinite, there is nowhere else it can be. It cannot ever be said of God that he is here but not there. This was not stressed in classical theology principally from the fear that the assertion of the omnipresence of God would imply identity of substance between creator and creation. What Whitehead asserted as necessary had previously been avoided as the erasure of an infinite, qualitative distinction. But in this case, since no isomorphism of being is posited, and God's absoluteness is inaccessible to us, the clear distinction between God and creation remains. Critical realism, moreover, is not open to characterizing all-that-is in terms of substance or essence because it is based on the relativity of its own perspective. Further, when creation is said to be 'in God', that may be more strictly expressed as 'within the circle of his relating', that is, in continuing relationship with God. That emphasis results in a theology different from both pantheism and panentheism.

A major theological implication is that God is present, meaning both alongside and contemporary. God-here-now is the primary affirmation, although present time includes the past which bears upon it and as much future as can enter planning, while present location includes such other space as is found to be relevant. Such theology will be grateful for much of the past and temperately hopeful for the future, but will find its area of responsibility in the present. Revelation is the vision of God in relation to present circumstance, and of the present in relation to God: theology is reflection on what this means in the midst of current Ambiguity. Information from the past and elsewhere is necessary, but only because it illuminates present relationship. In view of the diversity of judgment, however, it would be too optimistic to presume universal agreement on what is illuminating.

If God is present, then the old division between transcendence and immanence no longer obtains.[30] It may be that such dual locating was required when the 'three-decker' view of the universe was in force, so that God could be affirmed to be both in heaven and on earth. But it becomes redundant with a more unified view of space and of presence. Although God has been universally agreed to be both transcendent and immanent, exceeding as well as indwelling his creation, the existence of two locations for that presence has been a constant invitation to paradox, tension and one-sidedness. As with all paradoxes, equal force cannot be given to both parts simultaneously and the overwhelming emphasis historically has been on transcendence, located as spatially above, although sacramental views of nature have given some importance to immanence also. The Liberal Protestants in the nineteenth century, however, stressed the social immanence of God but were followed by the neo-Orthodox reaction towards extreme transcendence; contemporary theological writing is becoming increasingly immanentist. Now that immanence has been taken seriously, it seems possible that if the paradox is not challenged God will be for ever on a see-saw between the two, because each has its problems, and as these are felt in either case the opposite will be asserted. Transcendence and immanence therefore offer alternating locations with different values for the presence of God rather than a unified picture.

The difficulties of asserting immanence in an ambiguous world are legion. Nature may indeed become sacramental when the attraction of God's presence is felt through it. But that does not permit a general statement on nature, which includes competition for food and mates, depredation and parasitism as well as beauty, balance and benefit. Good and evil here, as in history, are so inextricably intertwined that it is not so much a case of perceiving God *in* states and events as of *relating* them to him, enjoying or grieving over them (as we perceive them) in his presence, assessing them as responses to his gift of freedom. Any particular instance of claimed immanence is also fragile because the world changes. Thus, although the Liberal Protestants were critical of the self-satisfied features of the progress of their time, their connection of God with that process was vulnerable to its upset in the horrors of the First World War. Immanence, therefore, is a difficult claim to sustain, and it has the further theological danger of becoming too cosy, of rendering God too domesticated within our world or our society. It therefore provokes a reaction in favour of transcendence.

But transcendence has bred even more difficulties for theology than immanence. Its impulse is understandable, Denying that God is comfortably to hand, is comprehensible or even potentially manipulable by humanity, theologians have located God in eminent superiority, found him worshipful because he is high and lifted up, exercising distant but forceful power. Such a God is over against us as well as graciously condescending to humanity below. The result is that transcendence on the one hand separates

God and humanity entirely, setting up distance and void between them which has to be crossed before any relationship can begin, and on the other produces the kind of above and below, superior-subordinate paradigm from which only hierarchical, dominating images can come. Distance and implied absence is explicit in much religious and theological language which may be metaphorical, but whose effects have solidified into fact and persist even through demythologization. God *sends* his Son or his Spirit from his remote location and Christ will *return* from it. Arguably the Holy Spirit became a necessary expression for divine presence because God was seen as distant in heaven with the risen Christ at his right hand. The Spirit then 'descends' in order to 'dwell'.

One way of understanding the Bible has been conditioned by the effects of distance. Across the void God is believed to have communicated, indeed created, by a word, a one-directional word from above to below which did not involve him in any loss of transcendence. Humanity's role is to hear it and obey. Because God on this view is thought to be distant, but we have his word here as Scripture, that proximate word may be invested with the properties ascribed to the far-off God and thus may acquire holiness, omniscience, omnipotence and unchangeableness of itself, as illumined by the Holy Spirit. One (insufficient) way of describing the Reformation is that it marked a change of proxy holy object, for the same kind of analysis can be made of some views of the church as the surrogate of the distant God. When God is conceived as remote, and a *fortiori* when his particular action appears to have ended in the past, his 'mementoes' – church, saints, Bible – all run the danger of being invested with a reified sanctity. When these become the objects on which attention is principally directed in their role as means to the distant God, no room is left for the here-now God in his present relation with all creation. And that alone can give point to church and Bible. Orientation towards distance and past produces the rigidity and incapacity to change, or even to acknowledge that change is the way of everything in the world, which was criticized in the previous chapter.

The other dubious feature of transcendence is its hierarchical implication. Hierarchies are undergoing severe criticism today. Women, blacks and the poor who have suffered from their effects are engaged in pointing out the deficiencies of such a substitute for mutual relationship, to put it no higher. But there seems little point theologically in attacking human hierarchies while leaving the vertical relationship between God and humanity intact. No relationship which involves above and below can be conceptualized in other than hierarchical terms. Presumably the imaging and hence the conceptualization of the vertical relationship with God arose from the projection on to his experienced presence of the greatest power, dignity and mercy known in an already hierarchical society. But projections have effects because they harden into perceived reality (not merely in religious matters) and the construct becomes the way things are.

The vertical relationship between God and humanity, although probably not the origin of hierarchies, could, when it was perceived as fact, give religious sanction to all other vertical relationships. These, as Sheila Collins insists, form a 'pecking order in which the direction of flow is from superior to subordi- nate, and not the other way round. At its best it is paternalism; at its worst, tyranny.'[31] Although in Christianity there has been some allowance for flow from the subordinate to the superior in prayer, George Herbert's 'reversèd thunder', the general picture holds, and, in the interplay between human experience and the conceiving of deity, God in his vertical relationship has also been seen to range from paternalism to tyranny. To leave God this possible range of relationship in a day when these are so heavily criticized, by Christians as much as by others, is to make him unattractive and alien in the world. It is at present a widely-endorsed Christian aim to work for freedom and opportunity among the disadvantaged. But to do so in terms of serving a God whose paternalism recalls the best ideals of the colonial age creates an impossible split for Christians who find themselves encouraging horizontal relationships on earth in the name of a vertical relationship with God. To put the matter rhetorically: Can we simultaneously enable people to *stand up* for their rights while calling upon them to *bow down* before the Lord their Maker? While any change in imaging God will have to be justified as Christian and as evoking worship, the presence of God *with* creation offers a far more attractive possibility of response than a God distantly sovereign in transcendence.

The *presence* of God has regularly been a sub-theme in religion, even if it has not been theologically dominant, and although descriptions have varied, the effect has always been to find God gentler, more persuasive than coercive, as in Brother Lawrence's *Practice of the Presence of God*. Power cannot be dramatized in the same dominating way in proximity, so old-style omnipotence and distance have gone together.[32] When the chief emphasis moves from omnipotence to omnipresence, however, a very different picture results. A God who is contemporary and alongside is still transcendent, but his infinite transcendence radiates out from every given present. His omnipresence means that he is fully present everywhere and that his presence at any point is the concrete instancing of his omnipresence. Transcendence in relation to humanity is thus moved from a long vertical axis, with all that implies, to a short horizontal one which makes mutual relationship possible. People can feel the attraction of a God alongside, drawing them to respond. To be in the presence of God therefore remains as worshipful as it ever was when expressed in images of traditional omnipotence. In the old picture of vertical transcendence, God was above and humanity below. Humanity in its valuation of liberation has gone through a ninety-degree shift to stand upright, as it were. An emphasis on God as present moves his location also through ninety degrees to find him alongside. Presence, moreover, implies no force and imposes no encroachment on me as a person. God is free in his relating to all; we are free to respond to him, not from the forcefulness of the above-below paradigm, but through the attraction which draws us freely to him.

Presence, however, has its own ambiguity like every other term. It could be seen as the stifling proximity of God. A Maori story illustrates this well. Soon after the beginning of the world, Rangi, the sky father, and Papa, the earth mother, were locked in continuous embrace. The children born of this union had to crawl between their parents with no space and no light. But Tane, one of the children, spirit of the forests and especially of the giant kauri tree, organized the others to push Rangi up and off Papa into the sky. He still weeps for her while she responds in mists, but the children and all Maoris have their feet planted in mother earth while their heads are in a space they have made their own. In a similar way the location of the world within God could be experienced as an oppressive blanket, inhibiting growth and free development. The only way to be oneself in that case would be to distance God by the exercise of power and acquire one's own space. Alternatively, presence could be interpreted as a judgmental kind of spying, much as the Victorians invoked a voyeur God by hanging framed texts on their walls like 'Thou God seest me'. The omnipresence of God is then intrusive and hostile like the secret police. An emphasis on the presence of God as fundamental to religion and theology will have to avoid both these unpleasant possible connotations although they may occur in individual interpretation.

Although creation is in God, although the world is permeated by his presence, no oppressiveness need be implied thereby. The God in whom creation lives is a God whose mode of being is relation, relation at its most sensitive and aware. Among humans the relationship which smothers is that which gives satisfaction to the smotherer, which enhances his or her ego at the expense of the other. If God could be said to have an ego it certainly does not require enhancing at the expense of creation. (That is not even the point of prayers of adoration which, with confession, have more to do with articulating the kind of relationship within which divine service takes place.) 'The art of loving seems to be the art of keeping a proper distance,' John Drury observes, and he finds humanity unable to maintain a golden mean between coming too close to another, and remaining too aloof, apparently unconcerned.[33] We know ourselves, moreover, to be variable, sometimes needing the close companionship of others, sometimes requiring space to be ourselves. God who is by definition eminently sensitive in his relating, eminently aware of the other as other, is going to relate at just that distance which allows us our own kind of autonomy, but does not imply lack of concern. His omniscience, his sufficient knowledge in every case, enables him to know the 'proper distance'. Moreover, the space which allows us to be ourselves also allows God to be God. His independence is also preserved by it.

His presence is something on which we can depend, even when there is no resonance of it within us. There is no fickleness in God, no absence in the abyss of heaven, but there may be times of bleakness in life when he seems absent and silent. 'Verily thou art a God that hidest thyself' (Isa. 45.15) expresses a well-known experience. There are many possible reasons for this appearance of absence, including human variability, our seeking God the wrong way, and our need to learn responsibility. Whatever the reason, the omnipresent God cannot be absent, cannot be other than relating to all creation since he has initiated this relationship. So even when God seems remote, human responsiveness and responsibility continue to matter to him.

God's close presence therefore does not stifle our growth but encourages it. The picture of a judgmental God whose presence is a fifth column comes from thinking that our sins and our state of sin define the only relationship possible between him and humanity. In that case it is our sins he is present to note. But the God whom we worship is fundamentally for us; his relation to humanity and all creation is positive.[34] Certainly we can do all manner of things on our side to grieve him, to ignore or spoil the relationship. But while these do have consequences they do not eradicate the relationship – they cannot, it is God's nature to relate – and they do not make God one whit less attractive to us. The love, patience and steadfast goodness which characterize his connection with creation as affirmed in the whole tradition of belief, are not wiped out by his evaluation of it, which can simultaneously find it wanting or positively perverse. On our side we cannot let our guilt hold us back from him as if that were the only matter of consequence in the relationship.

The appropriate preposition to use for presence is *with;* God is present with us and all creation. That represents a solidarity not found in God being present *to* the world as a subject of contemplation and worship only. He is certainly that, but the preposition 'with' conveys that he is on our side as we endeavour to make sense and value out of the world. The placing of presence is important. It is not immanence with God found in and through the things he has made. Rather, the world appears different, *is* different because it is experienced in his presence and seen to be related to him. Observers and observed are *coram Deo.* Because presence is alongside, it is not remote like transcendence. Yet the minimal distance preserved in presence *with,* which would be lost in presence *in,* is that distance which gives both God and us a measure of independence even in relationship. At all points, not just in the Christ-event, though paradigmatically there, God is Immanuel, God with us. There is clearly a sense in which the omnipresent God is *in* us and all creation, but he has chosen in his infinity to observe for our sakes the boundary which allows creaturely freedom for good or evil. He does not cross that boundary, but is beside us as a presence of good, justice and beauty whose influence and force attracts freely so that the boundary is not a barrier.

'Relationship', even when defined as sensitive caring awareness of the other, and 'presence' are unspecific terms to which I have so far deliberately avoided giving much content. For humanity that presence and relationship will undoubtedly be understood in personal images and characteristics, not because God is personal in his nature, but because this is how we apprehend God in categories we understand and value and can relate to him. This character of personal apprehension among humans does not, however, imply that the quality of his relating to non-human nature is personal. In his omniscience, knowing what needs to be known in any situation, God will relate with complete sensitivity in whatever is the best way to every particle of creation. The insistence that God relates directly to all creation is necessary, for an anthropocentric vein in theology has claimed that he relates to the rest of creation through humanity alone. Only because God was presumed distant, like the owner of the vineyard in Jesus's parable, could the notion have grown that humanity's stewardship in respect of creation included being the sole channel of communication between God and nature. This is perhaps more visibly wrong to a woman than to a man, since there was a time when women were included among 'the rest' for whom men were mediators: 'He for God only, she for God in him' (Milton). But male, female, dinosaur, sloth or electron, God relates directly to each with complete understanding.

When people speak of God they use personal terms, images and characteristics because we have no others of equal value. Formally this is the projection upon God of the terms which seem most appropriate. Projection is not a matter to be feared or denied, for we have come a long way from Feuerbach's description of it in religion alone.[35] It is the mechanism by which we understand what is going on by interpreting it in categories with which we are familiar. It is a much wider, less egocentric capacity than the distortion of perception identified by that name in psychoanalysis. If we have no categories of understanding to project we will not understand the other, as children miss nuances which are beyond their present knowledge. The danger, however, remains even outside psycho-analysis that projection may be premature, limited or overly rigid. The function is acknowledged in the critical realism of science, where an understanding is projected on to the material, and more pertinently in the analyses of interaction by social psychologists. Projection in this sense happens in any encounter, for participants as it were present themselves to each other, on their own side projecting a number of clues concerning who and how they are by the way they dress and behave, while simultaneously projecting an understanding of the other by reading his or her clues and interpreting how the other is contributing to the situation.[36] Our capacity to project is one characteristic which makes us able to sustain an encounter, for if we are not reading the other, albeit in terms we understand, we are engaged only in monologue.

The matter is not formally different with God since we interpret and react in the same kind of way. Experience and imagination are both required to understand what is going on. In human encounters the more one has of both, the better one will understand beyond the exchange of words the attitudes, connotations, reactions and total quasi-dramatic situation of interaction with other people. We similarly project on to the relationship between God and the world our understanding of both gained not exclusively by words but by a reading of present circumstance enlightened by experience and imagination. There are, of course, material differences in the case of God. God, being infinite, is in a class of one, so there is no basis of comparison with a general experience of gods. What takes the place of that is the accumulated record of experience in Scripture and tradition. That record is diverse, but then so is our experience of humanity. We select from both what we judge appropriate in a given situation. A further difference is that God's cues are not presented as a human being's are, although both equally require interpretation. Humanity acts in every word, nuance and posture. God acts in that his nature has effects, and it is the effects, past and present, which one reads as cues. These may not be cues to his existence, which is a matter of the judgment of belief, but cues to an understanding of what is to be thought or done, given that belief in that particular situation. Anything may then become a cue, not only the more obvious effects of God like the existence of the world, the Bible, or the church. Religious biography is full of 'ordinary' situations suddenly becoming divine cues to people.

It is an ambiguous world, however, and everything in projection remains ambiguous. The cues for the projection are diverse, changing and open to more than one interpretation. What is projected may be limited, egoistic or simply misconceived, but it may also be sensitive, comprehending and, within the limits of human capacity, appropriate. 'You will know them by their fruit' (Matt. 7.16) is the only possible human criterion, but itself is not above Ambiguity. The picture of God in his relation to the world which emerges from any particular projection may illuminate and enlarge Christian life and devotion, or it may curb these painfully, or it may be found irrelevant to them. No projection, however, is an invention *ex nihilo*. It is a response to a situation perceived as the presence of God, a response which will be more or less sensitive and imaginative, but will also be conditioned by the capacities and the society of the one who projects. Yet projection is not simply throwing images out into a void. We project our understanding on to the close presence of God as on to a screen. God is then the origin and end of our projecting, but the projections themselves are thoroughly contingent in their content.

A good example of this contingency of projection, which has implications for an understanding of God and begins also to hint at complexity in practice, is the way in which 'the world' has been valued differently in theology, even in the last fifty years. In the 1930s the perception of the world was to a great extent shaped by the dominant theology coming out of Germany. As Wingren describes it, the Confessing Church, to which both Barth and Bultmann belonged,

> was polemically opposed to National Socialism, which at that time represented 'the world'. The term 'world' had a negative ring; it was a case of cutting the church off from its surroundings, keeping its teachings pure. In the years that followed World War II the whole situation suddenly changed. The colonial period was over; African and Asian nations began to receive their independence, simultaneously discovering their frail economic situation. Under these conditions, to take on 'the world' and jointly shoulder responsibility for secular problems

becomes *Christian*, demanded by love. The term 'world' changes face and becomes something positive.[37]

Because projections are contingent upon present circumstances they share in the Ambiguity of the world. The presence of God with us does not remove that, but does give point to the struggle to understand and act. Things can be even more complicated than the situations Wingren describes, for he is concerned only with two dominant views in sequence. But his example is worth exploring. Each of these versions of reaction to 'the world' can be supported by biblical stances, not merely by proof texts. At one point the Israelites were called on to come out from among their neighbours and be separate, thus maintaining their identity: this can be given a 'spiritualized' interpretation. But at another the prophets insisted that economic justice was integral to the worship of Yahweh. Paul, concerned about the integrity of the infant church, warned against the world, but Jesus's practice is recorded as life and work among the poor and outcast of society. No definite conclusions can be drawn from the Bible which represents God in both types of relationship so a reading of the contemporary situation becomes essential.

Moreover, there is theological ambiguity inherent in each assessment, for withdrawal from the world means leaving it to the devil, so to speak, mutely supporting whatever *status quo* obtains, while engagement in the world of politics and economics runs the risk of losing the gospel in compromise and a social action which will always be limited and ambiguous. Further, each perception and decision is made in the midst of a host of other ambiguities running from the varieties of other people involved with their differences of judgment, to ignorance of the outcome or repercussions of any decision taken while the world changes and other decisions are made.

Any theological stance on any subject can be shown to be at least as complex as this. In theology as in epistemology it would be possible for paralysis to set in in a crisis of relativism which can display the variety but is incapable of direction among it. I have argued, however, in Chapter 3 that relativity, the responsibility of choice and action, rather than relativism, is the appropriate outcome of Ambiguity. Although we, unlike God, have no transcendent viewpoint from which to make a complete evaluation of better and worse, we do in fact make such assessments contingently. Our responsibility is to do it to the best of our capacity. The recognition of diversity does not preclude commitment to what we see as the right expression of faith and the right action in the present. It does, however, preclude sweeping judgments of absolute right and wrong. Intolerance is not a necessary corollary of commitment and cannot coexist with the perception of Ambiguity. What is appropriate, that is, what seems right for this time, situation, place and people, is seen from a particular point of view. But if that is found to work, to make God a here-now reality, to be satisfying and stimulating in Christian life, the response then is to share it, to persuade others.

Theology is not a demonstration of right belief as opposed to wrong, utterly independent of all human situations. It is a persuasive exercise, a recommendation of the satisfaction and value of a contemporary perception of relationship with God and the implications of that. 'I am persuaded' was Paul's expression of his conclusion that nothing could separate us from the love of God, and it is similarly the conclusion with which we endorse a particular understanding of God and his desires for the world. At the same time, the existence of Ambiguity does not permit us to forget our own contingency. For example, I find the second, positive evaluation of the world so immediately attractive that I require the first to give me perspective on it. My point of view and commitment have not changed, but I can see new ambiguous features of the belief, and I am forced to admit that if my 'world' were represented by National Socialism it is at least possible that I would feel differently and thus interpret the relationship with God differently. Diversity thus prevents us from a facile equation of our own preferences with the will of God.

The position is complex but not impossible. The Bible is ambiguous because, although it is orientated on God, and the New Testament on Christ, it records experience in such a variety of ways and societies. Tradition and theology have the same character. They are at the same time the product of an ambiguous world and what is needful in a world which continues to be ambiguous. If the contents of the Bible had been less diverse it could not have functioned in so many different societies to give content and meaning to the presence of God. Its Ambiguity is visible in the long view, and must never be forgotten, but chosen and justified examples illuminating current perceptions may serve relatively unambiguously in any particular present. In the same way we need to raise our eyes to see the Ambiguity of the world, but we also have to lower them to see what sense we make of our part of the world now in the presence of God. If we can divorce ourselves from ideas of finding *the* truth, *the* revelation of God, *the* way to live a Christian life or be the church, or from paralysis because none of these is available, we can get on with the proximate though critical business of finding and recommending the best we can know now in respect to God. We will not overcome Ambiguity, but that is not our responsibility: the production of the best possible order is.

The roles of God

The metaphor of 'presence' is intended to convey a good deal of suggestiveness about God with the minimum of definition. It is possible to dwell on it in such a way that neither God, nor the content and manner of his relating, become too solidified, particularized and local. Considering the otherness of God, this is a good thing, and satisfying to those who find it makes God a reality here, now and for them. It does, however, have a certain limitation, which becomes visible when it is compared with biblical images of God like father, shepherd or judge. These express a public, lived divine-human relationship which is a social reality enduring through historical vicissitudes. The perception of presence, valuable and fundamental though it is, does on its own tend to private and individual illumination. But in the process of proclamation and acting upon our belief that there is a relationship between God and the world we need accessible and relatively concrete terms which can stand public use and local definition.

This consideration sets limits upon recent theological interest in symbols and metaphors, and in some ways even on models. That interest has developed a sense of the variety and sheer imaginative expandability of language, while refining understanding of how it signifies. After the straits of verification and falsification such richness is welcome. But reality is not simply linguistically described, it is socially constructed. It is the need of theology to be social, to wrestle with such problems as the division of life into secular public work and possibly religious private family, to have something lively and immediate to say to society about its relation to God which means that linguistic and aesthetic categories have to be supplemented. There is a sense in which an emphasis on symbol and metaphor accepts and reinforces the exclusion of religion from the public domain.

From my point of view in any case, religious symbols are suspect if they are meant to represent the encapsulated mode of presence of something which is otherwise absent, as emperors scattered statues of themselves in their far-flung dominions to be symbols of their absentee lordship. We do not need symbols of a distant God, because God is not distant. Even if they symbolize 'the beyond', it is a beyond which is also present. They are intensifications or concretions of this presence for us, they do not stand in lieu of God. Symbols have all manner of values which I heartily endorse, but they also have a difficulty in relation to social reality, particularly our current, secular social reality, and for action and proclamation in the world. A symbol has to be private (to an individual or a group) and intermittently functioning in order to remain symbolic. When symbols become public and constant, as in the words of a language, they lose their symbolic force through sheer use and custom, and hence dwindle into literalness (the taken for granted meaning).

Exactly the same social difficulties arise with metaphors. Their extension into common currency normally means a loss of intension and thus an increase of literalness.[38] Who, now, thinks of a table leg as a metaphor? Many of Shakespeare's great metaphors ('The time is out of joint . . .') have become so common that it is only with effort that one can recapture their pristine tension. The implications of a metaphor and its psychological force may continue, but, as I argued in Chapter 3, they continue as 'fact'. The very success of a metaphor, then, is its own undoing *as metaphor*. It is arguable, moreover, that images of God in daily use need to be free from the particular tension metaphor embodies. Its character of 'is and is not' becomes a stumbling block in action.[39] How are we to act if we both are and are not the children of one who is and is not our Father? The linguistic (as opposed to the social) basis for *action* may well be the more positive analogy than the tensive metaphor with its negative component. Metaphor in theology is a reminder of God's ultimate ineffability and the finitude of language. This implies a necessary humility, but when it comes to public speech and action that humility may be better caught by knowing that what one is committed to is seen from a particular point of view to which one may persuade others. Everyone in the market place has a point of view, whether they understand the force of metaphor or not.

The case with models is different. The commonness of its use does not diminish a model, for it is not primarily linguistic. I take the *primary* use of models to be that in science and the social sciences where a set of working relationships is given comprehensibility by the metaphorical application of a term or family of terms from another context. Its use is then for observations and comprehension of how something functions, and in this respect it has limitations for the actual *engagement in relationship* with God. The difference is like that between using a computer model of the brain and being engaged in one's own thought. Although the observer is always involved in observations, in, for instance, the choice of what to observe, there is a difference between that kind of involvement and existential engagement in which all distance from the action is lost. Certainly Ian Barbour invokes a 'dialogic model' of 'the person-to-person character of God's relation to man'.[40] That is one way of understanding how God and humanity have interacted, but *qua* model I find it more theoretical than existential. Involvement with God may make one realize that one is in dialogue with him, but not that one is part of a dialogic model. Therefore, although models may describe and clarify the nature of the relationship in reflecting on it, they are insufficient to express its experience.

While models, metaphors and symbols all make a real contribution to theology, they will not do for conceptualizing the social, active, but no less personal consequences of belief in God. These consequences need not only conceptualization, but also a greater degree of structuring than a metaphor like presence can offer. It is one of the insights of sociology that structure and order is as necessary for the survival and transmission of a conception or value as for anything else. In an analysis of the 'expressive revolution' of the 1960s and 1970s Bernice Martin has noted that the concern to be free of structures either expressed itself in counter-structures or else faded with time for lack of cohesion.[41] Her case against the endurance of one-sided unstructured affirmation is well made. She begins from the point that humanity achieves meaning in the world by making classifications. But 'classification by its nature makes binary oppositions symbiotic and thus an ineradicable ambiguity of symbol systems rests in that symbiosis'.[42] Conceptions of order thus have to coexist with conceptions of disorder, freedom with restraint, spontaneousness with predictability. Where only one value is upheld, without even admitting the existence of its symbiotic binary opposite, the meaning of the value itself is destroyed. An emphasis on order which refuses to countenance that anything can be disorder in relation to it, is as meaningless and sterile as the proclamation of freedom when the existence of restraint is denied. Only by observing a relation between order and disorder, freedom and restraint, is there a way of retaining and transmitting the preferred value. That is going to involve some deliberate structuring and the result is indeed ambiguous.

> The cause of freedom must enclose and imprison itself in an institutional form; the message of individualism must be carried by a group structure; the opposition to boundaries must erect a new boundary between its adherents and the boundary-conscious structure outside in order to protect the open pattern inside. So the possibility of structurelessness is expressed as a structure; the aspiration to spontaneity takes the form of a group ritual. In order to acquire any social power, an anti-symbol must take institutional form and thereby contradict its own inner meaning.[43]

This quotation has evident relevance for the institution of the church, but is equally apposite for the construction of a doctrine of God. The unstructured, one-sided emphasis on God's presence has a vital and necessary part to play in that total doctrine, but the mode of that presence will require further elaboration in its public, preachable aspect. I take the point that presence without absence loses any identifiable shape for us and specialness of occasion, but that is precisely one of the things I wish to affirm about God. There is a sense in which his presence is as common as the air we breathe, and quite without vulnerability to changed circumstance. There is, however, *in our experience* a symbiotic relation between presence and absence, which makes his presence special on certain occasions and more remote on others. But that has more to do with our fluctuating consciousness of it than with a shadow of turning in God.

Presence, therefore, valuable though it is in its suggestiveness without making closures, has to be supplemented by some structure more public than metaphor or symbol which will make concrete the nature and content of that presence and define it against other possibilities. Because the structure is chosen and devised rather than thrown up hastily in the heat of opposition (the origin of much doctrine), it can be as light as will bear the weight of the message for the present and foreseeable future, and while closing the range of possibility need not dictate the complete picture. This, of course, will no more avoid Ambiguity than was possible in the ascent to abstraction: 'Man experiences ambiguity, searches to create order and certainty with cultural tools which are themselves shot through with ambiguity.'[44] But as Bernice Martin comments, ambiguity is not meaninglessness. Symbols, concepts and all the ways in which we achieve order form 'an imprecise code' which is neither timeless demonstration nor nonsense.

The type of structure which is required here is one which will make relationship explicit and public. On the assumption that relationship with God is at least formally and structurally analogous to that with other humans (otherwise we could not call it relationship), it seems reasonable to understand it by means of current analyses of what relationship is, allowing for material differences. The *public* aspect of human relationships has been fruitfully explored in social psychology by means of the dramaturgical model (that model by which one sees how relationships function, but which becomes accessible only when we detach ourselves from the actual process of relating). The role theory involved in this model offers both a tool for understanding the origin and continuing function of the social images we use of God, and a means of reviewing and expanding our way of connecting with God in the light of our own social experience.

Before turning to the positive benefits of role theory for expressing our relationship with God, however, it is necessary first to disarm some common criticisms of it. Constraints upon behaviour are implicit in roles which have therefore been seen as external, artificial, inhuman impositions denying spontaneity of being and doing. Social psychologists themselves have been

largely responsible for this exaggerated conception, for they
have emphasized the scriptedness of performance, that is, the
determination of behaviour by norms, rules and demands of
customary expectation. This is undoubtedly too rigid a conception
of social relationships as they are experienced, but before
softening it, it is as well to acknowledge the degree to which the
way we act is in fact determined by norms and expectations
without which behaviour would be anarchic. A role in social life,
like a part in a play, does set certain limits to the range of expressive
action possible. Just as one could not act Hamlet convincingly as
a devil-may-care libertine, so one cannot credibly take the role of
policeman with a frivolous attitude to law and order. Similarly a
university lecturer who broke into song in the middle of class
would be felt to have transgressed the acceptable bounds of that
role. Song is not part of the convention for lecturing performance.
Again, when one friend lets another down, the expectation from
the role of friend is disappointed.

So there is a measure of scriptedness or determination in roles.
But even that may be felt to vary. When a theologian commented
that he could skip along a public street with his daughter, but
could not skip on his own, the general reaction among his peers
was surprise that even the first was possible. An excessive
emphasis on determination may be countered by insisting on the
possibility of improvisation within a role, which is the freedom
to play a role one's own way, expressing one's own values
and responding to particular individual circumstances. Erving
Goffman, whose writing on roles has been very influential,
distinguishes between 'role', the normative demands of a
position, and 'role performance', which is what individuals actually do in that position.[45] When people are not totally immersed
in commitment to their present role as currently conceived by
society, there is room to manoeuvre the way it is played. And as
people are ambiguous they are free to change their performance.
A minister who does not wear a dog collar, for instance, is
signalling some distance from the traditional role and an area of
freedom within the general framework of expectation. As Robert
White has noted:

It is a virtue of the concept of role that it allows for the force
of social expectations without obscuring the part played by

individual wants and peculiarities . . . .Role expectations are
rarely specified down to the last detail. They consist of ranges
of behaviour considered appropriate for a given position.
Within these ranges the individual can perceive and perform
role behaviour in a manner quite his own.[46]

The positive benefit of a role is that it provides an accepted corpus
of behaviour which enables members of a society to relate to each
other in an orderly way without having to start from scratch at
each encounter. Society is not a chaotic aggregate of individuals,
so we have norms and expectations of what it is to act as a minister,
a policeman or God, but at the same time concrete instances of
behaviour are not totally dictated by such definition. So there is
freedom within a role, and it is possible to reject a role as given
and take on the massive task of changing conventions and
expectations, as Black Power and the Women's Movement are
doing. Every house husband, women engineer, black member of
the local constituency association or golf club is a sign that roles
can be changed.

The second common criticism of roles is that they deal only
with the external, public aspect of life and have nothing to say
about an authentic inner self. When actors perform a part on stage
it is known to be a role and not their 'real' life, and this distinction
tends to be carried over into conceptions of social roles as well.
Two things may be urged against this. In the first place, too
much theology, especially since the Existentialists, has been
concentrated on individual authentic inner existence, as if God
communicated only with the private soul, and not with life as it
is socially lived in the work place and at leisure. Role theory offers
a way to complement individual experience of God's presence
with public relationships in a way which reflects the social reality
which belief and religion must be. Secondly, too acute a division
between public roles and private life, which confines roles to
habitual occupation and employment, does not do justice to
the scope of our own role playing, nor its part in our self-
understanding. Roles are, in the titles of two of Goffman's books,
Th Presentation of Self in Everyday Life, and *Relations in Public*.[47] We
cannot encounter another person, – spouse, family, friend or
stranger – without adopting some role towards them. Our
performance is simply the way we act and the impression we give

to others. A consciously angry parent or an unconsciously well-behaved bus passenger is each taking a role, for whatever version of ourselves we are presenting or projecting to others, whether intending to or not, is our current performance. When we are not conscious of adopting attitudes or finding the right thing to say, we tend to think that we are not in a role. But that, says Goffman, is the ideology of the honest performer, and a poor analysis of what happens, for we cannot avoid presenting ourselves to others and receiving impressions from them.[48] In social life it is never the case that we simply *are*; we are always *in relation*, and hence in roles. We do not simply *act*, we *express an action* by the way we do it, and similarly we *express* our feelings. We understand bodily posture and the nuances of feeling given off along with words of a play because we enact and recognize such performances in our daily lives.

There have been some objections to this total understanding of encounter in roles. Victor Turner, for instance, has written that 'there are important modalities of human relatedness that escape the note of role-playing entirely and yet are susceptible of objective description'. He speaks of 'opting out of role-playing altogether in what might be described as "anti-structure", akin to Martin Buber's "I-and-Thou"'.[49] Turner, a social anthropologist, developed a conception of *communitas* from his study of the unstructured prelude to *rites de passage* in a Central African tribe.[50] For a brief spell social position and responsibilities are in abeyance, and in that kind of anonymity a free relationship occurs in community with others undergoing the same transition. He found Western equivalents on the margins and in the interstices of society, such as the early Franciscan brotherhood and the hippies with their 'happenings'.

Certainly the sense of enjoying an interlude between socially organized times may make people more free and open with others they encounter, just as people on a train may tell strangers their secrets. But the societies Turner had in mind 'structured' their unstructuredness, in that as a group they made deliberate time for it and had expectations of what it would be like. In that case even *communitas* has roles in Goffman's sense, as all shared experience does. The experience of being without a role may occur for individuals when social structures collapse unexpectedly with no foreseeable restitution, and the result may not be liberation or *communitas*, but the disorientation and sense of unreality Saul Bellow describes in *Dangling Man:* 'I had not done well alone. I doubted whether anyone could. To be pushed upon oneself entirely put the very facts of simple existence in doubt.'[51] So whether *communitas* develops without intention, as it may in some cases, or requires the expectation of deliberate and terminable freedom from social conditions, the experience of life within it may be freer, but it will still be in self-discovered roles.

The experience of worship as I described it earlier takes place in the same kind of unstructured undemanding time as Turner describes, when freedom from preoccupation with who we are in relation to everyone else leaves us open for God, although still in the role of worshipper. Yet the Ambiguity of such experience as expressed in Turner's and Bellow's differing accounts may mean that for some, discovery of openness to transcendence is enjoyed as communitas or worship (often, though perhaps not always, because that is the expectation and the concepts for rendering the experience are known), while for some others it is an unreal moment unassimilable to the rest of life.

As Turner himself observes, *communitas* can exist only in relation to structure: it is an intermission between those structures which are required for social life. When *communitas* is cultivated on its own, it 'soon develops a structure in which free relationships between individuals become converted into norm-governed relationships between social personae'.[52] Therefore such moments of free communion cannot form the staple of encounter with others, or even with God, so they do not make the consideration of more defined roles redundant. Turner in any case, as an anthropologist, is considering only two categories: the fixed roles of social status and the freedom from fixedness in *communitas*. In this duality he echoes and indeed quotes Martin Buber's two forms of relationship, I-it and I-Thou, the one instrumental and reifying, the other open and sensitive to receive the Thou. These categories were also shared by Existentialist philosophers and theologians who divided authentic relationship into the two possibilities of alienation and reunion, as Tillich, for example, described estrangement in existence overcome in the ecstasy and miracle of revelation. This duality, however, does little justice to the range of experienced human relationships, and appears to designate opposite ends of a spectrum of possibilities rather than exhaust types of relating. Friendship and companionship, for instance, need not be instrumental, but rarely reach the level of 'I-thou'. They preserve the small space needed for understanding and independence such as I have already described for the presence of God, while allowing for openness and warmth of relationship. These are roles, for they involve interaction and an expectation of how the other will behave, but they are much more loosely structured than many social positions. Again there is the possibility of personal improvisation in how these roles are played so that they express individual people, and they are open to development and change.

People therefore cannot be divided up with complete disjunction between some authentic inner self and external roles. We know who we are (and who we are not) by our roles in society and how we play them in relation to others. We may find a particular role objectionable and frustrating or congenial and satisfying, but in either case we come to self-awareness through roles. Social relationships are fundamental to our self-concept, as W.J.H. Sprott, among many others, argues, since social intercourse changes us from the 'featherless bipeds' we 'naturally' are into human beings.[53] Among the evidence he cites for this are two cases of illegitimate girls, each of whom had been confined to one room and fed, but kept from society. 'At six years of age Anna could not walk, talk or do anything that showed intelligence, nor could Isabella, who was of the same age and had been shut up in the dark with her deaf and dumb mother. Her behaviour was like that of a child of six months.'[54]

Without social experience, therefore, there is no sense of the self. Society provides even our range of possible interests and values, however personally we may have appropriated them. Yet Sprott can also write: 'When self-consciousness has developed, (the individual) is enabled to reflect on his behaviour, to recombine his experience, to question the standards put before him and to modify them.'[55] So although we come to understand ourselves in relation to the categories of our society, and thus in roles, the improvisation possible in performance and the critical, reflective detachment implied in role distance and role rejection suggest that members of a society cannot be totally described by enumeration of their roles and performances. Role theory becomes reductionist only if it is assumed that the areas it covers –

communication and interaction in society – are all that can be said of humanity. But it is valuable precisely because communication and interaction form such a large and necessary part of life.

Thus far the discussion of role theory has been in relation to misgivings about roles. But already points have emerged which can be translated into a theological context. When we speak of God in relation to humanity, we refer to the divine equivalent of the presentation of self in everyday life, and his relations in public, to revert to Goffman's titles. From all the argument above, it is clear that to speak of God in roles is neither artificial nor superficial, although the ascription of any particular role undoubtedly reduces the divine presence to local comprehension. Moreover, on the human side, if experience of God is to be other than amorphous and private, if it is to be comprehensible as a particular kind of relationship which is capable of transmission, it will be portrayed in reciprocal roles and their implications.

Goffman makes an interesting distinction between the expression one gives in any encounter, and the expression one gives off.[56] The first is verbal, the second the compound impression made by dress, action, deportment, gesture and so forth, an impression which may be intentional or involuntary. Thus someone uttering words of sympathy while keeping eyes and body alerted for a coming bus *gives off* lack of concern even while *giving expression* to condolence. The important points from this are that communication is not only verbal, and that non-verbal cues always require active interpretation. A similar distinction increases understanding of divine roles. The word of God is a long-standing description of the expression understood to be given by God. Centuries of New Testament criticism, however, have displayed the humanness of the rendering of that word. To allow for human construction without relinquishing the conception of encounter with God, attention may be focussed instead on the 'expression given off' in that experience; that is, the clues and feeling tone present in the encounter which are interpreted as we normally interpret those given off by others.

The cues, of course, are much more indirect than those in human encounters, as became clear in the discussion of projection. Attention to the expression given off by them will in no way demonstrate to the sceptical that it is experience *of God* and not simply reaction to the world which is being described.

Nevertheless, if God is believed to have a relationship with the world, the expression given off by encounter with him accounts both for the fact and content of human interpretation. Experience of God conveys not just *that* he is but *how* he is in relation to us, and how we are in relation to him. Isaiah's vision of the Lord high and lifted up and of his own unworthiness is a paradigm of this symmetry (Isa. 6. 1–5). The content and style of the roles will be according to the understanding of the age, but the perceived appropriateness will derive from the reading of the experience. A particular relationship is apprehended, and this leads to the ascription of roles which in time become traditional and dictate the norms and expectations of subsequent experience.

What happens in the process of time is that a repertoire of roles for divine-human relationship develops. Sundén, a Swedish writer on the psychology of religion, has noted how natural a process this is and he illustrates its action in 'role-taking' and 'role-adopting'.[57] Thus, for instance, when one applies for a job one *takes* the role of interviewee, and anticipates that the employer will *adopt* the role of interviewer. Similarly, when people perceive their situation to be comparable to one in the religious tradition, they 'take' the role of the original protagonist *vis-à-vis* God, expecting God to 'adopt' the role which he took in the first place. In Sundén's analysis, tradition therefore provides a repertoire of perceptual patterns in interacting roles by means of which a religious construction may be put upon virtually any situation. Thus not only have we a range of role motifs for God, such as judge or potter, we may also derive patterns of interaction from every incident in the Bible. The first is the ascribed role proper, the second taken to be instances of God's past performance, whilst both together demonstrate the dramatic element in belief.

It is a further virtue of role theory for theology that it allows for there being more to God than his self-presentation in everyday life, for Goffman makes another useful distinction between front and back stage.[58] The analogy may seem mundane to apply to God, but it is no more trivial than a potter's workshop. Goffman's concern is with the difference between the planning and assembling of props backstage before a dinner party, say, and the public performance of the host and hostess, on stage and in their roles. This is the point at which social psychology, concerned as it is with the *public* aspect of interaction, needs to be supplemented with more consideration of interior thought and disposition, for the concept of 'backstage' can be enlarged to include a good deal more than the assembling of props. The way in which a role is played, its style, sensitivity and awareness, comes from a background of experience, thought, self-understanding and judgment. Performance does not spring fully fledged from a job description any more than acting is a matter of reading the lines. Our role playing is qualified by who we are.

Where this has relevance for our understanding of God in roles is that he too may be said to have a backstage area while what we encounter and relate to is the public role. Although that role does not give information about or access to what is the case backstage, it nevertheless relates the two areas which are distinct but not unconnected. God's roles are not, so to speak, some unpremeditated departure from divine normality, but an outcome of what he eminently is through his relating nature, albeit expressed in limited and local terms. There is, however, a difference. *We* need to acquire experience which feeds into our backstage area and modifies or develops the way we perceive relationships, while God in his omniscience is by his nature completely and sensitively aware of all else and does not need to learn to relate by experience. Experience makes a difference to God, but it is a cumulative rather than a qualitative difference. With this proviso the dramaturgical model yields a less philosophically abstract understanding of God-as-he-is-in-himself and God-in-relation-to-us than the earlier description of absoluteness and relativity.

Inherent in the notion of roles is the characteristic of reciprocity, since they are our means of relating to each other. No one, for instance, can take the role of teacher unless there is at least one person prepared to take the role of student; a bus-conductor with no passengers does not behave like a bus conductor; one cannot genuinely be a friend of someone who does not return that friendship. There is the same reciprocity in divine and human roles. One cannot describe God on the one hand and humanity on the other as wholly separate entities, for we are bound together in mutual interaction and expectation. Conversely, it is only when this binding takes place that roles are functioning. Without that our descriptions may be metaphors, but they will not be roles which we can enact in our own world in relation to God.

This leads to the final important characteristic of roles, namely their capacity to change over time with new circumstances. As ideologies, philosophical conceptions, the means of production, the structures of society or any other great influence on life changes, so will the roles which give them social reality. The same is true of relationship with God in regard to humanity's changes in society, understanding and self-perception. A biblical paradigm here is the prophets' casting of Israel in the role of harlot, wantonly going after other gods, but with the possibility of changing to the role of faithful wife on her return to Yahweh. But there is more to change than this example, for if roles are not to be artificial and imposed they must have empirical fit and true reciprocity: that is, they must really mediate the divine-human relationship and provide us with a *modus vivendi* in his presence. At this point differences between our society and those of the Bible become acute and demand change, for reciprocity means that if God is to be king or lord in more than a merely honorific or aesthetic sense, then we must take on and live out the roles of subjects or vassals.

Such roles were undoubtedly vivid to Isaiah or David and could be worked out within their own social structure. But our social structure has changed, so that most Westerners in the late twentieth century have not known the total impact of absolute personal sovereignty in their lives. We may experience often enough the use of impersonal power, like that of the state, but its source and the relationships it engenders are much more diffuse. Only in the role of chief or boss or manager at work is there still the kind of power reflected in images of king or lord. Yet although people may still be 'subject' to others in this way, at least the style of dominion and subjection have changed. Autonomy has become a contemporary ideal and 'subjection' is not a popular concept. Monarchical notions of obedience have largely given way to democratic conceptions of responsibility – a theme which will reappear in a later chapter. Autonomy may be too strong a word for what is possible in our violent, bureaucratic and sinful society, but the preference for as great personal self-determination as circumstances allow appears to be increasing. If the power involved in being king or lord were indeed part of current Christian understanding of God, there would be no problem in giving it contemporary expression in terms of employers, for they still operate some personal sovereignty which affects life. The Ambiguity of such power in action would not be argument enough against the idea, for all human prototypes for God are ambiguous. In so far as such roles as 'boss' or 'manager', or for that matter 'general in the armed forces', are not perceived as appropriate roles for God, that is both a comment on these roles (to which I shall return later) and a concession that such power is not in view in the ascription.

The most we could produce today would be a partial, private subjection at odds with all our other public experience and with society at large. This would make for a two-world experience among Christians, with God in the private and esoteric one. King and lord are traditional norms of ascription which were once genuine roles, but have dwindled to metaphor and symbol because they lack a counterpart in society. They cannot be acted out in public life, and their continued use serves to underline the idiosyncratic, private character of modern religion. Sociologists of knowledge have long been emphasizing that reality is a social construct.[59] If, therefore, we describe God in superannuated social roles outwith our own experience we effectively remove him from that reality.

I have already argued, however, that an important way in which the Bible justifies its place in Christianity is by showing us what it is like to have a relationship with God, and the kind of response that provokes. That involves the consideration not only of the content but also of what might be termed the method of the Old Testament writers and their antecedents, although it is not a method they consciously adopted. Current events were interpreted in relation to God and the appropriate contemporary roles ascribed to him and the community. Their *activity* in discernment and role allocation thus becomes important. Continuing, practical interpretation of the relationship was involved and the roles had real meaning. In the New Testament the same impulse shows in the roles given to Jesus Christ in relation to the infant church, such as high priest. It is in keeping with that spirit if we depart from the letter in order to make active interpretation of our world in God's presence in what today seem appropriate roles. The older ones need not be superseded, but they would remain what they now are, images for private use in devotion. With new roles which have meaning in our society we can discover God to be a social reality. He must be that himself in his omnipresence, but our antique images disguise the fact.

Given the background of role theory, it becomes possible to accommodate changes in the understanding of divine and human roles without necessarily attributing error to any. The roles into which any relationship falls do alter as one or more of the participants change. A well known and opposite example is the change in roles between parent and child as the child grows older and becomes more independent. At the same time the parent becomes less of an omnicompetent authority and (ideally) more of an adviser and friend. The old role was not wrong, but suitable for both in its time, justifiable pragmatically as offering the best and most productive kind of relationship. But unless it changes to meet the new situation that relationship deteriorates, for reciprocity will have been lost.

In summary, then, images of God are more than private and personal apprehension of metaphor if they are to express a public lived relationship with consequences for action. Role theory, with its analysis of human encounters, provides insight into such relation. In an interpretation of experience the expression given off by the way the world is and the presence of God in it is crystallized into reciprocal roles which make social sense and offer a vivid contemporary understanding of what it is to be and to act in his presence. No relationship simply happens, or is the result of total activity on one side and total passivity on the other. Rather it is a continuing, dynamic matter of interpretation, self-presentation and interaction which changes over time as in a realistic play. Our relationship with God cannot depend only upon the traditional repertoire while the world changes or we exclude him from that change. Following the vivid examples of Scripture, and with increased comprehension of human roles, we need to discover what expression is given off today by experience of God's presence in the world we know, and to what roles that leads. Yet because roles are reciprocal, this analysis of God and humanity in relation will have to wait until something has been said of humanity itself.

6

The Response of Humanity

The capacity for response

The characteristic of humanity which enables it to survive, and indeed to thrive, in an ambiguous world is its capacity for response, in the two senses of *responsiveness* and *responsibility*. Although there is more to humanity than that, it has been vital for the species, and continues to be necessary for the societies of the world, to be aware of their surrounding circumstances, to take account of any change which requires action and to accept in the process the consequences of the adaptation. Response is, moreover, the basis of relationship, the building of bridges between individuals, groups or societies, or between any of these and the world around. Yet, like everything else, response on the part of individuals or groups is ambiguous and finite. It comes in a range from the merest registering to partisan participation, and its consequences are rarely predictable. It can take the form of appreciation or hostility, domination or co-operation, self-aggrandisement or self-abasement, egocentricity or concern for others. Even these alternatives are too clear-cut, for in the ambiguity of our motives and actions they may well be blended. Response, then, is not some hallowed or particularly virtuous part of human ontology, although what follows emphasizes its positive aspect. Its importance lies in the possibilities it grasps – possibilities of openness to what is going on, of relationship, of creativity and action which will have effects. God, who has made the world possible, relates to humans without overwhelming them by his power. What is important about humanity in general, then, in relation to him, is the quality of that response of which it is natively capable, and which may be influenced by his presence, a response which is consciously direct in worship, but includes also responsiveness to the world in his presence and responsibility for how things are in that world.

Responsiveness is the sensitive 'answering' to what is around one. It is an openness to the experience of people, nature, art, fun, disaster, beauty, ugliness and so forth as these are perceived. People will naturally have their preferences, their taste and their social conditioning, but they are not totally determined by these, for they always have the ambiguous capacity to change. If our preferences are not allowed to foreclose our response, they are no bar to sensitive consideration of what is new or different, even what is not at first appealing. Openness to experience, however, is not simply the endorsement of all that can be experienced, since judgment comes into play – a point to which I shall return. But it does mean that no facet of existence and no expression of relationship or creativity can be ignored or written off immediately.

Responsiveness in humans, even when it is no more than a flicker of awareness, is not a passive state. It is not the imprinting of experience but the interpreting and evaluation of it at first hand. It can mean, for instance, going beyond the words of another, the 'expression given', whether by someone inarticulately in distress or by a politician defending a decision. At the same time as the interpretation and evaluation goes on, responsiveness is also an activity of giving, the giving of, at best, one's whole attention and sensitivity. There is a sense in which responsiveness cannot receive unless it gives in this way, and certainly there will be no relationship without both giving and receiving. Erich Fromm asks, 'What does one person give to another?', and answers: 'He gives him of his joy, of his interest, of his understanding, of his knowledge, of his humour, of his sadness – of all expressions and manifestations of that which is alive in him.'[1] To give this whether the other person wants it or not is egocentricity and monologue: to give this and receive it from the other is responsiveness.

Carl Rogers has defined openness to experience as 'a lack of rigidity and permeability of boundaries in concepts, beliefs, perceptions and hypotheses. It means a tolerance for ambiguity where ambiguity exists. It means the ability to receive much conflicting information without forcing closure upon the situation.'[2] One cannot, however, play along with ambiguity for ever, for there are undoubtedly times when decisions have to be made and action taken in such a way that closure, or at least relative closure, of a situation becomes necessary. But there is a vast difference in quality between a rapid closure on what seems self-evidently right without further consideration, and the closure which seems best in the situation, given its character, our evaluation, and the need to respond. Responsiveness to the world and to others will have to be to some extent channelled in this way if it is not to be utterly diffused, but the continuing capacity for responsiveness is not thereby diminished. Openness to experience is the first and most important of Rogers' three 'conditions of constructive creativity'. But it is balanced by his second, which is the requirement of an internal locus of evaluation. We are aware of the whole complex of our judgment, including which values we prize and what we find satisfying or stimulating. That judgment prevents openness from being a simple succession of experiences without emphases or borders. Yet the openness prevents the evaluation from becoming rigid prejudgment. His third and minor condition of creativity is the ability to play spontaneously with elements and concepts: to do more, that is, than we have been taught to do, and to do it as play, instead of, say, as duty or the desire for promotion. While constructive creativity is not a possibility in the same degree for everyone, the balance between openness and personal evaluation is almost always a tenable aim for anyone, and may lead to more constructive creativity than was thought possible.

Responsiveness begins from the moment of awareness of what is 'not-self', the otherness in things and people. The sense of being a person grows along with that awareness through comparison and contrast, and the way it develops affects the capacity to relate. Personality, as Gordon Allport describes it, is 'an individual's unique way of perceiving his environment, including himself'.[3] It 'is never a fixed entity or pattern, but a complete system of potential ranges of behaviour that may be evoked (within the limits of possibility for the person) by the various physical, social and cultural conditions that surround him at any time'.[4] Responsiveness, then, is not something which one can have in addition to one's other characteristics, but, in its sense of interaction with all that is going on around, is fundamental to having a personality at all.

This point, like the one concerning the sense of the self emerging in social roles, is important to underline against that tradition in theological anthropology which has concentrated on the unrelated individual or on humanity in essence to make an ontological analysis. The description 'in the image of God' for created humanity, which occurs only in Gen. 1.27, has been interpreted to mean that by virtue of being human, individual men and women possess some faculty, such as reason or morality, which differentiates them from animals and makes them in one point like God, although even that point is distorted by the fall. As I do not believe that God created humanity in the sense of forming it ontologically, I cannot use the picture of the image of God in that sense, nor do I have to debate whether the image was defaced or lost in a subsequent fall. I am about to suggest that the way we relate to God is through the responsiveness characteristic of humanity in general and which God evokes in relation to himself. To that extent I am still concerned with an ontological feature in humans, but in their capacity to be more than isolated units. If image-of-God language is to continue to be used after the overwhelming weight of evidence for our evolutionary history and our social nature, it may have to take the form that as it is God's nature to relate eminently, so humanity in its ambiguous and finite way naturally relates to others.

Personality, then, is elicited by response to the conditions surrounding us. Yet in a world characterized by Ambiguity these conditions will bear the marks of diversity, polyvalence and change. For some people in certain situations that removes the security which makes openness to experience possible. Allport describes this as 'cognitive crippling . . . where men and women have not yet learned to accept the uncertainties of life, nor to be confident of their own identity and worth'.[5] In an analysis of prejudiced children he concludes that it is because they are inwardly insecure that they demand outward order and control. If the upbringing is repressive, with emphasis on control and rigidity rather than the encouragement of autonomy, conformity to authority may come to stand for security, for knowing where you are. In extreme cases perceptions then become rigid in, for example, the dichotomy of sex roles or ethnic prejudice. 'It seems as though they cannot tolerate ambiguity of any sort: neither in their perceptions, in their categories of thinking, nor in "taking chances" with ethnic groups other than their own.'[6]

Such people are disadvantaged in an ambiguous world which must seem one continuous threat to the security of their order and the patterns they grew up with. Further, they are disadvantaged in relating to others, for they can do so only on their own terms, in their own black-and-white categories. So response may be a universal human potentiality, but it is also a continuous possibility for humans to curb or indeed quench their own responsiveness or its manifestation in others. It is a capacity which can be undeveloped, withered, warped or deliberately neglected by our own choice or by the effects of other people or circumstances upon us. For this reason even the area of responsiveness is included in our responsibility, if we perceive it, like relationship and sensitive awareness, as a value to be promoted. I don't wish to suggest that people may interfere in the bringing up of prejudiced children by prejudiced adults, but that we are collectively and individually responsible for the kind of conditions which make people insecure and unsure of their worth or identity, and we ourselves may blunt the responsiveness of others by the way we are.

While complete rigidity is an extreme case of cognitive crippling, we are all attached to our views and values. They are, after all, ours, part of us and part of that framework without which we could not understand the world. It is to the extent that the attachment becomes wedlock that we shall be less able to respond to others, for such response involves sympathy, if possible empathy and the risk of change. Our own locus of evaluation will keep us from changing with every person we meet, but to be responsive to others makes us (positively) open or (negatively) vulnerable to seeing things their way, sharing their values and pursuits. But it is equally possible that we shall change others, and in regard to our finitude, that is another kind of risk. That, however, is how life-in-relation appears to be: two self-sufficient people, who want neither to give nor to receive, cannot relate.

Responsiveness, then, is openness, imaginative comprehension of the other, and the giving of oneself, all of which is balanced by a locus of evaluation within, and a sense of identity and worth.

Our responsiveness to God, and to the world in God's presence, is not different. 'What makes man good or bad before God is in truth not the qualities which can be noticed or measured, or the consequences of his actions, but the response of the free person which takes shape in these actions. To be sure the outer and objective structure of his activity is important, very important, but the deepest value lies in the response of the heart.'[7] There will be no worship where there is no openness to God's otherness, no giving of oneself to it and no endorsement (Amen) of the judgment. In worship, moreover, we discover that God is also open to us, offering us relationship.

Further, one cannot see the world in his presence without responsiveness to it as world. Relationship with God need not lead to premature closure and judgment on the world, but may rather stimulate a more demanding openness than one might otherwise have chosen. Nothing and no one can be written off as beyond the pale of God's presence, outside the possibility of his grace. The whole of experience is given us to be enjoyed, suffered, deplored or repented of in his presence. But there is again a balance to our openness, a balance which orders and weighs experience for us from our Christian stand-point. Belief in God's love to the point of costly forgiveness through Christ, for instance, makes a difference to the quality of our patient responsiveness. There is diversity among Christian standpoints, so that evaluation will not always be the same: but some values like love, joy and peace transcend these particular differences at least as ideals. Yet if Christians over-define these values independently of the situations in which they are to be exercised, where they form the basis of our valuation, then again the possibility of response and interaction with others is curtailed. That in its turn will curtail the good side of the ambiguous change we risk in openness, whereby we may learn more of what these values can mean in the diverse situations of the world, situations in which God is also involved.

For God is pre-eminently God present in a particular situation, drawing us on to respond to it. It is when relationship with God is not itself presently responsive, but has all the rigours of an unambiguous given from the past, that categories harden, responses become stock and openness closes. Change and ambiguity in the world then become threats to be met by an insistence on divine or ecclesiastical order as given. While this rigour may give the impression of tremendous theological or religious assurance, it bears remarkable similarity to Allport's 'cognitive crippling', which, to give security, required the safety net of external order and fixed categories of the acceptable and the unacceptable. Yet the relationship with God can itself give a sense of identity and worth which needs no such external rigidity since it is a living, open matter in process, even though it will need some form and order for transmission to others.

Nor do people need to repress their present responsiveness out of a sense of obedience, for it is precisely obedience as it functions in relationship which stimulates that response. Two of Luther's emphases come well here. First, he argued to the effect that Christian action in society, compromising though it might be, is better than leaving the world to the devil. Christians could 'sin bravely' in that respect, for they had a gracious God. Further, Luther insisted that faith is primarily trust; it is a quality of relationship rather than the certainty of order in any form. It is in that *fiducia*, that relationship of trust, that Christian openness and evaluation are possible.

Responsiveness to other people and to the world around cannot be separated from *responsibility*, since we are not primarily a world of contemplatives, but a world of actors. At the most basic level, 'structures of mutual responsibility appear to be built into human experiences; they provide the framework within which orderly interaction between persons and groups takes place . . . We are at least irked, and at times thrown into chaos, when this fabric of mutual responsibility breaks down.'[8] This is the responsibility which goes with our roles in society and which almost everyone practises most of the time in such matters as turning up to work on time or obeying the rules of the road. These are obligations which we are responsible for fulfilling, and we become accountable to the appropriate authority when we fail to observe the expected form. Although this orderliness may occasionally be depressing, or unduly rigid, so that many people feel at times a wild desire not to conform for once, such institutionalized practice, when it is legitimized by the consent of society, does in general provide for common responsibilities in an unproblematic manner. It should not be made to appear too unambiguous in practice, however, because 'the consent of society' is not a simple notion.

Everyone also encounters individual occasions where responsibility is not as agreed or codified as the examples above, and where personal priorities among competing claims have to be assigned. It is a common experience to find responsibility to one's family and the demands of one's job vying in complex ways for one's time and attention. The claims of an invalid mother (whether she makes them or not) have to be balanced against those of spouse and children. Loyalty to workers and to shareholders is not easily attained in a business decision. Moral dilemmas arise in all the permutations of our various responsibilities to different people in different ways. Ambiguity is fully felt here, for in these situations there is no single continuous 'right answer' to what is to be done, and opting to meet one responsibility means lessening or even excluding another, so that the choice carries consequences.

In these more complicated experiences the nature of responsibility becomes plain. It is not a thing, as duty was thought by the Victorians to be something relatively well-defined according to one's status which had to be shouldered. Nor is it an objective imperative independent of any constellation of circumstances. Rather it is a matter of relationship and the moral aspect of such relationship in action. That responsible relationship may be with a thing or an ideal ('my father's memory', 'company standards', 'my country') but it will work itself out in relationships among people. Indeed, in so far as the impersonal thing or ideal is promoted without respect of circumstances or persons, it is likely to cripple other relationships which are forced to conform to it. The primary question of responsibility is what may be the right and good thing to do in this relationship, given these circumstances. It demands all the responsiveness of which we are capable. H.R. Niebuhr put the matter thus: 'Teleology is concerned with the highest good, to which it subordinates the right; consistent deontology is concerned with the right, no matter what may happen to our goods; but for the ethics of responsibility the *fitting* action, the one that fits into a total interaction as response and as anticipation of further response, is alone conducive to the good, and alone is right.'[9] Thus the search for appropriateness and applicability in the epistemological field is paralleled by a search for what is fitting in the moral field, so that both reflect the change and process of the world.

No one can decide on what is fitting, however, without the same 'internal locus of evaluation' which weighed experience even in responsiveness. Their values and purposes give people commitment to some things more than to others. Although decisions in some cases are agonizing because the same values, or equally prized values, are in play in different forms, some are comparatively simple because certain possibilities and avenues of action do not reflect our aims and values. At the same time, however, it is possible to be myopic about the extent of responsibility, focussing values and purposes too narrowly upon the immediate vicinity. Responsiveness, and the responsibility which acts upon that, is not only to our local neighbour, our professional colleague or fellow worker, but to the whole organization of society and its relation to the world. Responsibility of this wide nature has been hammered home by such publications as the Brandt Report, which shows what the rich North, and every consumer within it, is doing to the poor South. As Martin Luther King expressed it in his *Letter from Birmingham Jail:* 'Injustice anywhere is a threat to justice everywhere. We are caught in an inescapable network of mutuality, tied with a single garment of destiny. Whatever affects one directly, affects all indirectly.'[10] This may be an unwelcome message for those of us who are comfortable, for whom 'the system' has worked satisfactorily, or who find their responsibility fully enough exercised at home and work. Yet that 'network of mutuality' does require of us responsibility for our own society, and for how that society itself relates to others.

It is the human capacity for response which has meant that the orderable world is indeed ordered by humanity. People are responsible as its architects for both its better and worse aspects. No system, for instance, is simply a system. It is a conglomerate of values, decisions, practices and power ordered by men and women and received by others. It is a contingent artefact and could be otherwise. 'Artefact' is the opposite of a natural object and the use of that term stresses that society is the doing of humans. By itself it is a neutral word, since artefacts are experienced as diverse – beautiful, useful, ugly, hostile. Our social structures, then, as artefacts, may in some cases dominate us as machines or technology may, but we can at least dissolve the impersonal mystique which surrounds them, in order to discern the benign and malign effects as we responsibly see them. They may be judged better or worse on various counts by those involved with them, undergoing pragmatic criticism or justification. Further, artefacts are capable of change or modification or over-throwing, as the history of machines, architecture and social structures all show. 'Structure' and 'system' are impersonal words, further evidence of machine thinking applied to human situations; they seem to 'emerge' inhumanly to support or restrain. The very terms, then, breed a sense of impotence in individuals. Humanity, however, is responsible for the artefacts within a society. It is relatively responsible for the present state of its own relative artefacts. As Bonhoeffer put it: 'One's task is not to turn the world upside down, but to do what is necessary at the given place and with a due consideration of reality.'[11] Starting 'at the given place' does not conflict with wider responsi-bility, but rather puts its seriousness to the test. It seems, for instance, an undemanding romanticism to be indignant over apartheid in South Africa while ignoring the causes of racial tension in Britain.

Society curbs individual freedom sufficiently for people to live together in general order. Its artefacts, the social conditions to which our freedom is relative, are changeable, so our responsi-bility is to see that what changes and what endures are as good as we can make them, given our own relativity and the Ambiguity of the world. Responsibility is a matter of relationship in action, and we are caught up in a network of mutuality in our society. If, therefore, the way society is organized works systematically against one sector – the poor, women, blacks, religious or ethnic minorities – we may use the orderability of the world, which made the predicament possible in the first place, to change things for the better in their respect. By 'better' I mean such things as having sufficient income to prevent one's whole horizon being occupied with the struggle for survival; having a wider range of possibilities through, for instance, education or travel and enough freedom to follow some through; acquiring enough space, both physical and psychic, to be relatively independent and discover what capacities of response one has; and to do all of this by virtue of being human as sufficient reason. Of course that definition of better cannot be advanced without counting the cost in the process of change, and it represents one version of late twentieth-century

Western liberal thought. It would not, for example, be enough in those places where political representation or an end to torture would be part of the definition. But the responsibility of twentieth-century Western liberals is to that time and place, and the best vision of which they are capable. If it is persuasive beyond that, well and good. If not, the immediate responsibility is not diminished.

Every page of this book should have written across the top: 'This does not remove Ambiguity', and that is as much the case with relative responsibility as with anything else. The Women's Movement is a good case in point. Women are divided on the issue of their self-definition in more ways than can be dismissed as pre- and post-consciousness raising. Even those who see injustice and wish to act against it have to decide 'whether they want to "get into the man's world", defined as an evil world but also the "real world", or to hold out for a better but non-existent (utopian) world represented by the still unempowered "feminine" principles'.[12] Methods, direction and style of action are then variously assessed for the diverse situations in which they will be used by very different women. Moreover, 'conflict and disturbance cannot be avoided if there is to be change. In fact, that is the main problem of change – it upsets things',[13] There is plenty of evidence that at home and at work, conflict, disturbance and upset are experienced in both male and female reactions.

This perspective, however, in no way invalidates the Women's Movement, for the homogeneity of any human enterprise is apparent only when one has little acquaintance with it. The example serves to show diversity in the decision whether responsibility is to be exercised for change in a certain area, and that even when the decision is taken, the complexities are only beginning. What is striking about the Women's Movement, on the other hand, is that it began from a position of little power; it has worked by persuasion far more than by force; its general viewpoint has become known and proved attractive in many parts of the world; by reasoned articulateness and concerted action it has challenged and frequently changed male and female perceptions of women; it is organized to implement social change. Humans work in Ambiguity with Ambiguity, but some degree of achievement (from the protagonists' point of view) is still possible.

Relationship with God does not offer the believer an alternative world from what often appears as the misery, grubbiness, compromise and unfinished nature of the world we know. Rather it sets that whole ambiguous environment in the wider context of his infinitely relating, caring and attractive presence. In that case the responsiveness and responsibility with which we relate matter not only for our own good and that of the other; they matter further because God is part of every relationship, and it matters to him in the pleasure and pain all creation brings him. The world, Ambiguity and all, has infinite importance because of this omnipresent relationship, and that makes a difference to the response of those who experience creation in this perspective. Oppression, for instance, may be judged as not only humanly bad but an abuse of relationship with God, in whose presence both oppressor and oppressed conduct themselves.

Feuerbach once objected that Christians were unable to value other people simply as people. Christian love, he complained, is exercised because it is commanded by God who first loved the world, and not because of the intrinsic worth of humanity.[14] In this way humanity's value *as humanity* is denied. There is some point in this objection, for Christians cannot respond to people independently of any reference to God: their point of view, their vision, is wider than to see humanity on its own. But this does not mean that they cannot see worth in others, that they cannot enjoy responsiveness and creativity or appreciate responsibility nobly borne wherever these occur. Nor can Christians believe that such achievements are irrelevant to the God who relates to all unless they are preceded by an affirmation of belief in Jesus Christ as Lord. If anything, the Christian can value human worth more highly than others because it has a significance beyond the temporal. But then, so do all our failures, an aspect of humanity which Feuerbach in his optimism passed lightly over. Responsibility is largely accountability – first in our local relationships, then to our society and that society's relation to the rest of the world, but also at every stage to God who lets creation be. God in his eminently sensitive awareness knows better than people do themselves what their possibilities are, what difficulties they face, what evasions they make and what success they have. He knows it not only to evaluate it, but to draw us on with the support of his strength, wisdom and goodness to take on action for humanity and nature at which we might otherwise blench.

Possibly no one has won through to a finer expression of Christian responsibility than Dietrich Bonhoeffer in his *Ethics*. The context of Nazi Germany in which it was written gives the book greater poignancy, but its vision of what it is to be Christian and responsible applies far beyond its origin and has resonance even in my own different theology. Responsibility, he writes, is part of God's call and comes to us first where we are: 'The calling is the place at which the call of Christ is answered, the place at which a man lives responsibly.'[15] A doctor, for example, has a responsibility to take public action against any measure which threatens medical science, human life or science as such. 'Vocation is responsibility and responsibility is a total response of the whole man to the whole of reality; for this reason there can be no petty and pedantic restricting of one's interest to one's professional duties in the narrowest sense.'[16] The two dangers Bonhoeffer sees here are an enthusiasm which extends responsibility arbitrarily to the point of irresponsibility, and a diffident caution which restricts it to a narrow field. In either case it is possible to confuse one's 'natural impulses with the call of Jesus Christ'.[17]

We act responsibly in a tension between obedience and freedom. Obedience alone leads at best to duty, at worst to slavery; freedom alone breeds irresponsibility and self-will. 'Obedience shows man that he must allow himself to be told what is good and what God requires of him (Micah 6.8); and liberty enables him to do good himself . . . Obedience acts without questioning and freedom asks what is the purpose . . . In obedience man adheres to the decalogue and in freedom man creates new decalogues (Luther).'[18] Obedience to Christ is radical in Bonhoeffer's understanding, and that frees us from the law of God, if a responsible deed lies outside it – not, of course, without extremely serious consideration, but a consideration which does not separate the law from its giver, and which sees in the deed a higher fulfilment of the aim of the law. 'The man of responsibility stands between obligation and freedom; yet he finds his justification neither in his obligation nor in his freedom, but solely in him who has put him in this (humanly impossible) situation and requires this deed of him. The responsible man delivers up himself and his deed to God.'[19]

Bonhoeffer's last years and death form a parable of responsibility. The Nazi régime under which he suffered dented considerably the belief that secular power is exercised by lieutenants of God who are to be obeyed unless they interfere with church life and doctrine. Even where the belief is still held that worldly authority is given by God, the church's vision of the area of its activity has so expanded beyond the walls of the churches to include justice that some conflict is likely. Karl Barth gives consideration to this in his discussion of whether a Christian can refuse conscription in time of war.

> The state is not God, nor can it command as he does. No compulsory duty which it imposes on the individual nor urgency with which it presses for its fulfilment, can alter the fact that the attitude to all its decisions and measures . . . is limited and defined by his relationship to God, so that, although as a citizen he is committed to what is thought right and therefore resolved by the government or the majority, he is not bound by it finally or absolutely'[20]

This does not mean that a Christian is automatically subversive, for, 'his relationship to God will not absolve him from his obligation to the state; it will simply pose it in a specific way'.[21]

The Christian 'internal local of evaluation', in Rogers's phrase, does not merely criticize the state on occasions, it desires the best for the state, it desires what Barth attractively calls 'the better informed state of tomorrow', and works towards that.[22] This in turn implies that Christians have sufficiently thought through what 'the better informed state of tomorrow' may be like, and are ready to take on the responsibility of changing values and priorities where that is necessary.

Ambiguity, however, remains the condition within which thought and action are taken. Bonhoeffer saw this clearly, for after the ringing affirmation of responsibility whose obligation to God and our neighbour gives us freedom, he continues: 'At the same time, (the responsible action) is performed wholly within the domain of relativity, wholly in the twilight which the historical situation spreads over good and evil; it is performed in the midst of the innumerable perspectives in which every phenomenon appears. It has not to decide simply between right and wrong and between good and evil, but between right and right and between wrong and wrong . . . Precisely in this respect responsible action is a free venture; it is not justified by any law; it is performed without any claim to a valid self-justification, and therefore also without any claim to an ultimate valid knowledge of good and evil.'[23] Such action, as Bonhoeffer also knew well, involves one necessarily in guilt. 'Before other men the man of free responsibility is justified by necessity; before himself he is acquitted by his conscience; but before God he hopes only for mercy.'[24]

Sin and guilt

It is arguable that in much traditional Christian doctrine a Christian was not thought of as an adult except in the matter of sin. Although growth in grace was expected, the posture of Christians before their Father and Lord was understood to be that of children and subjects, receptive and dependent. Only on these conditions would all that is good flow from God to humanity. Had Christians been considered equally child-like in sin, there would have been no more need of the punishing power of traditional omnipotence than a boxer would need to knock out a wayward four-year-old. Instead of that, whether sin was seen in terms of concupiscence or rebellion, it was the work of an adult with sensual or conative power and independence (or an incipient adult, flexing future wings). Perhaps that is why sin has been attractive, and its portrayal so much more interesting than that of goodness.

Behind the notion of concupiscence lies the dualist Platonic tradition of the regrettable earthy body and senses on the one hand, and the transcending soul and spirit on the other. When the church fathers were in the process of interpreting the fall as a permanent character of human existence, they used these categories to express an inherent ontological defect. Spirit, including intellect and will, was universally impaired by the sensual appetites. As James Mackey describes it, the fathers 'saw in the sense appetites agencies that of their very nature prevented the higher flights of the human spirit. They found in the very structure of human nature a propensity for falling away from its true goal.'[25] And if men considered themselves weakened to some extent in this fashion, they held that women were far more damaged. Even in Eden, they noted, the devil aimed his temptation at Eve, and inferred that Adam was too strong to be tempted directly. The Reformers interpreted sin differently, but still 'it was by use of this exaggerated concept of concupiscence that they explained how it was that man could go no distance toward the rational discovery of God'.[26]

Mackey observes how tenacious has been this idea of an inborn tendency to the temptations of the flesh. Its endurance is understandable, for within its own frame of reference it accounts for our finitude. But the sad results of its negative attitude to the body and its pleasures are only too well known. Especially to those who know little else of religion, the prohibitions on carnal matters have often become the stereotype of what the church stands for. Moreover the conception reduces all the complexities of actual motivation to one inborn negative compulsion. Its implication of the ineradicable inferiority and weakness of women, together with the social consequences of that idea, are being vigorously combatted by women today with a determination and intelligence which themselves contradict the traditional picture of the weaker vessel. But indeed it is questionable whether sin can be an ontological state of humanity; the most fundamental difficulty with the whole conception is the irrationality of holding humanity responsible for the results of its own inescapable innate orientation. There may still be a state of sin, a state of the rejection of all relation, but that is not an inborn ontological characteristic. If we are born with an inherent tendency to evil, our responsibility is vastly diminished; if we are indeed responsible, we must have made our own choice to close ourselves off from others and from God.

Responsibility, however, does loom large in the conception of sin as rebellion. Brunner characterizes this as 'the revolt of the creature against the Creator' and the 'presumption of the son who rebels against the Father'.[27] The cause of such rebellion is pride and the belief that one knows better than God. Brunner's forthright prose is worth dwelling on further:

Sin is defiance, arrogance, the desire to be equal with God, emancipation, a deliberate severance from the hand of God . . . this is the very origin of sin: the assertion of human independence over against God, the declaration of the rights of man's freedom as independent of God's will, the constitution of autonomous reason, morality and culture . . . where reason refuses any longer to apprehend, but wants to give and to have, where.it no longer reflects upon existing truth, but desires to 'think things out for itself', to initiate, to create, to produce its own thoughts in its own way, a human self-initiated creation made by 'man in his own strength'.[28]

The God who is here envisaged is one who has created an order in which humanity at large and each individual human has a place like a school with its pupils, as in my earlier illustration. Freedom, somewhat as in Kant's view, lies in committing oneself to growing conformable to that ideal position. Given that background, obedience is virtue and fulfilment, thinking for oneself is error and sin. To the extent that God is believed to be ordering the world, the disruption of order, or a refusal to accept the order as given, will be seen as sin. But God, I have argued, has not ordered the world: instead he has given it possibility. In so doing, he has given creatures a freedom bounded only by their own finite natures to order it themselves. As all order is creaturely ordering, then, the disruption of order is no longer necessarily sinful, and thinking for oneself becomes a positive virtue in the sight of God as a condition for devising the best possible order. People are not schoolchildren with a syllabus to follow, but adults with responsibility to and from God for what they do. We have Christian ideals by which we value and assess what is done or needs doing, but we have to wrestle responsibly with putting these into effect.

A further difficulty with sin as rebellion is its inherent conservatism. Rebellion against God and rebellion against his order as traditionally conceived are easily confounded. Moreover, since omniscience was interpreted as God knowing everything from all eternity and having laid down the order of creation, no change could be ascribed to him. This view at its most rigorous leads to the position that any change which cannot be squared with order traditionally understood is to be resisted: anyone who suggests change in doctrine or church order is guilty of rebellion and sin. In this way whatever is, is not only right, but divinely sanctioned, apart from the effects of sin. And in principle there is nothing outside God's ordering. Although the churches insist on this a good deal less now, it has meant in the past that any independent thinking had to take place outside rather than within them. The kind of difficulties the Women's Movement still has with certain churches, however, demonstrates that although churches have largely given up attempting to legislate for the independent secular public sphere, in the private and family sphere which they still regard as their own, as well as on ecclesiastical matters, conservative conceptions of a given order still hold sway, and change may be seen as rebellion.

The churches indeed have been the locus of the discernment of order. It is arguable that the consuming self-concern which cuts us off from all others was interpreted specifically as *rebellion* only when the church was in a position of authority and control. One does not rebel against the weak, but against a concentrated power base. After Constantine had declared Christianity to be the official religion of his empire, the church had an order to uphold, an establishment to maintain and the power to enforce this. At that point and thereafter rebellion against the church's order, modelled on the hierarchy of God and creation, was sin against God's order. Several circumstances combined to continue the identification of sin with insubordination at the Reformation, such as Luther's difficulties with Muentzer, Calvin's with Servetus, the peasant uprising, the spread of the radical reformation and the general need of the Reformers for state support. Since that time, however, independence and change have established a secular sphere outside the church and on the traditional model it appears as if God's power of ordering and control had shrunk with that of the churches.

Harvey Cox has pointed out how Promethean a conception of sin rebellion is. 'Man the sinner is wrongly pictured as the fist-shaking, contemptuous insurrectionary. . . . who storms the heavens with such audacity that God must constantly summon the host to quell the revolt.'[29] Brunner's description ('defiance, arrogance') would certainly give substance to that criticism, although his description of what constitutes the revolt ('to initiate, to create, to produce its own thoughts') seems much more mundane. Indeed 'fist-shaking insurrectionaries' against God have been rare since the Romantics, for whom it was a daring act to challenge him. There is little in our society to support such a stance today. Further, the Lucifer figure, the sinner-as-hero, merely makes sin more interesting than conformity (which is how goodness has to appear on this model). Authority, if not God, is still challenged for this reason by the young. As Cox himself argues, we need a conception of sin which will bring it down to the level of our daily reality and make it evidently unappealing and undesirable. What the churches have too often succeeded in doing, against their best intentions, has been to make God unattractive in his distant judgment, and sin alluring in its proximate freedom.

Cox proposes apathy as a current interpretation of sin, with Eichmann as paradigm. Eichmann was no towering Lucifer, asserting himself over against God, but an ordinary, indeed trite, little official, whose like can be found in bureaucracies the world over. Yet his efficient office work got the cattle trucks of Jews rolling through Germany in the Third Reich even when troop trains had to be held up. By doing his own work without ever considering or caring for its nature and implications, Eichmann made a distinctive contribution to one of the most terrible episodes of human history. In him evil loses its grandeur and becomes banal. In that case sin is apathy, the abdication of all responsibility for what goes on around us 'keeping your head down and your nose clean', however the rest of the world may be. This was also the sin of Adam and Eve, as Cox tells the story, for they also departed from the responsibility God had given them to look after the garden, and let the snake tell them what to do. Irresponsibility and timidity, then, are as much a manifestation of self-concern as rebellion, and much closer to most homes. When a screaming women is murdered within earshot of a block of flats and no one moves to help, apathy is again demonstrated. When people take no concern over the planning of their cities, the size of the defence budget compared with that for housing, or measures to lessen unemployment, they again abdicate their responsibility. Apathy indeed will prevent even the most ordinary relationships from enduring.

There is an odd phenomenon called diffused responsibility. When only one person is present to take responsibility, he or she often does. But in a group where no one person is obviously responsible, the effect of diffusion is frequently that no responsibility is perceived or conceded. Bureaucracies are notorious for this; groups of onlookers don't want to get involved; and crowds may manifest the diffusion to vanishing point of responsibility for action. In the same kind of way we may try to absolve ourselves from responsibility by holding that society is organized by 'them', not 'us'. The result, however, is the kind of apathy which lets be whatever happens. Responsibility is not dissolved because it is diffused. Dorothy Emmet has described similar evasions of responsibility made possible by the constitutional and insti- tutional arrangements of a liberal democracy: 'Those of us who distrust the *Fuehrer-Prinzip* (we have seen what it can mean) will look on these evasions as a risk to be taken for the sake of a system in which powers and responsibilities can be spread. Yet the temptation to pass the buck is a real one; this is yet another instance of how there is a catch in everything, so that no institutional arrangements will produce Utopia.'[30]

It need not be a sin to be an adult with sensuality and a mind of one's own. Much nearer to the point is what one does as an adult with these and other powers, and the degree of independence possible. As Mackey comments: 'No one starts out with responsi- bility for the tradition which made him, but he inevitably ends up with responsibility for the tradition which will continue to form him, and that will make succeeding generations.'[31] Responsibility will not even be perceived, however, unless one's horizon is wider than one's own well-being. Like responsiveness, the joy or sorrow at what one encounters, it demands an awareness which goes beyond the self. And with that perception we return to the traditional and still valid conception of sin as consuming preoccupation with oneself. The difficulty in the traditional view is that this egocentricity was called 'self-love', and the recommended alternative was self-denial or even self-hatred. This was a natural enough move when the self was thought to be ontologically defective, but it so concentrated attention on the self which was to be denied or hated that it became another form of inverted egocentricity and could produce psychological disaster. As Gabriel Moran claims: 'The preaching of self-hatred as the way to Christian holiness produces the worst narcissistic illusions while it accentuates dangerous neurotic tendencies deep in the human personality. Selfishness and self-love have often been equated whereas in fact they are opposites.'[32]

This is Erich Fromm's conclusion also. One cannot love others unless one loves oneself. '*The affirmation of one's own life, happiness, growth, freedom is rooted in one's capacity to love*, i.e. in care, respect, responsibility and knowledge. If an individual is able to love productively, he loves himself too – if he can love *only* others, he cannot love at all.'[33] Conversely, a selfish person loves him – or herself too little. 'He seems to care too much for himself, but actually he only makes an unsuccessful attempt to cover up and compensate for his failure to care for his real self.'[34] Selfish people cannot love – either themselves or others. Loving oneself does not mean being lost in admiration at one's own qualities and goodness and thus oblivious to all else. That indeed would be as narcissistic as the constant search for one's sins. Instead of that, loving oneself means the recognition of the human being one is, with all one's potentialities, with the result that 'respect for one's own integrity and uniqueness, love for and understanding of one's own self cannot be separated from respect and love and understanding for another individual'.[35] This is Allport's 'sense of identity and worth', and part of Rogers's 'locus of evaluation' which makes anyone able to face the world, respond to it, but not be entirely confounded by its diversity and its need.

In the Christian case respect, love and understanding for oneself and others are all bound up in our universal relationship with God who desires the best for all his creatures, including ourselves. Our worth to him, signalized by Christ's death, establishes our sense of worth. Fromm quotes Meister Eckhart to great effect: 'If you love yourself, you love everybody else as you do yourself. As long as you love another person less than you love yourself, you will not really succeed in loving yourself, but if you love all alike, including yourself, you will love them as one person and that person is both God and man. Thus he is a great and righteous person who, loving himself, loves all others equally.'[36] Such love, however, is not a vague and impulsive benevolence, for the recognition of one's own identity and uniqueness in the presence of God leads to the use of that identity in responsible action with God. For this to happen effectively self-love will mean, as V.A. Demant describes it, 'a right ordering of all my activities, physical, mental, occupational, cultural, in an order which ministers to the response of my whole being to God and to all things in God. This rightness or *justitia* is an essential ingredient in charity according to the Catholic Doctors, and . . . where it is absent in persons or peoples solidarity does not arrive in spite of all good will.'[37]

If love has the same characteristics in loving oneself and

another, it follows also that loving God and one's neighbour are not two different activities separated out by the 'and'. Nicholas Lash is scathing on those who speak as if 'the fulfilling of each commandment occupied distinct areas of their time and energy. At our best we talk as if these two loves could conflict (which, if it were true, would prove the atheist's point that the existence of God restricted human development). At our worst we talk as if formal prayer was "loving God" and sticking elastoplast on the knees of a screaming child "loving our brother". Then we spend a great deal of time discussing how each of these two apparently contradictory commandments can be fulfilled without detriment to the other.'[38] The two cannot be held together, however, unless God is present in all situations and unless it is seen to be his desire for the world that the best possible in human, social and natural terms be achieved in it. In that case to respond to the other is simultaneously to respond to God, and to share responsibility for how others are is to accept the purpose of the freedom he gives us.

Thus far sin has been described as apathy or egocentricity, which shows lack of responsiveness and abdication of responsibility because of preoccupation with the well-being and security of the self. Such curvature of the self in on to itself is a different thing from self-love, that acceptance of the self which makes possible openness to God's influence in all the matters of living responsibly with other people. Nevertheless there is more to life in an ambiguous world than that. Even when sin as loveless self-centredness is not primarily at issue, the manner and scope of our responding are. Kenneth Burke puts the matter with an air of inevitability: 'In their societies they will seek to keep order. If order, then a need to repress the tendencies to disorder. If repression, then responsibility for imposing, accepting or resisting the repression. If responsibility, then guilt.'[39] There is no way out of incurring guilt. One may understand the timidity of the individual before the powers that be, but to accept quietly and without question the way things are is to reproduce Eich-mannian apathy and collusion with the *status quo*, for no order is likely to work in everyone's favour. On the other hand, to advance a preferred version of social order, which will still be finite, and therefore imperfect, will involve conflict and upset, if nothing more, for an uncertain result. Action of this kind, intended for the good of others and not for self-advancement, would come under Bonhoeffer's description of 'bearing guilt for the sake of the neighbour'.[40] His own instance was the telling of a lie to save another's life, but his life illustrated the width of the concept in his complicity in the plot to kill Hitler. The guilt in such cases may seem to some extent excusable, but it is still there, as it is in any situation where a choice between two imperfect courses of action is all that is available. None of us can know what effect our actions or our passivities will have in an ambiguous world of diverse interests, changing circumstances and plurality of vision. So neither action nor abstaining from action absolves anyone.

These instances form what might be called public guilt, and to them may be added the guilt we participate in by membership in our occupation, class or country. To be a manager, for instance, in an industry where concern for people is lost in the drive for profit, or to be a citizen of the rich North, consuming on favourable terms the products of the poor South, is to share in that collective guilt. Further, there is our individual and private guilt, for all our relationships are ambiguous. Parents, for example, may damage their children without realizing it and despite their best intentions, simply by being the kind of people they are. We may destroy another person's ideals or self-image in a few careless words, or spoil a relationship by inattention. When we intend to be vicious to each other, the possibilities are endless. We are capable of wrongdoing also in the way of theft, arson and so forth, but here again, although it is no mean thing to be the victim, the chief damage is the absence of relationship within society which makes it possible for one to steal from another. It is in absence and failure of relationship that we sin, when something better is possible.

This is the merest sketch of the dimensions of guilt in every life. No one can avoid the tragic element which includes but also transcends our own personal fallibility. That conclusion cannot be passed over easily in self-acceptance, and may indeed keep self-love from being indulgent. By ourselves we can only recognize that guilt is part of life. We cannot cure our own, nor absolve other people from theirs.

It is in the perspective of our relationship with God, to whom we are constantly responsible, that this guilt, wrongdoing or failure in relating becomes sin. Sin then takes two forms. First there is the refusal to respond, which is 'a No of the human person, who shuts himself off and hardens himself when openness and self-donation are expected. As the Bible puts it, it is the human heart turning to stone.'[41] Then, second, it is our failure, even in openness and self-donation, to understand, to respect, to care in the right way at the right time when something more sensitive was truly open to us. Apathy, egocentricity, insensitivity and finitude are all bound up in the meaning of sin. In so far as these attributes hem us in and isolate us, we are in a state of the absence of relation, a state of sin. In so far as they characterize our relationships, we fail in relating and thereby commit actual sins. Since love of God and love of the neighbour cannot be separated, what we do to others, we do to God. If we cannot relate to others, we do not know how to relate to him; if we are not sensitive to others, we will not be sensitive to his influence either.

If we are sensitive, however, and aware of our failure, we see in his presence what sin is, for all failures are also failures in relating to him. In his love he has given us freedom, and in that context our sin becomes grievous, undesirable, a blot on the relationship as well as having contingent effects. A 'sense of sin' in that case is not the recognition of disobedience and the fear of retribution – a child's reaction. Instead it is the adult acknowledgment that certain thoughts or actions have been utterly unworthy of our relationship with God, so that God has been 'let down'. But sin does not remove the relationship, for it is God's nature always and everywhere to relate. We do not 'clear the way' to God, as it were, by our repentance and confession, but in our repentance we find his forgiveness already there, waiting for us. When we open ourselves to any experience we find God already there, prevenient in it, and this is true of remorse and admission of failure also. We still have to live with the consequence of our actions, but there is no need for an accumulation of guilt to corrode our capacity to respond, since we are forgiven.

At this point it becomes particularly difficult to discuss God's forgiveness without consideration of the death of Jesus Christ which gives dramatic form to the loving and costly nature of that forgiveness. Part of what Christ's death portrays, however, is that God's forgiveness is not a mere indulgence of his creatures, for he is wounded by our sin. We cause pain to God. What that pain can be like to one who relates with eminent sensitivity we can hardly guess. Yet his love accepts the pain within the relationship, so that when we turn to him in repentance, the estrangement on our side is overcome, and the reconciliation overcomes the cause of the pain.

Even when sin and guilt are taken with full seriousness, however, they are not the whole description of humanity in relation to God and the neighbour. In the ambiguous world there is better as well as worse among women and men. We not only cause God pain, we also bring him pleasure. We can hardly credit God with the partial vision which allows sin to register while our better actions are filtered out as irrelevant. Humans are capable of relationships which contribute to their mutual growth in love and understanding; they are sometimes capable of creating social structures in which people may go about their business in peace and comparative freedom; in many countries ideals of fairness have been erected to which businesses and public officers must be seen to subscribe if they are to keep face and custom. None of this may be unambiguously good, but even our worse acts are not entirely and unambiguously bad. God with his complete realism knows the mixture in our actions and does not measure us against a perfection of which we are not capable and from which we have not fallen. This perception does not make our coldness and self-sufficiency any less serious, but it does mean that there is more to our relationship with God at all times than sin.

7

The Companionship of God

What transforming light, then, is cast on humanity in its achievement and predicament by a sense of the presence of God in its midst? The answer is both that it makes no difference and that it makes all the difference. The one thing which cannot be said is that such awareness makes *some* difference, either quantitatively, as if he added a little to experience here and there, or in quality, as if the world looked only a little different in his presence. The difference God makes is simultaneously all and nothing; nothing has changed but nothing is the same. Expressed less elliptically, the result of awareness of God's presence is that although the world is as complex as before, the perspective on that process and the value given to every part of it have changed completely.

The sense of God's presence does not make the world any less ambiguous in all its circumstances and in its impact. Valleys are not exalted for us, nor are hills laid low. As Peter Baelz has observed: 'When the Psalmist declared that he had never seen the righteous forsaken, either he was living a very cloistered existence, or else piety had got the upper hand of honesty.'[1] God has let creation develop as it could and did. That freedom is bounded only by each creature's contingent limitations in natural or human history. To remove Ambiguity for any, even intermittently, would be to moderate that freedom and also to take away the condition of an active response to life, and thus to God himself. If the way in which we respond matters to God he will not from time to time remove the conditions for that response. Moreover belief that God can, in traditional omnipotence, and will remove *some* Ambiguity (particularly what causes us trouble) but not all;

that he will, for instance, cure some diseases at our behest but not all, makes God appear capricious or given to favouritism. An appeal to his inscrutable will in such cases provokes the same kind of moral outrage as Dostoevsky expressed in Ivan Kara-mazov. There is, as Stewart Sutherland has noted, 'a distinction to be drawn between what brings intellectual puzzlement [and is thus indeed the mystery of God to us]. . . . and what gives rise to moral uncertainty and even confusion. . . . There is an element of doublespeak in discussing God's attributes quite plainly [traditional omniscience, omnipotence] while insisting upon the mystery of evil and the incomprehensibility of his goodness when confronted with evil or suffering,'[2] or, for that matter, when confronted with a cure or the settlement of a difficulty.

Although it is the tendency of humanity to cry to God in extremities of sadness, war, destitution or death, and indeed frequently to find him there, if that practice represents only the desire for divine eradication of our particular difficulties, it gives God the status of a problem-solver. It appears then that what people can manage they manage. When they can no longer cope they call in God, just as they would call in a plumber or an electrician when necessary. God then becomes the celestial repairer of boundary situations and hence a skilled artisan. Undoubtedly boundary experiences, when human finitude is painfully clear, have brought people to God. But when this becomes the expectation of God's role, it gives rise to a number of undesirable implications. One is the notion that God will somehow intervene in emergencies to alter circumstances in our favour. Quite apart from the theoretical difficulties of an act of God already mentioned in Chapter 4, there are the religious difficulties of a God who appears to exist for our benefit when needed. Practically, moreover, experience would suggest that on the tradesman model God appears unreliable, since compara-tively few distresses and diseases are healed. Another difficulty with this view is the implication that a life without insoluble problems is a life without need of God. In that case also, every human advance in understanding and problem-solving, say in the medical field, is a retreat for God. He grows increasingly superfluous.

Instead of this picture of intermittent action by God in the world which makes empirical differences here and there, I have argued that God acts by being who he is and eliciting response. It was Oman's valid insight that we project on to God our own impatient desire for prompt and efficient action, so that we have scarcely begun to understand his tolerance, his patience which waits for response rather than imposing a solution.

> He will not force his mystery upon us. He will lead us up to it. Violence is the destruction, the contradiction, the absolute opposite of this mystery . . . God's tolerance is not like man's. It is not mere endurance of what we ourselves think right or not very far wrong. It is real tolerance – the recognition of the freedom of the possessor of a mind and conscience to err, the determination not to replace man's own dim search for light and man's own vacillating discipline of a wayward will even by omniscient wisdom and omnipotent righteousness.[3]

The difference God makes, therefore, lies, not in his spinning of circumstance nor in his removal of difficulty, but in the quality and force of his relationship. Even when this is unrecognized and uncultivated, the creature has a different status and worth because of it. Recognition, however, alters one's whole perspective: the world no longer fills the horizon but is contained within his relating, indeed exists because of that relationship. In that case action, thought and being have point not only as a struggle for survival, the making of order or the promotion of pleasure or justice, but as a response to divine possibility. Because that possibility is offered through a relationship which God has with every part of creation, the sense of his presence changes conceptions of all relationships such as those with nature, in industry, in politics, in marriage and personal friendship, and thus makes all the difference in detail as well as in general. What this chapter is concerned with now is the roles into which such relationship can fall and the effects of these roles in some areas of life which show how that difference can work out in practice.

For ourselves in the presence of God there is first the relief of being utterly understood in all our personal complication and fluctuation among the diversity and variation of circumstances in which we live and act. We need no fig leaves of explanation to cover our nakedness. Nakedness is not shame, however. It is who we are in our particular mixture of good and bad, order and disorder, responsiveness and egocentricity, responsibility and apathy. The one aspect in complicated, harassed and dissembling lives when people may be truly themselves is in relation to God. Moreover his presence does not have the daunting neutrality of a recording angel with two columns (positive and negative) to every name, nor the covert hostility of a suspicious criminal investigator. God is fundamentally for us, his steadfast love is with us before, during and after anything we may do. To find ourselves in his presence, then, is like returning to a mother who has allowed her adult children to go free, but whose interest, love, enjoyment and pain is intimately bound up in all that happens to them. God's presence combines that kind of love and comprehension. He does not know our future except in its possibility, and his continuing love stands by us as that possibility becomes actuality. This does not mean that God indulgently endorses all that we do, but it does mean that whatever we do, access to his relationship of love is not blocked off. Our wrongdoing takes on a new aspect precisely from that fact. Given the relationship with God and in its context, sin is out of place, mean, thankless, hurtful to others and to God.

Already roles for the relationship have emerged which make it possible imaginatively to realize and enact it. There are few who do not know what it is to be an adult with parents, and many who know what it is to be the parents of adults. I have used the more maternal picture thus far largely because in our society it is the mother who is expected to follow her children's fortunes with that kind of concern. A father is stereotypically permitted pride in his offspring's success, and some such pleasure at least must be ascribed to God. But in our achievement-orientated society it is not clear how fathers are supposed to relate to the less successful of us. A mother, on the other hand, is more typically affected by the person, while success or failure in the world's terms is of little import. There are no prior conditions to the constancy of her love. It is given, not won, and in this way expresses what we want to say of God.

The human side of such relationships involves neither a child who is dependent nor an adolescent unsteadily making sorties into the world, but an adult who has established his or her own base in a career or home. That corresponds to the freedom God has given us, and the space to be ourselves which is part of the relationship. It is possible for adults to live as if neither the parental home nor the presence of God existed, yet that home or that presence is very much aware of the grown, independent offspring and is permanently available as a place or an acknowledged relationship of love, understanding and acceptance. Of course it can happen in real life that a mother cannot bring herself to allow a child true independence, or that parents in their old age may have to be supported. Some children indeed are only too glad to leave their parents' home behind. But the actual human failings or weaknesses in the role do not invalidate it as a prototype for the divine-human relationship. No father has ever matched up to what has been ascribed to God the Father. What is seen to be irrelevant or negative is continually sifted out. But then, also, a kind of inversion takes place, so that the qualities of the divine role become Christian ideals for human living as well. In that case parents and children who have not arrived at that quality of relationship in which the independence of each is recognized, but love and friendship still unite, are moved to endeavour for it, since that is how God relates to us.

Love and thankfulness and contrition are usually all learned in the family, but take on a different and, as it were, more horizontal character in adulthood. One's decisions are then one's own and one is responsible for them. But a parental influence which has tended the person one way rather than another may be gladly acknowledged without surrendering independence. In this kind of way our relationship with God influences us, although our decisions and actions remain ours. One of the ways in which the analogy fails, however, is that God is always our contemporary. There is no generation gap of values and style to overcome.

The family pattern in one way or another has to be invoked to express the quality of love in God's relation with humanity, because that is *par excellence* the locus of love among humans in a continuing relationship. Yet to have only family roles for God is insufficient. That reflects and on its own reinforces the divide we make between work and leisure, between morality and values at home and in business. It is understandable that religion has been part of private rather than public life, because so often it is only at home that people feel they can 'be themselves'. As Margaret Kane has noted of a manager: 'Perhaps it is because he feels the pressure of his work situation upon him to become a certain type of person who is single-minded in pursuit of industrial efficiency that he tries to protect one part of his life and personality from this all-consuming demand.'[4]

If church and theology simply acquiesce in this dichotomy, however, they seem to confine the presence of God to suburbia and to relinquish all belief that they have a responsibility in shaping society. In that case 'the inevitable consequence of a view of mission which does not take seriously the church's role in the shaping of society must be that the church will itself be shaped by society'.[5] Work is such a large part of most people's lives, and unemployment is so devastating, that they cannot simply be ignored by reiterating religion's familial roles. Nor can the ethos and structure of business and factory be of no concern to a church in industrial society. What is needed in that case, then, is a perception of our relationship with God which will cut across this divide between home and work, with point in both areas. Then, by its inversion, that relationship becomes a Christian ideal which provides a pattern not only for personal relationships, but for those in industry, technology and commerce as well.

Companionship is a relation which has this effect, for the role of companion can be taken in any external circumstance, from the most propitious to the downright bleak, and also at home, at work and in leisure. One could hardly find a more wide-ranging role for the omnipresent God. Everyone has known companions and what makes for companionship, so positive content can be given to the roles. Although 'companion' has overtones of warmth and sharing, it is a relatively unspecific word, blessedly exempt from any necessary connection with a sex, colour, class or culture. One is free, therefore, to discover for oneself in one's own life what particularities of companionship mediate God, making him a lively presence with whom one can live and act. This by no means supersedes all that has already been believed of God. What happens is that our individual experience interacts with our understanding of God from Scripture, church and tradition to emerge as a relationship which we can live out in the ambiguous conditions of our own part of the world. In describing these roles and how they function I have once more set aside for the moment the tensions of Ambiguity in order to convey their potential scope. Actual experience of relationship with God is likely to be less simple and consistent, yet the roles express a real possibility.

By its derivation, 'companion' means 'one who shares bread', implying a relationship of trust and mutuality. It has come to mean someone who is with others, who works or plays alongside them, who goes with them as they travel, whose 'company' is enjoyable. It expresses a relationship which has also been found appropriate in marriage. The Church of Scotland rubric includes: 'Marriage is appointed that there may be lifelong companionship, comfort and joy between husband and wife.' In all these senses it is eminently suitable to express God who is present both as contemporary, the one who understands people where they are, and as the one in solidarity with men and women, basically in their favour, however critical from time to time. All God's promises to be with his people expressed in Scripture, from the Exodus to Christ as Immanuel and the sending of the Spirit, are caught up and acted upon in this relationship. Images of life as a journey or of the church as the pilgrim people of God are illuminated by divine-human roles of companionship, for in any pilgrimage the quality of hopeful travelling is as important as the intention to arrive.

Alastair Campbell has written of the similar case of friendship: 'There is no such thing as being *efficient* at friendship (not genuine friendship), since it is not an activity which aims at achieving something . . . Although my friends and I may do things together, the heart of friendship is a *way of being*, not any particular activity.'[6] Similarly, the heart of companionship is God's way of being with us and our way of being with God, sharing what happens *en route*. We may achieve things in God's company, but the relationship itself is discovered/revealed as grace rather than efficiently brought about. The roles of companions require the minimum of prior structuring and definition, for they will emerge and change in process as individual understanding and circumstances change. I have chosen 'companion' rather than 'friend' because the more general term has a wider range of possibility today. Moltmann has commented on how 'friend' has moved entirely into the private sphere compared with its old corporate use reflected in the sentry's question, 'Friend or foe?'. 'The friend has become the personal friend, the 'bosom' friend; friendship has become individualized and emotionalized. Inner agreement, natural affection, mutual goodwill and free choice have now become the determining factors in friendship.'[7] While companionship in private lives is likely to have many of these warm qualities, they are not usually to be found in the same way in public relationships such as those in business. Therefore, although John's Gospel portrays Jesus saying to his disciples, 'I have called you friends' (John 15.15), and in spite of the attraction of such roles for the divine-human relationship, the scope of friendship in modern society is too limited to express the totality of relationships implicit within the individual connection with God.

The God who is our companion is not omniscient in the old style, knowing all the future before it happens. Such a God would lack one of the qualities of staunch companionship, that of 'seeing it through' with the other. But God who knows the actual as actual and the possible as possible has both the interest and concern to companion us through life, wise but not impossibly knowing in all the changes. God is not the map-maker who designed the route, and then observes our progress; he is not even the guide who has been that way many times, for in a changing world each way is different. But he is the companion, of eminent experience and loyalty, whose wisdom is an ever present help.

'Companion', moreover, expresses in a role the power of God which is attractive rather than coercive. People who force themselves upon us are not companions, even if we have to be in their company. Nor does one set out to select a companion deliberately with a list of desirable values. What happens is that one person *gravitates* to another who is attractive for some reason: someone who shares one's interests or sense of humour; someone who is good to be with. Similarly one gravitates spontaneously to God by the attraction of who he is and the effects he has created. All the old hierarchical, vertical images of God, like king and lord, have built into their connotations and sometimes explicitly stated, the kind of power which works by subjection. That use of power which I have already described is now seen to assault and diminish the one made subject, strictly curtailing his or her free response, and it is unlikely to evoke worship today. God has our attention and devotion by the lure of his goodness rather than by the command of his sovereignty. His power is not lessened. God is not weak. But the power which rules, subdues, dominates, is rejected for the power of attraction which will not overwhelm the other. In his freedom, he gives us ours. Yet in the relationship of companions there is both dependence and independence.

Because both are present simultaneously, 'companion' is a better role than 'adult child', where dependence is followed by independence. Dependence in companionship, however, is not like that of children on a father nor of subjects on a king. We depend on those whose opinion and experience we value and whose company we enjoy, since we are social beings. Unless it is pathological, this dependence coexists with independence, for we are responsible for our own decisions and actions, however much we may be influenced by our companions. Religion is often criticized for arresting personal development at the stage of infantile dependency and moral development at the stage of heteronomy. Again hierarchical roles reflecting a vertical rather than a horizontal relationship would, at face value at least, give grounds for these criticisms. But on the other hand freedom is never absolute. No one arrives at moral decisions in a vacuum, as if no one else had ever considered or advised what ought to be done, and no one can live a balanced life independent of all others, taking each decision and action *de novo*. The kind of relationship one has with a companion, open to influence from the other, yet still responsible for what we in fact are and do, provides a model for the degree of dependence and independence we need psychologically, morally and in relation to God.

The pattern of dependence and independence in the relationship between God and ourselves is not symmetrical. Indeed it rarely is among human companions, for we have different things to give to others and to receive from them. Yet dependence and independence may be predicated of God. Because he knows the world by relating to everything in it, he is dependent on the relationship for that increase in experience. Further, the gracious character of his relating makes him vulnerable to joy or suffering over the quality of response. And because he will not force acknowledgment of his presence, its felt quality of companionship is dependent upon our responding to his attraction. On the other hand God's independence of us, established by his absolute centre to which he alone relates, and typified by the small space between him and humanity, leaves him free to be critical or encouraging, consoling or rebuking. That small space implied by his presence *with* us, which would be lost in thinking of his presence *in* us, gives us both freedom. We are not God's puppets dancing as he pulls the strings, but neither is he our friendly

neighbourhood deity, a cultural artefact and a source of undemanding support. Neither manipulates the other, although each
contributes to the companionship.

Kings and lords are served, but one does not habitually serve
a companion. Yet there remains a transformed version of this,
even on the horizontal plane. One could scarcely be the continuing
companion of someone with whom one had nothing in common.
Sharing and like-mindedness, even allowing for differences, are
part of the conception of companionship. Similarly, 'companionship' would not be the most appropriate term for the relationship
with God unless ideas and priorities which on the human side
lead to action, were held in common, although people hold them
from their finite point of view and their stance within the Christian
tradition. We do things for our companions because they are our
mates, friends or whatever, as sufficient reason. We do not let
them down. In the same way, companionship with God, a
continual source of pleasure, fellowship, standards and perspective of the world, is reason enough to inspire action. The result
in practice is likely to be the same as with the model of service,
but the rationale has altered together with the basic image of
relationship with its reciprocal roles. Action is no longer the duty
of humanity's servant status, but the moral responsibility arising
from companionship in process.

There is pleasure and fellowship in companioning God, but
there is also the pain of failure in the relationship and the daunting
scope of its responsibility. For God as well there will be pleasure
and pain in all relationships. In his eminently sensitive relating
God may be seen as responding with pleasure to human responsiveness and the endeavour to implement common aims and
ideals, but all ruptures of relationship will cause him pain. As sin
is absence or failure of relationship, and God relates to everyone
and everything with a sensitivity and realism beyond human
comprehension, he will suffer from sin far more than humans do,
although his joy is also greater. Relationship is never without
vulnerability as well as delight. The same is true of relationship
with the world. When God is known as companion, we are not
only responsive and responsible *to* him in the world, as everything
is; we are responsive and responsible *with* him. To have pleasure
in a poem or a film, to enjoy the sight of parents with children, to
be moved by the beauty of mountain or river or to rejoice when

the destitute are housed is to share that pleasure with God, to be glad that such things can be, while knowing that they are not the whole story. But to see poverty, disease, all that hinders and cripples life in nature and humanity is to feel with God on our own small scale the pain of the world. In an ambiguous world the two aspects indeed are often blended. The sharing of such pleasure and pain with God is a form of prayer; when it finds expression in speech it articulates God's presence as part of the situation with which we have to do. God is not the intermittent problem-solver who may then put matters right, but his unco-ercive support and influence are available in tradition and in present receptivity as we take responsibility for alleviating the pain and increasing the joy.

Companionship in church and society

The discussion thus far has been concerned primarily with a personal individual relationship, but has implications also for the obvious communal connotations of companionship. Clearly no full study of the church can be undertaken in a book which has for the moment set aside discussion of Jesus Christ. What I am concerned with here are the effects on church life and structure of relating to God (or to God in Christ) as companion.

God is the companion of his pilgrim people in their worship and in their wandering through history. Worship is not different from the rest of life in that he is present there and absent elsewhere. It is humanity's inability to sustain awareness of the quality of that presence which makes particular set occasions and observances necessary, when people communally renew their sense of relationship with him and its implications. There is also the delight of coming together to worship. Worship at its heart is an encounter with the attraction of God, while a service of worship contains both a presentation of such relationship and a response to it. Responsibility in this case is not to disguise the warmth, beauty and wisdom of his presence, nor to truncate responsive-ness by the way worship is conducted or followed. This emphasis on the attraction of one who is with us and for us does not mean that there is no place for the confession of sin. But that confession comes, not as we prostrate ourselves before the Almighty in glory, but because as we attend to his sensitively aware presence our lives look different to us. Some parts we may share gladly, or in the fellowship of pain with him, but some will appear wanting in their loveless self-centredness. It is in the context of his companionship and not as an abstract datum that the fresh perspective on ourselves arises. For worship in the first place takes our minds off ourselves and fixes attention on God. We accord him his worth, his worthship. All else follows from that not only individually and collectively, but also for the world at large.

The dependence and independence which companions have with each other is true of the church and God as well. God depends on the church for experience of what it is for creatures communally to worship and companion him. But he does not depend on the church for his recognition as a presence in the world, and God is no more manipulable by humanity communally than he is by individuals. He is as free to judge the church as to rejoice in it. The church on the other hand depends on God for its *raison d'être;* it is the locus of the communal recognition of his loving and wise presence here, now, and could not be the church without that. It could be an institution dedicated to a past belief in God, but to continue to be the church it has to be engaged in what it is *now* to recognize him and the world as related to him. Otherwise it is cut off from present revelation. There will be continuity in the church as well as change, but it requires responsiveness both to tradition and the present to see what endures and what no longer mediates God as a lively presence.

The church's independence of God (qualified always by its concurrent dependence) lies in its need to achieve its own order like everything else in creation. God has not ordered the world, he has not guided creatures into pre-formed patterns, and that is true of the church also. There is no divine givenness about any church order and the varieties already visible in the New Testament witness to that. We are free, therefore, to find what works best, what mediates the divine presence effectively, what makes companionship with God and our neighbours a lively reality. Because we ourselves are diverse, there is not likely to be one single order which achieves this for everyone, but the aim transcends individual differences. We are also free to get it wrong, to make the limitations of our own view come between us, other people and God.

Although there is no one divine order for the being of the

church, it is understandable that the roles of divine-human relationship should become the pattern to be followed within it. When these roles are seen on the vertical axis, implying a superior and a subordinate, such relationships tend to be reproduced again within the church in a variety of hierarchies, including the relation of clergy to laity. Even when no ontological distinction is made between lay and ordained members, it is still possible to fall into patterns of clerical authority regulating those under authority. The shift to the horizontal axis changes the perspective. God, although omnipresent and transcendent of time and space, relates to human beings horizontally, encouraging them to be the best selves possible and using no force but attraction to draw them to him. Just so in church, no matter how large the denomination or how much organization it requires, relationships among the members which reflect the divine relating will be horizontal, not vertical, so that each may be the best possible, the most responsive and responsible. Minister and congregation are companions on pilgrimage, through all changing circumstances responsive and responsible to each other in the presence of God. When companionship becomes impossible between members of the church, that may indicate a want of responsiveness or an abuse of power, a return to old-style omnipotence put into action on the human stage. The ideal distance among companions is again that intermediate point between crowding the other and seeming unconcerned, even though in practice such distance becomes difficult to gauge and maintain among a variety of people. The ideal, however, would argue for no church office which put its occupant at too great remove (physical or psychic) from his or her companions, and no manifestation of the trappings of power which have distancing effect. A church companioned by God is not there to impress by its power but to attract. Admittedly, Ambiguity strikes even here, for some people are attracted by power. But from my point of view that kind of attraction is undesirable in a church.

The churches have wielded power in the past, and have seen themselves as the power of God visible in the world. Like God, the church was sovereign, parallel to and competing with other political powers. But if God's power is reinterpreted from sovereignty to attraction there is no need for the churches to continue to reproduce ancient structures of monarchical authority in order to represent that power. Such structures indeed will contradict their message and make it incredible. Power in the old fashion assumed vicariously for God has also the danger of becoming power for the sake of power and the maintenance of a powerful institution. Much of this kind of political power has been stripped from the church, not because she gave it up gracefully, but because alongside her in society, but outside her domain, there grew up in independence another vision of how things are which by its success assumed command, leaving the church with increasingly hollow words of power, dominion, obedience. That development may now be reversed, since it is time for the church, alongside society but independent of its this-worldly perspective, to set up and struggle for its alternative vision where power is the lure to goodness, wholeness and companionship in dealing responsibly with the ambiguities of the world.

When God is seen as a distant force acting from without on society at large the church again takes on that colouring in mission. Sacred and secular are then divided absolutely and the holy church is called upon to act as an external power upon unholy society. All the old bellicose hymns of mission bear witness to the dualism which is fundamental to this viewpoint. Christian soldiers march as to war on the enemy; they are asked, 'Who will leave the world's side, who will face the foe?' However much the emphasis may be on loving the sinner and hating the sin, that distinction in practice is not so easily made, and the attitude turns society at large into an enemy who must be conquered as a manifestation of the devil.

But if God is present everywhere, 'the world' cannot be our enemy and nothing can be secular as opposed to sacred. Mission is not the battle of one power against another, the earthly arm of God against the arm of Satan. Things are never as black and white as that. And if God is not an external force, neither is the church, for it can offer and experience companionship with the world in all its variety. As a companion it is alongside others with attraction as its chief power, yet with that element of independence which prevents the church from being simply identified with or lost in the aims, aspirations and standards of the world. It is not so much fighting a war as sharing a journey with the world at large and contributing to the quality of the journeying, 'leavening the loaf' in biblical terms.

Worship and mission are two activities of the church which, like love of God and love of the neighbour, may for some purposes be distinguished, but cannot be separated as if they were two totally different activities. The one motif of companionship covers both. We companion God as much in a protest about poor municipal services as when we gather to worship on a Sunday. God is a lively presence in the sacraments, but equally he companions the dole queue or difficult business decisions. There is no wall between the church and the world, for the church makes the *omnipresent* relationship articulate, comprehensible and vivid in picture, reading, sermon, song and prayer. In that case the image of the church as an ark, a house of salvation in a sea of perdition, will not serve. The image of the bride of Christ undergoes enlargement, for husbands and wives are now seen to be companions, so the purity of the church in action does not lie in withdrawing from the world, but in working wholeheartedly within it. To be the bride of Christ the church must also marry the world he came to minister to, in the same sense as a farmer's bride, say, also has to marry the farm her husband cultivates. One could also say that as the physical body of Christ was to be found regularly in the company of tax-collectors and sinners, so the ecclesial body cannot cut itself off from such companionship. Paul's emphasis on the interdependence of the members of the body of Christ ('The eye cannot say to the hand, "I have no need of you"', I Cor. 12.21) is exactly what the discovery of companionship is about.

Companionship is an ideal which is already inspiring action in current society, even when the name is not used, among basic communities of various interests and ideals which have been founded as an alternative to the social or religious *status quo*. These illustrate both the benefits and the difficulties of the move to the horizontal. Basic communities have their difficulties like any group of humans. They may give rise to endless arguments over the communal rearing of children, the sharing of duties, involvement beyond the community and so forth. Many who go there import expectations which may be incompatible with the group ethos – expectations, for instance, that women will take on all the domestic running, or that priests and ministers will automatically be accorded a status of authority. Nevertheless, even when everything negative has been said, 'at least something tangible is happening and is visible,' as David Clark insists. 'People are now *seen* to exist in our time who do not go along with the norms of consumerism and affluence; . . . people *do* exist who refuse to take as inevitable the organization of work on authoritarian and socially divisive lines; and we *can* observe groups determined to throw off the weight of impersonal, bureaucratic structures.'[8] For this reason Rosemary Haughton is right to call such communities 'a "sign of contradiction", as effective symbols are bound to be . . . The numbers are so far tiny, the resources ludicrously small, but the symbolic value is potentially enormous.'[9] That symbolic value and their practical encountering of problems make basic communities matters of concern to churches. I do not wish to suggest that churches become communes, but that the basic communities, which are already struggling with the realities of companionship have much relevant experience to offer churches with this view of their role.

'With' is once more an important preposition in such communities. Just as God is *with* us, rather than over or in us, so community members live and work *with* each other. L'Arche, for instance, 'creates home life and work situations with mentally handicapped . . . adults. That "with" is an important key word because the handicapped persons who come to the community are as much members of the community as the assistants and young volunteers.'[10] No one in that case is discounted. Each member has significance and a role to play in the decisions and practices of the group.[11] For the same reason there is often resistance to classical group structures with a director who lays down rules. Such resistance, however, carries with it its own responsibility for the community to co-operate in its decision-making in such a way that the group can continue to function with effect and without undue hurt to any. Sensitive awareness of others in an interdependent relationship is a precondition of success in such a case. Communities find it hard to carry permanent passengers, while those who are there only 'to do their own thing' are constantly disruptive of community. Acceptance of responsibility for one's decisions and actions is part of the individual autonomy aimed at in basic communities, an autonomy which yet has to function within a group.

This raises questions of leadership and authority which are rarely settled with ease in actual situations composed of diverse and changing people. In general, however, Clark observes two forms of leadership. One concerns the group as a whole, where 'each member is recognised as having leadership potential, given the appropriate situation, and the aim is to come to decisions through a common mind if at all possible'.[12] While this process makes for a high level of involvement from each person and draws out individual capacities for responsibility, it takes place as a group activity. In this way 'leadership potential' is not the possibility of acquiring personal power over others, but a way to empower the 'common mind' so that the group moves together. This coheres with the other leadership Clark discerns, that of the skilled co-ordinator of resources and information, the 'low profile enabler' who has more to do with making it possible for groups and individuals to take responsibility for their own development than assuming control of what is done. 'Leadership of this kind is as determined to prevent immature dependence as it is to encourage and support when really necessary . . . It does not do away with words like "should" and "ought" but helps to make them adult words by choice.'[13]

Clearly the practice of such models of leadership is continuously demanding, so basic communities on the whole will value the process of individual participation, horizontal relationship and communal responsibility, whatever the difficulties, more highly than the speed and efficiency which are (sometimes) possible in a hierarchy or bureaucracy which passes down a decision to be implemented. Indeed their foundation was inspired by reaction against the alternatives of passive consumerism or individual self-promotion found in society and to some extent reflected in church structures. Their foundation and continued existence is a symbol of the possibility that in spite of all Ambiguity, finitude and sinfulness it is possible for people to live as companions. One cannot therefore say: 'Companionship is a pretty ideal, but it will not work.' The question is rather whether it is valued highly enough to be allowed to work.

Yet churches are not the same as communities. In one sense church companionship is a more gentle introduction, since one does not actually live and take every domestic decision with the same group of people. In another sense, however, it is harder, for churches have a long tradition of vertical relationships which everyone has grown to expect. Moreover, unlike the small bodies of communities, churches are inclusive, with plenty of passengers, individualists and indeed all of society within their ranks. Communities are made up of these already persuaded of the value of the venture (or persuaded at least to try). In churches the process of persuasion has only just begun.

The beginnings are seen in those parishes which 'are taking genuine steps towards collaborative local ministry'.[14] That both a need and a desire exist for such wider forms of ministry is demonstrated by the explosion of literature on the subject.[15] Because so much has already been written, I am not taking up particular questions of the shape of this ministry. Companionship with God and companionship as the form of the church, in itself and in relation to the world, express roles in which these new forms may be enacted and carried further. The minister in such a parish has been described in words which echo the form of leadership in basic communities: he or she is 'working with (people), bringing the best out of them, giving full value to each one's contributions and ensuring that a spirit of cooperation flows through the common life'.[16] On this understanding the minister is less of an isolated professional omnicompetent in all church affairs, and more of a companion with others of different experience and skills. This does not deny the roles of ordained ministers or their training, but has more to do with how that training is put to use in empowering rather than 'governing' or even 'managing' a parish.

To the extent that this is happening in any denomination, the present becomes a period of transition and reform within and alongside existing structures and concepts. Like all such periods it has its tensions, likened by J. Milton Yinger to,

> the rebuilding of Grand Central Station while keeping the trains running. One must avoid waiting so long that the building collapses, yet build so skillfully that traffic may continue. In religious matters, for fear of 'stopping traffic' many people resist the building process; others, dismayed at the shakiness of the ancient structures, try to halt all traffic until a new structure can be built. (This cannot be done. The customers buy a ticket on some other route to salvation.)[17]

No reformation, however, can take place without opposition and hurt. This case involves a redistribution of power and greater participation from all, neither of which is an uncomplicated process. Margaret Kane has noted how difficult redirection can be: 'Much of the church's life assumes that the clergyman is the shepherd of the "flock" whose job it is to follow him, and some people among both clergy and laity like it that way. Any change causes considerable confusion and uncertainty.'[18] There are certainly some ministers who are only too happy to be the source of wisdom and authority in a church. On the other hand, even ministers convinced of the need for change find it hard to implement among parishioners who are used to the old and less demanding ways. It is much easier for them to leave planning and virtual decision-making to the minister. Oman observes the consequences: 'Not without reason, therefore, he comes to regard himself as the origin of all right direction and the bulwark against anarchy.'[19] Members and minister may in that case collude in leaving the vertical relationship within the church intact.

Yet by the very nature of the roles no one can be coerced into companionship, or the things which companions do together. These have first to be found attractive, for to some people in a world where everything is changing it may sometimes seem like the last straw when the church changes too, and is no longer what one has been used to from childhood, a safe refuge of the familiar. People may then be bereaved of their old ways and require companionship and persuasion in the introduction to new experience. They may need to lose the anxiety which reduces responsiveness and see for themselves the attractiveness of what is happening, see its connection with Christian values and worship, and that all comfort will not be lost by it. Some may never change: those 'parishioners who have a long tradition of regarding shared decision-taking as weakness and who yearn for a remote figure on whom they can be totally dependent'.[20] For many it will take a generation of trial and error to work through. It will not happen at all, or at all happily, unless everything is talked through by clergy and laity together, so that companionship may come into being in the process and thus be persuasive.

A ministry in local parishes which takes the role of companion has evident implications for other church offices, committees and commissions. One can hardly have parish ministers acting as co-ordinators, encouragers, a source of spiritual support while others fulfil their vocations, when they themselves are part of a vertical structure based on rule and obedience. Undeniably there has to be organization in any denomination: business decisions have to be attended to, decisions taken on what counts as disorder, pastoral care of ministers exercized, and so forth. But if God companions creation in its struggle with Ambiguity to bring about the best possible order, and if the church likewise understands itself under the motif of companionship, the manner in which these functions are fulfilled is likely to change, in order to enlarge the area of responsiveness and responsibility among all. This is a critical point, for it is only when the churches are seen to be taking companionship seriously to the point of their own restructuring that they may convincingly address the world on 'unjust structures' or the evils of hierarchical relationships in business and industry.

If the church actually demonstrated companionship in its local presence and its denominational organization, it would form what sociologists call a 'plausibility structure' or a counter definition of reality. That is, by its very existence it could show that relationships which are different from those normally presumed necessary in society can work effectively and attractively. Without that demonstration the church is in no position to criticize anyone. Given the reality of companionship, however, a whole way of being with the world becomes possible.

The companionship of the church and the world

A church which was clearly committed to companionship would have its first effects simply by being what it is, a visible, attractive alternative. In that sense it would be acting like God on the world. Further, those who share in its companionship already would come from all varieties of occupation and employment so that news of that way of life could percolate through society. Then in the very process of experimenting with companionship and erecting its plausibility structure the church would be having effects beyond its own organization.

Companionship with its connotations of being alongside in unoppressive solidarity, open to influence yet remaining independent and responsible, is a relationship opening up many possibilities which can only be indicated here as its potential scope and function. Creature-companionship, for instance, with the rest of nature, which is itself companioned by God and has intrinsic, independent value on that count, gives religious point to concern with the environment and expresses the limits of possible human action. (What cannot be construed as companionship with non-human nature is an abuse of human power.) Since humans have to eat, intervention in nature is necessary, but in the role of companion the mode of that intervention, its intention and extent, are not those of the vertical imposition of power, but those of responsible relationship. Such perception will not of itself settle all questions concerning the use of chemicals or machinery in farming, nor will it give instant priorities among conservation, farming, forestry, tourism and industry in relation to land use. Ambiguity remains, and the need for present local responsibility in the different issues as they arise. But to see God companioning creation, human and non-human, in its efforts to bring about order and balance, gives a rationale for Christians to be involved in environmental questions, together with a metaphysic and an ethos to bring to their discussion.

Although companionship is in the first place a relationship among humans, its projection upon nature, like its projection upon God, need not be anthropocentric since it allows for the independence of the partner. But because it is a human relationship, it has a much wider range of potential mutuality among humans than with nature. This is clearly the case where attraction draws people together to discover and enjoy the other, much as I have described companionship with God. Yet 'companion' as a role within a church or for a church in society cannot be limited to the company of those to whom people are instinctively drawn. Personal companions are usually those to whom we feel attracted by disposition, but when the divine-human relationship becomes the model for *all* relationship in church and world, then the limitations of emotional attraction are superseded. It is still the case, however, that companionship as a mutual way of being will work only if it is found attractive and satisfying, so that people take responsibility for the relationship.

Companionship can be sought, for instance, between races, or between any other classifications which divide some persons or groups from others. It is also a possible way of being among fellow-workers, or any other group in which humanity is thrown together without choice. As in the case of nature, the notion works as a reason for being involved, an ideal to work towards and the provider of roles to take in relation to others. Companioning is a way to act in the midst of Ambiguity rather than a way to transcend it, for each situation will be different (and situations themselves are not clearly-defined *loci*) with changing circumstances and diverse membership. Yet with the companionship of God as sufficient reason, Christians individually and in churches may endeavour to bring about an order in society in which a relationship is valued which respects the individuality and integrity of the other, yet offers the warmth of fellowship.

One area of society where companionship might alter vividly the quality of life is in business and industry. For here also the pattern of divine-human relating is possible. It may already occur occasionally but is frequently denied by existing structures. 'Division' often seems only too accurate a word for the division of labour into units and hierarchical structures which scarcely need to be described here. Just as churches have to be organized so too has industry, but the matter at issue concerns the quality of relating which the organization brings about. To relate is to be sensitively aware of the other, and this kind of awareness in our society has for the most part been relegated to private life; yet 'from the point of view of the social psychologist, the need of the individual for status and function is the most significant of his traits, and if this need remains unsatisfied nothing else can compensate for its lack.'[21]

From this point of view, therefore, the introduction of recreational facilities and canteens are only cosmetic changes if there is no trust in the work relationships, if the worker has no opportunity for response and responsibility, initiative and intelligent participation. In his powerful study *Beyond Contract: Work, Power and Trust Relationships*, Alan Fox describes 'low discretion roles' where a worker is closely supervised in action with no respect for his or her skill and capacity to make constructive suggestions.[22] It becomes clear to such workers that they are not trusted. From sociological research Fox documents the resulting suspicion and jealousy, the difficulties when co-operation is needed or differences have to be settled, and the absence of community.

His description of 'high trust relationship' on the other hand, reads like a prescription for companionship in action:

Participants share certain ends and values; bear towards each other a diffuse sense of long-term obligations; offer each other spontaneous support without narrowly calculating the cost of anticipating any equivalent short-term reciprocation; communicate freely and honestly; are ready to repose their fortunes in each other's hands; and give each other the benefit of any doubt that may arise with respect to goodwill or motivation.[23]

These possibilities are equally documented by research; they are not mere wishful thinking. Just as in some churches there is a perception of the desirability of a different, more communal ministry, and some have moved away from individual vertical management, so here and there in industry and business there is some acknowledgment that relations could be better and some experiments with greater worker participation made in diverse ways, from a variety of motives and with mixed results.[24] Again the questions are whether power will be shared on the one hand and responsibility taken on the other. Time and patience will be needed if involvement and consultation are to take place on every level.

First would come a change in attitude and practice, such as this: 'Authority is delegated all down the line, and all levels of management feel sufficiently secure to consider the well-being of their subordinates instead of constantly looking up the line to make sure they are being approved.'[25] Trust is not just an issue between shop floor and management but in all relationships. A rationale which should be acceptable to industry for such change to treating the manager or worker justly as a person is that 'justice in industry will lead to trust. Hereby better industrial relations will be created. These will lead to higher productivity. All will benefit.'[26] This undoubtedly is an appeal to enlightened self-interest on the part of employers from the self-interest of the workers. Yet self-interest is the interest of the *self* which is not simply an economic unit but an identity capable of response, responsibility and companionship. Arguably indus-trial relations have so often failed because that sense of the self was not in view. If such common humanity were to become part of the understanding on which business and in-dustrial relations were based, the rigidities of hierarchical structures and working practices might well become more fluid and open to change.[27]

Much more might be written of the ills and possibilities of industry. No mention, for instance, has been made of trade unions. But this sketch serves to indicate that companionship is a valid, indeed needed form of relationship there. What then is the church's relation to all this? In the first place it would have to see industry and commerce as the place of the presence of God, since God companions all creation. There is no area from which he has withdrawn his attractive, uncoercive presence and therefore nowhere that revelation, the perception of God in relationship with the world, is impossible. The church is not concerned with 'enemy territory' in industry, but with making explicit the effects of what is already implicit and possible in God's companionship. Then the church would need to be well-informed on what is happening, for a proffered companionship of amiable ignorance will not help anyone. 'The first job of Christians and the church is to know what the real issues are and to be in touch with the people and areas of life where disturbance is greatest. In order to do this the church must be close enough to the different areas of life to be able to identify the crucial issues and to distinguish them from what is merely "newsworthy".'[28] Such a process will involve clergy and laity working together.

When this has been achieved in regard to specific issues or to make a general case, the church then has a persuasive role to play. In an ambiguous world there is no such thing as a demonstration which will convince everyone from every point of view. An argument advanced is a recommendation to see things in a certain way, put as persuasively as possible. Although persuasion can come in a variety of strengths and the word has been abused by torturers, it remains sufficiently moderate to exclude the possibility of the church attempting to dictate to industry like an external power (a power it no longer has in any case). The power involved in the church's persuasion is the power of changing minds, not the power of telling others what to do. The distinction may sometimes be lost in practice, but it shows in the manner of proceeding.

To begin with, the church is unlikely to be persuasive if it is not plausible, that is, if it does not know what it is talking about or if the kind of relationships advocated for industry are not already functioning, albeit in Ambiguity, in its own area. They can then be seen to be achievable and attractive. The church could then show the nature of its interest in industry in such activities as organizing conferences to disseminate its knowledge and point of view, being ready to make informed comment in emergencies (as church leaders were called upon in the miners' strike of 1984–85), encouraging and supporting industrial chaplains and church members in industry to work for change, and allying themselves with others who wish such changes. None of this is unambiguous. Words may be just temporary sound and others who wish change may not have quite the point of view of the churches. Nevertheless it is through such ways as these that the church can promote and actualize the values and perspective of companionship.

Since companionship is the form of the church's being in the world, the ideal relationship between church and industry would be dialogue in companionship. Yet if the church shows a reforming interest, and even more if it begins to be persuasive, it is likely to meet opposition. There will probably be a number at all levels of industry who are not going to be impressed by ecclesiastically advanced alternatives and will tell the churches to stick to their spiritual last. In organizing themselves into companionship the churches may be seen as priestly: in perceiving the need for and urging moves toward companionship in society and the world at large the churches become prophetic. And prophets are rarely appreciated in their own time. The case against restriction is founded on belief concerning God's omnipresent relationship, but the likelihood of opposition raises a question which cannot be avoided. Upset, opposition and conflict are frequent reactions to change when people are accustomed to the status quo. How can such a positive role as companion be taken in the midst of a conflict which the very notion of companionship has generated?

Companionship and conflict

It could be a danger with a motif like companionship that it will be construed only in terms of comfort, viewing comfort as what we receive from God and offer to the world. Companions certainly do comfort, but there is much more to the role than that. A ski-instructor companions learners into more difficult manoeuvres; a companion may be the one able to tell us securely and effectively when we appear wrong-headed; by confronting a painful issue which lies silently between them a friend may breach one form of companionship in order to arrive at something more profound. While these actions would be undertaken companionably, they show that the relationship is much more robust, much more full of all kinds of giving and taking than one based exclusively on comfort.

It is from this sturdy view of the role that the question of conflict can be approached. It remains fundamental that what the church does is to offer and share an alternative vision of the world and society which has its own attraction and works in that way. Yet it would appear Utopian in an ambiguous world of varying and competing values to expect to achieve anything, within the church or outside it, without some degree of conflict. Conflict is not to be welcomed, since it can confuse or hurt, nor is it the only way to progress, as Hegel and Marx believed, such that it should be sought for that reason. Nevertheless hostility is likely to occur until change is really understood as the way of the world, so that it is expected and assessed rather than resisted almost on principle through insecurity with the unfamiliar. Outright conflict comes from those who enjoy or profit by the *status quo* enough to overlook its faults, whether these are, in industry, autocratic managers or workers whose aggression is exercised in the confrontation of 'us and them'.

God who acts through eliciting response to himself is not caught up in Ambiguity, but his effects take part in the competitiveness of the process whenever they challenge the way things are. For that reason his followers may have to act with more force than God himself, however reluctantly and while remaining within the role of companion. The Ambiguity of symbiotic opposites recurs here too. Just as freedom has to express itself in structures in order to gain a place, so the aim of companionship will have to be expressed in the midst of opposition and hostility which it has itself generated by pointing to the absence of companionship. This can be experienced even within the personal relationship with God when conflict arises between a sense of the responsibility such relationship leads to and a disinclination to take such responsibility. That kind of inner conflict has long been recognized as a common experience. Matters seem to become more controversial only when the *same* kind of conflict becomes outward and social. Yet to the extent that Christianity is itself outward and social, it would appear that conflict there is as likely as inner disturbance.

'When justice is too long delayed someone has to become impatient and indignant', Siefert and Clinebell write in their consideration of the churches and conflict.[29] To refrain from action because of the possibility of conflict is one way of breaching companionship with those who need it. On the other hand companionship with those who profit from a situation deemed unsatisfactory may have to be breached in the name of a more profound relationship. Yet each situation and each action needs careful assessment: 'Love often must express itself in honest confrontation which creates conflict . . . Yet this should never cloud the realization that, ethically speaking, this is a concession to the imperfections of the situation.' For 'compassionate concern is most fully expressed in cooperation rather than conflict'.[30]

Siefert and Clinebell urge that any action should be kept to the minimum essential for change, confined to the least destructive forms and resolved as rapidly and constructively as possible. These are certainly desirable aims, even though any actual situation of conflict is unpredictable and not easily controlled because of the diversity of people involved and the momentum such action can acquire. As John Habgood has warned concerning one kind of protest: 'The problem about civil disobedience is that although it may begin with very limited aims, it tends to feed upon itself. The excitement and the publicity generated by it, and the unreal expectations roused by it push it into more and more extreme forms of confrontation. It unleashes forces which are difficult to control.'[31]

That description can be only too accurate, and to it may be added the possibility of the hardening of attitudes on both sides until they become embattled, engaged in fruitless attack and defence. Such dangers have to be balanced against the likelihood of the effectiveness of more peaceful procedures and the gravity of the injustice at issue – a process which is more easily indicated than achieved or agreed. Siefert and Clinebell offer some practical advice: 'On major matters (the churches) should not stop short of alienating extremists, nor go so far as permanently to alienate the middle group on whose support change depends.'[32] They express concern lest 'those churchmen and clergymen who are trying to make amends for years of unrealism, utopianism or apathetic inactivity may move to the other extreme of uncritical acceptance of exaggerated and irresponsible uses of power and conflict'.[33] I have described the absence of relationship as sin, but failure in relationship when something better is possible is sin also. There is then in the relationship with God and the world a responsibility *to* action to establish companionship and a responsibility *in* action so that its character does not deny the good it seeks. 'God calls us always to act carefully and deliberately, yet nevertheless positively to express creativity within ambiguity.'[34] All action and the results of all action are ambiguous, but one may work in and through the difficulties because companionship is a vivid and valid relationship whose achievement expresses in human terms the relation between the world and God.

The tensions, the variety of opinion, the unpredictability of the effects of social action are all typical of life in an ambiguous world whether one perceives its relationship with God or not. The world is not ordered by God so that there is one correct way to see or do things against which all else is error. Knowledge in the changing and polyvalent world is not fixed or timeless, but relative to the epistemic order which gives it meaning and endures while that order endures. That is one instance of how God, without any diminution of his own power and freedom, has let creation be to bring about its own varieties of order, balance and achievement. The exercise of such finite freedom gives rise to the Ambiguity of the world, that is, its experienced character as varied, polyvalent and changing.

But God does not remain aloof from all this activity. His presence permeates the world which lies within the circle of his infinitely sensitive and aware relating. That presence, however, is neither a comforting blanket against reality nor a stifling blanket against initiative. Instead it is attractive, uncoercive, preserving the independence of the other, but intensely concerned in all the variables of the world that the best possible balance may come about. All creation has this value for God and each part responds to him by the way it is with whatever range of potential it may have. Humanity with its self-awareness has the greatest potential of response and therefore the greatest responsibility for how things are in people's own milieu, in their society and through that for the world. From a theistic perspective this is response to God even when his presence is not recognized.

Recognition of God's presence where it occupies the whole attention is worship. Recognition of his relationship with the world and how the world appears in his presence is revelation. With that enlarged perspective, given definition by the tradition of religious awareness and present experience, come values, direction and a way of acting in the world. As God's relationship can be seen in terms of companionship in its solidarity with, yet its respect for the other, so Christians may take the role of companion in their own communal worship and way of being. That role they may then take further into all the confusing, complex issues of the day, assured of the wise companionship of God, responsive to what is better and worse around them, endeavouring however fallibly to make visible the attractiveness of God and his desire for the best possible present order in creation.

Ambiguity will remain as long as the world endures, so that any revelation of God and the world in relation will be *timely*, effective at points in time, rather than timelessly beyond all historical conditioning. Moreover, all religious thought and action will be caught up in the polyvalence and change of the process. The very description given here of metaphysical Ambiguity, of God as absolute and relative, of the divine-human relation of companionship is no exception to this condition of existence. The only constant is God's continuing relationship with creation. Yet in and through and by means of Ambiguity, at every contingent place and time, among people of any age and culture, this relationship may be apprehended, God may be worshipped and all conceptions of the value and significance of experience transformed.

Notes

1. Introduction: The Interpretation of Experience

1. E. Ashby, 'A Second Look at Doom', Twenty-first Fawley Foundation Lecture, University of Southampton 1975. Philip Stewart, 'What Carrying Capacity for Planet Earth?', unpublished paper 1985.

2. John Oman, *Vision and Authority*, Hodder and Stoughton ²1928, p. 19.

3. A. O. Lovejoy, *The Great Chain of Being*, Harvard University Press 1957, p. 328.

4. David Lodge, *How Far Can You Go?*, Penguin Books 1983, p. 239.

5. Plato, *Timaeus*, 29.

6. I am by no means the first theologian to recognise ambiguity. Tillich, for instance, was well aware of it, but for him that was only another example of the world estranged from its true being. Barth, in discussing Nothingness, describes a dualism, a Yes and No in creation: 'not only clarity but also obscurity; not only progress and continuation but also impediment and limitation' (*Church Dogmatics*, III.3.50, T. & T. Clark 1961, p. 296). But this perception has not been made central.

2. The Ambiguous World

1. David Hume, *Dialogues Concerning Natural Religion*, Hafner Publishing Company 1969, p. 46.

2. Albert William Levi, 'Bergson or Whitehead?', *Process and Divinity*, ed. William L. Reese and Eugene Freeman, Open Court Publishing Company 1964, p. 144.

3. Although this can be said to be Plato's most usual conception, he does also write in *The Sophist* (249C-D) that reality is simultaneously all that is unchangeable and all that is changing.

4. Dorothy Emmet, *The Nature of Metaphysical Thinking*, Macmillan 1966, p. 3.

5. Oswald Spengler, *The Decline of the West*, London 1926, 1929; Arnold Toynbee, *A Study of History*, Oxford University Press 1934, 1939.

6. Pieter Geyl, *Debates with Historians*, Fontana/Collins 1970, p. 203.

7. Jonathan Cohen, *The Diversity of Meaning*, Methuen ²1966.
8. Doris Lessing, *Memoirs of a Survivor*, Picador, Pan Books 1976, pp. 19f.
9. Mary Douglas, *Purity and Danger*, Routledge & Kegan Paul 1966, p. 36.
10. Ibid., p. 39.
11. Suzanne Langer, *Philosophy in a New Key*, Oxford University Press 1942, p. 287.
12. David Attenborough, *Life on Earth*, Collins/British Broadcasting Corporation 1979, p. 248.
13. Louis MacNeice, 'Snow', *Collected Poems*, Faber & Faber 1966, p. 30. The theme recurs in MacNeice: 'World is other and other, world is here and there', 'Plurality', ibid., p. 243.

3. Knowledge and Judgment

1. Jerome Kagan, *The Growth of the Child*, The Harvester Press 1979, p. 65.
2. Max Black, *The Labyrinth of Language*, Pelican Books 1972, pp. 184f.
3. Robin Gill, *The Social Context of Theology*, Mowbray 1975, pp. 102ff.
4. W.B. Gallie, *Philosophy and the Historical Understanding*, Chatto & Windus 1964, p. 154.
5. T.H. Newcomb, *Social Psychology*, Holt, Rinehart & Winston 1950, p. 280.
6. Max Black, *Models and Metaphors*, Cornell University Press 1962, p. 236.
7. I.G. Barbour, *Myths, Models and Paradigms*, SCM Press 1974, p. 6.
8. Ibid., p. 30. Author's italics.
9. Richard Rorty, *Philosophy and the Mirror of Nature*, Basil Blackwell 1980, pp. 12f.
10. Ibid., p. 163.
11. D.O. Edge, 'Technological Metaphor', in *Meaning and Control: Social Aspects of Science and Technology*, ed. D.O. Edge & J.N. Wolfe, Tavistock Publications 1973, p. 47.
12. E.H. Gombrich, *Art and Illusion*, Phaedon Press 1960.
13. M.L. Johnson Abercrombie, *The Anatomy of Judgement*, Pelican Books 1960.
14. Antonin Artaud, *The Theatre and its Double*, Grove Press 1958, p. 78.
15. Edge, op.cit., p. 31.
16. David Hume, *An Enquiry Concerning Human Understanding*, The Open Court Publishing Company 1902, pp. 171ff.
17. See, for example, N.R. Hanson, *Patterns of Discovery*, Cambridge University Press 1958; T.S. Kuhn, *The Structure of Scientific Revolutions*, University of Chicago Press 1962.
18. Kuhn, op.cit., p. 24.
19. Anthony Quinton, *The Nature of Things*, Routledge & Kegan Paul 1973, p. 131.

20. Op.cit., p. 273. Nicholas Rescher, *The Primacy of Practice*, Basil Blackwell 1973, p. 103.

21. A.R. White, *Truth*, Macmillan 1970, p. 109.

22. J.L. Mackie, *Truth, Probability and Paradox*, Clarendon Press 1973, pp. 22, 26.

23. D.W. Hamlyn, *The Theory of Knowledge*, Macmillan 1971, p. 117.

24. Ibid., p. 125.

25. Frederick Copleston SJ, *A History of Philosophy Vol. VII, Fichte to Nietzsche*, Burns & Oates Ltd 1963, p. 410.

26. Ernest Gellner, *Legitimation of Belief*, Cambridge University Press 1974, p. 49.

27. Richard J. Bernstein, *Beyond Objectivism and Relativism*, Basil Blackwell 1983, p. 9.

28. Ibid., p. 86.

29. Ibid., p. 15.

30. H. Stuart Hughes, *Consciousness and Society*, Paladin 1974, p. 429.

31. Gellner, op. cit., p. 48.

32. Ibid., p. 47.

33. Ibid., p. 50.

34. Ibid., p. 204.

35. Ibid., p. 13.

36. J.G. Herder, 'Ideas towards a Philosophy of the History of Man', in P.G. Gardner (ed.) *Theories of History*, Free Press of Glencoe 1959, p. 35.

37. L. von Ranke, 'The Idea of Universal History', in F. Stern (ed.), *Varieties of History*, Macmillan 1970, pp. 57–9.

38. E.H. Carr, *What is History?*, Penguin Books 1964, p. 19.

39. Herbert Butterfield, *The Whig Interpretation of History*, Penguin Books 1973, pp. 180f.

40. E.H. Carr, op.cit., p. 24.

41. R.G. Collingwood, *The Idea of History*, Oxford University Press 1946, p. 244.

42. A. Marwick, *The Nature of History*, Macmillan 1970, p. 21.

43. 'Objectivity' is sometimes used to express the force with which a conviction or an idea strikes an individual. He or she may have so little sense of having contributed that the idea appears to have come from 'out there'. Nevertheless one lone person with a compelling conviction will be generally regarded as holding it subjectively until it has been communicated and shared. The inter-subjectivity of a group raises the status of an idea, and the greater the group, the greater the status of the idea. The most inspired prophet has to persuade others before his or her conviction will have effect.

44. D.W. Hamlyn, op.cit., p. 69.

45. I.G. Barbour, op.cit., p. 92.

46. A. Quinton, op. cit., p. 43.

47. A.J. Ayer, *The Problem of Knowledge*, Penguin Books 1961, p. 35.

48. A.D. Woozley, 'Knowing and Not Knowing', in *Knowledge and Belief*, ed. A. Phillips Griffiths, Oxford University Press 1968, pp. 82,85.

49. Cf. N. Rescher, op.cit., chs 1 & 2.

50. I have retained the term 'metaphysic' in this chapter although the aspect I am concentrating on here, namely the way in which a metaphysic promotes values and guides behaviour, resembles 'ideology' in its sociological use. Ideology, however, has so often been a term of abuse that it tends to carry undesirable connotations and I have therefore retained the more neutral term.

51. W.J.H. Sprott, *Human Groups*, Penguin Books 1977, p. 186.

52. Kuhn, op.cit., pp. 199f.

53. W. James, *Pragmatism*, Longman, Green & Co. Ltd 1907, p. 7.

54. Carl Rogers, *On Becoming a Person*, Constable 1974, pp. 216f.

55. Ibid., p. 216.

4. Theological Order

1. David E. Jenkins, *The Contradiction of Christianity*, SCM Press 1976, p. 14. Pluralism in theology today is something more fragmented than the previous existence of 'liberals' and 'conservatives,' as Lonnie D. Cleaver insists in *The Shattered Spectrum*, John Knox Press 1981. Yet pluralism has been mooted in theology at least since James Ward's Gifford Lectures of 1907–10, *The Realm of Ends, or Pluralism and Theism*, Cambridge University Press 1911, which, from his different philosophical and historical stance, raise many of the issues addressed in this book.

2. Wilfred Cantwell Smith, *The Meaning and End of Religion* (1963), SPCK 1978.

3. John Hick, *God has Many Names*, Macmillan 1980, p. 5.

4. Edward K. Harrison, *Cosmology: The Science of the Universe*, Cambridge University Press 1981, p. 113.

5. E.L. Mascall, *Christian Theology and Natural Science*, Ronald Press 1956, p. 132.

6. George S. Hendry, *Theology of Nature*, The Westminster Press 1980, p. 111.

7. William G. Pollard, *Chance and Providence*, Charles Scribner's Sons 1958, p. 71.

8. Cf. Maurice Wiles, *The Making of Christian Doctrine*, Cambridge University Press 1967.

9. Gustavo Gutierrez, *A Theology of Liberation*, SCM Press 1974, pp. 3–15.

10. Joseph Butler, *The Analogy of Religion Natural and Revealed*, George Routledge and Sons, nd (first published 1736).

11. Anselm, *Proslogion*, Clarendon Press 1965, p. 117.

12. Hume, *Enquiry*, p. 42.

13. Cf. James Barr, *The Bible in the Modern World*, SCM Press 1973, pp. 156–67.

14. William James, *The Varieties of Religious Experience*, Longmans, Green and Co. 1928. p. 35.

15. Martin Thornton, *The Function of Theology*, Hodder and Stoughton 1968. p. 28.

16. Dietrich Bonhoeffer, *Letters and Papers from Prison. The Expanded Edition* ed. Eberhard Bethge, SCM Press 1971, p. 360.

17. Robert H. King, *The Meaning of God*, SCM Press 1974, p. 97.

18. I am indebted to Elizabeth Templeton for this example.

19. Only after this chapter was completed did I realize that there could be a question here concerning whether worship transcended the Ambiguity of experience. I do not believe that to be so. Undoubtedly reflection on the experience is polyvalent and the experience itself may be ambiguous in its affects while it takes place, as the varieties of description of religious experience indicate. God, to be God, transcends Ambiguity, and our experience of God removes our attention from our ambiguous selves, but because even then we remain ambiguous in ambiguous circumstances, the experience does not so much transcend Ambiguity as place it in the larger setting of God's relationship.

20. Thomas Fawcett, *The Symbolic Language of Religion*, SCM Press 1974, p. 97.

21. Gabriel Moran, *Theology of Revelation*, Burns and Oates 1967, p. 120.

22. Ibid. p. 145.

5. The Presence of God

1. Martin Buber, *Between Man and Man*, Collins/Fount 1979.

2. H.P. Owen, *Concepts of Deity*, Macmillan 1971. p. 1.

3. Gerhard Spiegler, *The Eternal Covenant*, Harper and Row 1979.

4. Ibid., p. 188.

5. Nelson Pike, *God and Timelessness*, Routledge & Kegan Paul 1970, p. 110.

6. Spiegler, op. cit., p. 190.

7. Charles Hartshorne, *The Divine Relativity*, Yale University Press 1948. I find it difficult to say to what extent I am indebted to process theologians. Some conceptions, like that of God's perfections as potential and abstract, have come from them directly. Others, such as the 'attraction' of God, I had arrived at before reading process theology seriously. But I may have picked up ideas by osmosis beforehand. Whatever I have derived from process theology, however, has changed its character by being blended in with other beliefs and arguments advanced in this book.

8. Karl Barth, *Protestant Theology in the Nineteenth Century*, SCM Press 1972, p. 432.

9. Thomas C. Oden, *The Structure of Awareness*, Abingdon Press 1969, p. 4.

10. Barbour, op. cit., p. 156.

11. Hartshorne, op. cit., p. 121.

12. John Oman, *Grace and Personality*, Cambridge University Press 1925, p. 15; id., *Vision and Authority*, p. 245.

13. Oman, *Grace and Personality*, pp. 16f.

14. Ibid., p. 22.

15. Ibid., p. 47.

16. Ibid., p. 53.

17. Ibid., p. 61.

18. G.W.F. Hegel, *The Philosophy of History*, Dover Publications 1956, pp. 30–4.

19. G.W.H. Lampe, *God as Spirit*, Clarendon Press 1977, p. 17.

20. Gordon Kaufman, *God the Problem*, Harvard University Press 1972, p. 134.

21. Daniel Day Williams, 'How Does God Act?', *Process and Divinity*, p. 171.

22. A.N. Whitehead, *Process and Reality*, Cambridge University Press 1929, p. 488.

23. Hartshorne, op. cit., p. 135.

24. Whitehead, op. cit., p. 314.

25. Norman Pittenger, *Picturing God*, SCM Press 1982, pp. 68f.

26. Charles Birch, *Nature and God*, SCM Press 1965, p. 99.

27. Op. cit., p. 101.

28. Whitehead, op. cit., p. 43.

29. Ibid., p. 486.

30. I have argued this point and much of what follows more concisely in 'Human Liberation and Divine Transcendence', *Theology*, Vol LXXXV, May 1982, pp. 184–90.

31. Sheila Collins, *A Different Heaven and Earth*, Judson Press 1977, p. 67.

32. Erving Goffman makes this comment on businessmen who add to their stature by distancing themselves from their subordinates, in *The Presentation of Self in Everyday Life*, Penguin Books 1976, p. 234.

33. John Drury, *The Pot and the Knife*, SCM Press 1979, p. 36.

34. There is, however, more than one way of interpreting God's presence positively in theology. John Baillie, for instance, who stressed the close presence of God even while Barthians were emphasizing transcendence, found that presence 'haunting'. 'No other challenge that has ever reached us has been so insistent or so imperious,' *Our Knowledge of God* (1939), Oxford University Press 1963, p. 156. Baillie's view is closer to that of Ps. 139 ('Whither shall I go from thy Spirit?') or Francis Thompson's 'Hound of Heaven' than my description of God's drawing us by attraction. The presence of God could have both these effects, but Baillie assumes a universal God-consciousness which is not universally attended to and is therefore troubling, while I do not.

35. Ludwig Feuerbach, *The Essence of Christianity*, Harper Torchbooks 1957.

36. Goffman, op. cit., passim.

37. Gustav Wingren, *The Flight from Creation*, Augsburg Publishing House 1971, pp. 79f.

38. This danger has been noted by Sallie McFague, *Metaphorical Theology*, Fortress Press 1982, p. 41.

39. The 'is and is not' character is described by McFague, op. cit., p. 19.

40. Barbour, op. cit., p. 157.

41. Bernice Martin, *A Sociology of Contemporary Cultural Change*, Basil Blackwell 1981, pp. 25ff.

42. Ibid., p. 37.

43. Ibid., p. 41.

44. Ibid., p. 35.

45. Erving Goffman, *Encounters*, Penguin Books 1972, p. 75.

46. Robert W White, *The Enterprise of Living*, Holt, Rinehart and Winston Inc 1972, p. 65.

47. Erving Goffmann, *Relations in Public*, Penguin Books 1971.

48. Goffman, *The Presentation of Self in Everyday Life*, p. 77.

49. Victor Turner, Foreword to Dorothy Emmet, *Function, Purpose and Powers*, Macmillan ²1972, p. x.

50. Victor Turner, *The Ritual Process*, Penguin Books 1969.

51. Saul Bellow, *Dangling Man*, Penguin Books 1977, p. 158.

52. Turner, op. cit., p. 120.

53. Sprott, op. cit., p. 23.

54. Ibid., p. 27.

55. Ibid., p. 187.

56. Goffman, op. cit., p. 14.

57. H. Sundén, *Religionen och rollerna*, Stockholm 1966, cited by Johan Unger, *On Religious Experience*, Acta Universitatis Upsaliensis 1976, p. 19.

58. Goffman, op. cit., pp. 110,114.

59. Cf. Peter L Berger and Thomas Luckmann, *The Social Construction of Reality*, Penguin Books 1966.

6. The Response of Humanity

1. Erich Fromm, *The Art of Loving*, Unwin Books 1962, p. 24.

2. Rogers, *On Becoming a Person*, p. 353.

3. Gordon Allport, *Pattern and Growth in Personality*, Holt, Rinehart and Winston Inc 1961, p. 274.

4. Ibid., p. 181.

5. Ibid., p. 274.

6. Ibid., p. 270.

7. Piet Schoonenberg, *Man and Sin*, Sheed and Ward 1972, p. 19.

8. James M. Gustafson and James T. Laney (eds), *On Being Responsible*, SCM Press 1969, p. 4.

9. H.R. Niebuhr. *The Responsible Self*, Harper and Row 1963, pp. 60f.

10. Martin Luther King, 'Letter from Birmingham Jail', in Gustafson and Laney, op. cit., p. 257.

11. Dietrich Bonhoeffer, *Ethics*, Fontana Books 1966, p. 233.

12. Rosemary Radford Ruether, *To Change the World*, SCM Press 1981, p. 53.

13. Margaret Kane, *Theology in Industrial Society*, SCM Press 1975. p. 47.

14. Feuerbach, op. cit., p. 266.

15. Bonhoeffer, op. cit., p. 256.

16. Ibid., p. 258.

17. Ibid., p. 259.

18. Ibid., p. 252.
19. Ibid., p. 253.
20. Karl Barth, *Church Dogmatics*, III/4, T. & T. Clark, 1961, p. 467.
21. Ibid.
22. Ibid.
23. Bonhoeffer, op. cit., p. 249.
24. Ibid., p. 248.
25. James P. Mackey, *Life and Grace*, Gill 1966, p. 155.
26. Op. cit., p. 157.
27. Emil Brunner, *Man in Revolt*, Lutterworth Press 1939, pp. 129f.
28. Ibid.
29. Harvey Cox, *God's Revolution and Man's Responsibility*, SCM Press 1967, p. 39.
30. Dorothy Emmet, *Rules, Roles and Relations*, Macmillan 1966, p. 203.
31. Mackey, op. cit., p. 191.
32. Gabriel Moran, *Vision and Tactics: Towards an Adult Church*, Burns and Oates 1968, p. 116.
33. Fromm, op. cit., p. 47, author's italics.
34. Ibid.
35. Ibid., p. 46.
36. Ibid., p. 49.
37. V.A. Demant, *Theology of Society*, Faber and Faber 1947, p. 25.
38. Nicholas Lash, *His Presence in the World*, Sheed and Ward 1968, p. 4.
39. Kenneth Burke, *The Rhetoric of Religion*, University of California Press 1970, p. 314. The quotation continues: 'If guilt, then the need for redemption, which includes sacrifice, which in turn allows for substitution.' The christological argument, however, lies outside the confines of this book.
40. Bonhoeffer, op. cit., p. 244.
41. Schoonenberg, op. cit., p. 20.

7. The Companionship of God

1. Peter Baelz, 'Is Prayer still Valid?', *Christianity and Change*, ed. Norman Autton, SPCK 1971, p. 93.
2. Stewart R. Sutherland, *God, Jesus and Belief*, Basil Blackwell 1984, pp. 28,30f. My comments in square brackets.
3. Oman, *Vision and Authority*, pp. 225f.
4. Kane, op. cit., p. 6.
5. Ibid., p. 75.
6. Alastair V. Campbell, *Rediscovering Pastoral Care*, Darton, Longman and Todd 1981, p. 93 (author's italics).
7. Jürgen Moltmann, *The Church in the Power of the Spirit*, SCM Press 1977, p. 120.
8. David Clark, *Basic Communities: Towards an Alternative Society*, SPCK 1977, p. 108.

9. Rosemary Haughton, *Community*, no.14 (Spring 1976), p. 3. Cited by Clark, op. cit., p. 258.

10. Elizabeth Buckley, *Community*, no.11 (Spring 1975), p. 4. Cited by Clark, op. cit., p. 173.

11. Communities are varied and some, especially those officially connected with churches, do not display this egalitarian ethos. Generally speaking it is the new autonomous communities who are experimenting in group decisions.

12. Clark, op. cit., p. 239.

13. Op. cit., p. 15.

14. Robin Greenwood, 'Presiding: A Parish Priest's Work', *Theology* Vol. LXXXVII, November 1984, p. 413.

15. For example: Stephen Mackie, *Patterns of Ministry*, Collins 1969; E. Schillebeeckx, *Ministry: A Case for Change*, SCM Press 1981; John Tiller, *A Strategy for the Church's Ministry*, Church Information Office 1983.

16. W.D. Horton, 'The Pastor's Problems: Administration', *Expository Times* Vol. 95, no. 4, Jan. 1984, p. 102, cited by Greenwood, art. cit., p. 413.

17. J. Milton Yinger, *Religion, Society and the Individual*, New York, The Macmillan Co. 1968, p. 312.

18. Kane, op. cit., p. 113.

19. Oman, op. cit., p. 263.

20. Greenwood, art. cit., p. 417.

21. J.A.C. Brown, *The Social Psychology of Industry*, Penguin Books 1970, p. 281.

22. Alan Fox, *Beyond Contract: Work, Power and Trust Relations*, Faber 1974.

23. Ibid., p. 362.

24. The variety and possibility of such moves now taking place as well as the need for them are documented in Peter Mayhew, *Justice in Industry*, SCM Press 1980. An instance of how an authoritarian management can abort the reality of joint consultation while appearing to cooperate is given in Brown, op. cit., p. 297.

25. Brown, op. cit., p. 228.

26. Mayhew, op. cit., p. 155.

27. As this section has been concerned with *human* relationships I have not included in the text another notion which has been with me since my training as an industrial chaplain, namely that theology should have something to say about machines, processes, etc. and not only about those who use them. Since the theology in this book concerns the transvaluation of all relationships, it is not the machine ontologically, as to an engineer, but the machine in relation to its users which is primary. Many workers already have a relationship with their machines which could be described as companionship, even though it is often expressed in curses (as I have heard a farmer fiercely but fondly swear at his cows). Although machines are inanimate, they are not identically passive under use, so the relationship between worker and machine is not wholly different from that of farmer and animals. Some workers at least,

therefore, in a sense companion the instruments and even the components they work with as well as each other. Since machines, unlike animals, are artefacts, if that relationship were then inverted, 'companionability' could become a prescriptive criterion for the design of industrial equipment, technological assembly and so forth.

28. Kane, op. cit., p. 90.

29. Harvey Siefert and Howard J. Clinebell, *Personal Growth and Social Change*, Westminster Press 1969, p. 171.

30. Ibid., p. 167.

31. John Habgood, *Church and Nation in a Secular Age*, Darton, Longman and Todd 1983, p. 171.

32. Siefert and Clinebell, op. cit., p. 162.

33. Ibid., p. 170.

34. Ibid., p. 159.

Index